FIX&
FLIP

FIX&
FLIP

THE CANADIAN HOW-TO GUIDE FOR BUYING, RENOVATING, AND SELLING PROPERTY FOR FAST PROFIT

MARK LOEFFLER & IAN SZABO

John Wiley & Sons Canada, Ltd.

Library and Archives Canada Cataloguing in Publication Data

Loeffler, Mark
    Fix and flip : the Canadian how-to guide for buying, renovating and selling property
for fast profit / Mark Loeffler and Ian Szabo.

Includes index.
Issued also in electronic formats.
ISBN 978-1-11818105-8

        1. Flipping (Real estate investment)—Canada. 2. Dwellings—Maintenance and repair—
Economic aspects--Canada. 3. Real estate investment—Canada. I. Szabo, Ian, 1976– II. Title.

HD1382.5.L63 2012   332.63'240971   C2012-906363-0

ISBN 978-1-118-23993-3 (ebk); 978-1-1182398-0 (ebk); 978-1-118-23988-9 (ebk)

Production Credits
Managing Editor: Alison Maclean
Executive Editor: Don Loney
Production Editor: Pauline Ricablanca
Assistant Editor: Brian Will
Cover Design: Adrian So
Cover Photography: Cover Image: Painter © Hemera Technologies / thinkstock; Agent © Hemera / thinkstock; Carpenter © istockphoto / thinkstock; For sale sign © istockphoto / thinkstock; Wooden board © ihoe / istockphoto
Composition: Thomson Digital
Printer: Dickinson Press

Printed in the United States

1 2 3 4 5 DP 17 16 15 14 13

Mark Loeffler
To Fiona

Ian Szabo
To the Szabo men and the Hickey men, creating generational change.

Contents

Acknowledgements

Mark Loeffler

I have to thank our editor Don Loney and his fantastic team at John Wiley & Sons for all of their hard work and dedication putting this book together. As always Don, your patience and guiding hand were much appreciated.

I'm always grateful to Don R. Campbell and the Real Estate Investment Network (REIN) for providing world-class real estate investment education and providing the place and reason for us all to meet and learn. Thanks.

I'd like to thank all of the contributors to this book. Donna Ragona, Thomas Beyer, Gary McGowan, Wade Graham, Cindy Wennerstrom, Jeff Reed, and Sean Greene, your stories, successes, and difficulties have added much depth to the book. The readers will have a much richer experience because of your contributions.

Finally, I'd like to thank my wife, Mary, for her ongoing support. Without you this book and my whole career would not be possible. Thank you so much.

Ian Szabo

I'd like to thank my father, Tony Szabo. Dad, you got me into the renovations business, and I learned many practical strategies from you that I use today. More importantly, you taught me about work ethic and determination. Thank you.

Thanks to my father-in-law, Gary Williams. I know my actions don't always make sense to you, but you always support me and know I'll pull through. Your support means everything to me.

Thank you Adam Rosborough, you've always believed in me and trusted my path. Thanks for being a steadfast friend and supporter.

Huge thanks and much love to my wife, Tanya Williams, and my daughter, Brianna Szabo. Because of you two, I know that my life is complete. I don't need anything else to be happy in the world. Thanks for showing me what contentment looks like.

To my mentor, Philip McKernan, your Everest Business Mentoring program has helped change my life drastically for the better. Thanks also to the whole crazy crew of Everest participants. We've come a long way together, haven't we?

Introduction

The Most Common Perceptions of Fixing and Flipping

Thanks for reading our book! *Fix and Flip* covers a topic that is commonly talked about, but very little understood. There seem to be two common views about fixing and flipping real estate for profit:

Common View Number 1: Flipping Houses Is Not a Sound Investment Strategy

There are those who believe that flipping houses is fraught with risk. To some degree, they're right—if you don't know what you're doing. We've heard from people who think that fixing and flipping is some kind of scam—the flipper makes huge returns for little or no effort. But rest assured—the fix-and-flip strategy is far from a scam. It requires the same amount (or more) of due diligence and effort as a buy-and-hold or rent-to-own investment.

Our advice: ignore the naysayers. Fixing and flipping houses is not impossible, nor is the strategy a scam. It truly is possible to profit by fixing and flipping houses. What you'll learn from this book is that it's not a "fly by night" undertaking, and that there are some excellent reasons to fix and flip rather than buy and hold, even if you want to profit from real estate over the long term. One of the biggest revelations you may have is that fixing and flipping can be a long-term investment strategy, even while it provides a fast return.

Common View Number 2: Flipping Houses Is Easy

This attitude usually arises during a major boom in a real estate market. As with all real estate investments, fixing and flipping is easier to do in a strong real estate market (where purchasers exceed inventory) than a weak one. However, as we will teach you, successful fix and flippers will not rely solely on the market for their success. You can never outsmart the market, and we always recommend fixing and flipping strategically, in any market. A successful fix-and-flip investor will not *rely* on a strong market to turn a successful fix-and-flip project.

The misconception that fixing and flipping is easy is somewhat like a disease. Whenever people start to believe in this falsehood, the appearance of "easy money disease" causes people to do silly things. We've seen people buy properties at fair market value, spend tens of thousands fixing them, and then expect to make a profit. It defies all logic, because if you spend too much buying and renovating, and then can't exit for more than you've spent, it's the antithesis of profitability. Yet when people believe in the easy-money approach, they will make this most cardinal of errors.

A hard-charging market deludes people and, inevitably, there are fix-and-flip newbies who get stuck with an unsellable property on their hands. In the game of musical chairs, eventually the music stops, leaving someone without a chair; just like in musical chairs, some flippers are left out of the game when the music stops.

The Middle Road

The truth is somewhere in the middle of the two views we just discussed. Some people *are* full-time fix-and-flip experts. Of the two of us, Ian is a good example of that. Others use flipping as a supplement (or an accelerant) to their overall real estate investment strategy. Mark is a good example of that.

But even Ian, who flips houses full-time for a living, did not start out that way. He started out the way that we suggest you do it—slowly. First Ian was a full-time contractor doing the odd fix and flip, and then he was a part-time contractor/part-time flipper. Finally, he became a full-time flipper. How long did the entire genesis take? Eight years! This is not an overnight endeavour. We're not saying you can't build your business faster than that if you desire to be full time as a fix and flipper. But it will not happen overnight, nor should it. Take your time and make sure you have the right deal and that you're executing your strategy step by step. Use fixing and flipping as a supplement, and at the same time, keep your eye on the long-term horizon. You may or may not want to do it full-time. There are strong reasons for both, but for the most part the supplementary strategy is the best one.

This may be one of the most important themes of the book. We really want you to "get" this, because some of you may have bought this book with the idea of jumping from a different job in a different industry to becoming a full-time fix-and-flip professional immediately. We strongly caution against that.

Fixing and Flipping - The New Model

Most people consider the fix-and-flip model to be like this:

1. Purchase house.

2. Renovate house.

3. Sell house for a profit.

It's true that this is *one* strategy for fixing and flipping, but what will become very apparent to you throughout this book is that this traditional model of flipping is just one of many models.

Our model of fixing and flipping is the following:

1. Purchase property.

2. Renovate Property (unless you wholesale).

3. Exit property, removing all or most of the initial cash invested.

4. Move on to the next deal.

Notice that the new model does *not* demand that you sell the asset. Through the value that you create as a fix and flipper, there are ways to remain the owner of the property and not leave any of your own money in the property. You can leave the bank's money in the property, and in certain circumstances you can leave an investment partner's money in the property too, but as a fix-and-flip investor, you will do everything you can to remove all of your own money from the property.

The new fix-and-flip specialists are sometimes selling and sometimes retaining ownership of the asset for future gain. Thus, when we say "exit," we don't always mean to sell a property. Keep that in mind as you move through this book. Exiting a property does not necessarily mean selling. However, it does mean that you've removed all or most of your initial investment in the property, either through a sale or a refinance.

Is This Investment Strategy for You?

This kind of real estate investing is not easy. In fact, no model of real estate investing is easy, and it's not a quick path to wealth. There is no easy or quick path to wealth.

But in particular, fixing and flipping is very intense. There are strict deadlines—not the kind of deadlines that you may be accustomed to. Not the kind that come from a boss or a co-worker. These kind of deadlines are very real. They are the kind of deadlines that will cost *you* real money if you don't meet them.

There is generally more real cash put at risk when you start a fix and flip, so there's more of a chance of losing real money. Real cash means money from your own (or your investor's) pocket as opposed to financed money. The reason there's typically more real cash involved in a fix and flip is the added renovation expense. Carrying costs can also be higher, as you're working on the project before it hits the market.

We need you to ask yourself very carefully if this is for you or not. There is no shame if it's not. Treat it as a gift if you discover that it's not for you, and move on to what will work for you and what will make you happy.

By the same token, we don't want to scare you away from trying fix and flips. Doing it well is a matter of following the recipe and developing expertise. If you truly want it, you *can* do it. But, just telling you that you can do it is a simplistic formulation. There are considerations of time, family support, and money for such an endeavour as fixing and flipping. What we want you to know is that if you want it badly enough, you can develop the skills to do it. We never promise it will be easy.

If It Is for You . . .

If, after some soul-searching and research, you find that fixing and flipping is a strategy you would like to put to use, or if you have already done some fix and flips and want to get to another level, we suggest you think of it as a supplement or an accelerant to your existing career, or to your existing real estate investments. Especially at the beginning, don't try to make it your sole career. Do at least five fix-and-flip projects before you make that kind of decision.

Fixing and flipping *can* be a wonderful supplement to your existing career or your real estate investments. It *can* provide you with the one thing that most long-term buy and holds don't: significant cash in a relatively short time frame. And it *can* allow you to own a property long term with little or none of your own money in.

All this is possible only if you get the fundamentals right. Without a doubt, the two biggest fundamentals of fixing and flipping are the following:

1. Buying for the right price

2. Renovating to add value without too great an expense

You will see these themes recur over and over in this book, and many of the other topics we discuss in some way relate to these two fundamentals. The truth is that if you keep focused on these two fundamentals, and if you execute these two fundamentals correctly, then you will likely do well at fixing and flipping.

Through patience, practice, and focus, you can develop "the knack" for finding, fixing, and flipping properties. The knack is something you'll notice when you can look at a property and see potential that many others, perhaps a hundred others, have overlooked. The knack is that sudden insight that says that $10,000 worth of renovations can create a $20,000 lift in value. The knack is not understood by many, and that's why fixing and flipping is not for everyone. In reality, the knack is just practised focus on the fundamentals. You can develop the knack as well as anyone else.

Go Slow, Focus, and Relax

Enjoy this book, learn from this book, and most of all learn from yourself. Take whatever you read with a grain of salt. Remember that for us to do what we've been able to do, and for the people profiled in this book to do whatever they've been able to do, a certain level of experience had to be attained. Each of us has a different background.

Consider that Ian ran a renovation company for eight years before he became a full-time fix-and-flip expert. Consider that Mark had many successful years in sales and rent-to-own real estate investing before he started doing a lot of his fix-and-flip projects.

We invited Thomas Beyer to contribute a section in this book for you because we think he has one of the wisest and most balanced approaches to starting out in real estate of any we've seen. Heed Thomas's advice about getting started, and we promise, you'll enjoy the journey a lot more.

In case you don't know Thomas, he's a full-time real estate investor whose company, Prestigious Properties, manages around $100 million worth of real estate, mainly across western Canada, but also in the United States and eastern Canada. He started off a mere 15 years ago with only one property worth $80,000.

Thomas preaches patience and incremental progress. That's why we wanted him to contribute his wisdom to the book. Thomas always says, "Real estate isn't a get-rich-quick scheme; it's a get-rich-for-sure scheme." Heed these words, and take it slow and steady.

Enjoy the book and please interact with both of us on our websites, or through Facebook, Twitter, YouTube, live events, and wherever else you might find us. Our contact information can be found on page 245.

Part 1

The Basics

1

What Is a Fix and Flip?

In this chapter, Ian talks about the fix-and-flip basics and how he came to understand it's not an easy path to wealth.

To put it in simple terms, a fix and flip is the process of:

- buying a property at the right price;
- adding value through renovations; and
- exiting the property with a profit.

You'll notice that I did not say "sell the property," and the reason for this is that you won't always sell the property, although selling is one exit strategy I regularly use.

Adding Value

People often get into this game to "get rich." Oftentimes they even think they'll be able to "get rich quick." The truth is that *if* you're able to create wealth at this, it will be a direct result of how much value you add—value to your end user, value to renters, value to investors, value to lenders, and even value to your spouse and children. These are all necessary to create a successful life as a fix-and-flip investor. The creation of wealth is always a by-product of providing value.

Fixing and flipping, probably more than any other method of real estate investing, is the art of creating value and of problem solving. If you can solve a problem, then you're on your way to adding value.

When you go into a nice neighbourhood in a high-demand town, you're starting in the right place. From the beginning, you're working with a product that people will want. Now, you take a house that has been neglected, it's an eyesore, and it doesn't fit into its surroundings, and you've got something even better. You already know that people will pay a certain amount of money for a certain type of house in a certain neighbour-hood in a certain town or city. So all you have to do is *be the solution* by providing that type of property. The raw material is the house that has been neglected, and your skill and expertise are the catalyst for turning that undervalued property into something of value. You are *adding value* by taking that property and bringing it up to the standard of the neighbourhood.

The world is in desperate need of people who can add real value. The economic collapse and uncertainty in much of the world, especially the United States, is a perfect example of the creation of false value. People believed that false value was real value. Eventually the movie ended and the acting stopped. All that false value was wiped out and along with it the savings of a lot of hard-working people. Be a creator of real value and you will do very well at the flipping game.

What's the Trick?

People often ask me, "What's the trick to flipping houses?" The reality is that there is no big trick or secret to it. There are a million small tricks that you will learn as you go along, but there is no single big trick.

People often get hung up on the money. They think they need a ton of money to get going in the business. Money doesn't hurt, but it's definitely not the key ingredient. In fact, if you start with a bunch of money but no skill, you'll probably end up with no money! You're better off looking at this as a game of skill rather than a money game.

There is a simple truth to this business that you may have heard elsewhere before: there is a lot more money out there looking for the right deal than there are deals looking for money.

Now, if you have the deals but no money, you'll need the skill in presenting that deal to get the money. You'll also need the skill to find the deals, and a certain set of skills to pull off the renovation aspect. I could list off a bunch of skills that make this business work (and I will below), but the fact is that it's skill, not money, that makes this business work.

Focus on having or finding the skills necessary in order to successfully flip houses, and the money will come. If you focus on the money instead, you will have a harder time finding the money.

There's a good chance you will have to use your own money to start off, but if your goal is to fix and flip regularly, you will find that money will be attracted to you. This is the truth for both Mark and me. We have a harder time finding the deals than the money, but the money comes because we bring the deals.

Fixing and Flipping Is about Putting on Hats

To do a flip successfully you need to focus on skill rather than money, but you don't need to have *all* the necessary skills in order to do a flip. However, you will need to supplement your own skills by leveraging the skills of others.

I don't personally possess all the necessary skills to do a flip myself, so I utilize other people's skills in order to do the job that I need done.

What the successful fix and flipper does is put on a few different hats to pull off a flip successfully. Putting on hats just means you're employing skills (your own and others'— in which case, you have to put on the management hat) to do the very unique job of fixing and flipping a house. Some of the hats include:

- **Deal Finding:** This is the skill of sourcing a property and purchasing it. You need to know if you can buy it at a low enough price and exit it at a high enough price.

- **Project Management:** You have to manage a team whose members have their own special capabilities and skills. You have to understand your team and work to keep your team motivated and working well together. You also have to take care of the planning and scope of work necessary to complete the job. This is all under the banner of project management.

- **Analyzing Your Exit Plan:** You need to be able to analyze the deal that's in front of you and know what your exit strategies are. You have to know which one is Exit Plan A, Exit Plan B, and Exit Plan C. Then you have to have the skill and knowledge to execute your exit.

- **Financing:** This one forms a part of deal finding and analyzing your exit, but knowing how and where to get the money is a skill unto itself.

- **Design:** This is the skill of knowing what will truly raise the value of the property. It's also the skill of doing the renovations in such a way that your costs will not kill your profitability. The design hat is integrated with the project management hat to a large degree because only the skill of project management will allow you to carry out the design aspect with any success.

Everyone Wants to Be a House Flipper

Whenever I'm in the company of a real estate crowd, I'm always amazed at how many people really want to be house flippers, or so they say. Flipping houses conjures up something romantic about buying and restoring a property for a large profit and the independence of being your own boss. I've actually seen people post photos online of themselves holding their big cheques. (I find this funny because a big cheque at the end of a job doesn't mean a big profit; there are still the bills to pay at the end of the job, after all!)

But the problem is that most people don't know what flipping houses is all about. In truth, there is nothing glamorous about the business at all. Just like any business, it takes commitment and determination, and the right blend of knowledge and skills to make it work.

My experience tells me that this business is not as easy as it seems. In spite of the fact that the definition provided at the beginning of this chapter is quite a simple one, and in spite of the fact that perhaps it's simple to grasp the concept that adding value is all you have to do to be successful at this business, the reality is that many people are not successful. Simple and easy are two different things. Often the simplest things to do are the hardest. Some people can't say the simple words "I love you" to their loved ones. Simple does not equal easy.

Take, for example, a guy I know who was trying to get into flipping. I'll call him Paul, although that's not his real name. He got into the flipping business with the best of intentions, and he even had a skill background that I highly respect. He was a renovator! Of all the skill sets to take into the house-flipping business, I think this is one of the best.

The problem with his first flip was that he couldn't get past the fact that he didn't have to take responsibility for what was behind the walls. In spite of the fact that he doesn't have X-ray vision, and he couldn't possibly know what was behind the walls, he still felt an obligation that if he was going to put his name to the flip, that he had to take responsibility for what was behind the walls.

Please don't misunderstand me here. If you know there is a problem behind a wall (mould, electrical, etc.) you absolutely have to fix it before you can sell it. In fact, not only is not doing it highly unethical, it's also illegal.

What I do mean to say is that you don't go ripping out walls when it's not necessary! Paul couldn't get past the fact that without him pulling apart the place, there was no way to know for certain that everything was up to snuff.

The lesson here is that flipping a house is about renovating what must be renovated at the lowest possible cost to you. It's not about having absolutely everything perfect so that your overactive imagination can rest.

Don't be like Paul! Please understand that although the definition of flipping seems very simple, it actually requires you to employ a bunch of different skill sets, or at least have a team that can employ their skill sets toward your cause. Paul had all the abilities and tools to do the job well, but he wasn't able to employ his "flipping muscle" to override his "renovator muscle." His renovator instinct took over and he overbuilt—and overspent— on this particular flip.

Don't Get Discouraged!

Paul is a wonderful guy and a very talented renovator, but only time will tell if he's a flipper or a speculator (see the next chapter for a discussion of the difference). In the example I gave, he made a critical error, and it caused his project to suffer. But if Paul is able to use that experience to learn and then change some of his behaviours, he will be fine. If he doesn't, or if he throws up his arms and gives up, he'll never receive the benefit of that lesson.

I learned the same lessons as I got better and better at fixing and flipping houses, and so can Paul. The same words will apply to you as you develop your skills and learn how to employ them.

The Fix-and-Flip Success Formula

Fixing and flipping is an art that involves a) creation, and b) fixing a problem (that someone else created), specifically the problem of a house that has zero curb appeal. As a fix-and-flip investor, it's your modus operandi to make money solving that problem and creating something beautiful in the process. A well-renovated house that's ready to fulfill a family's dream is a beautiful thing, and I hope you never forget that.

When you add enough value through your work and expertise, you'll make a profit and have the recipe for a winning investment strategy. But there's a hidden risk to fixing and flipping. People often get deluded about what it means to be a fix and flipper, and they actually don't know how to do it. They often throw themselves in without getting the fundamental piece first and foremost. The most common mistakes people make are: a) overspending on the purchase of a fix-and-flip project; and b) overspending on the renovation of a project.

Fixing and flipping is a formula that takes practice to perfect, and you can improve at it just like I did over the many years that I've been working at it.

2

What Are the Differences between Flipping and Speculating?

In this chapter, Ian looks at the two very different approaches to fix-and-flip investment.

Some people hold the view that flipping is akin to speculating. In my opinion, if a flip is done right it is very different from speculating. It is a business like any other: if you successfully add value, you can make a consistent profit.

Speculating, on the other hand, is the activity of the get-rich-quick mindset type. Speculators will do well in a quickly rising market, simply because they bought at the right time and will sell at the right time. But they will get crushed over the long term. The long term favours the savvy fix-and-flip expert.

It could be argued that there is a certain skill to timing a hot market correctly, but the sad truth is that most of these speculators will only do really well at their "speculation flips" when the markets are up, and will get crushed when the markets are flat or down. Why? It's simple: because they're not adding any real value. Speculation flips are the equivalent to the experience of unskilful day traders who are successful at the stock market when the whole market is charging forward, but who are destroyed in a flat market.

Let's be honest—in a really hot market, you don't even have to add value through renovations to turn a profit. Just buying and selling a couple months later is good enough.

Being a flash in the pan might seem fun, but the real goal of fixing and flipping should be to create long-term success. Spend time becoming a true expert instead of a speculator. Below, I will discuss some of the key items that you will need to master in order to avoid being a speculator.

Have Multiple Exit Strategies

Successfully flipping in a flat market is very different from speculating. It requires work, study, and knowledge rather than dumb luck. When you undertake a fix and flip, you're essentially doing a whole case study about a specific property. It has to fit all the criteria that you *know* will allow you to add value and therefore consistently make a profit. You're basing your decisions on the past performance of a particular property and area, and you're going forward with a plan based on the criteria involved.

A speculator needs to sell a property at a much higher price in order to make the project a success. But a flipper actually doesn't have any attachment to a certain exit strategy because he or she will always have numerous possible options that will make the deal work. A successful flipper can do at least two of the following on any fix-and-flip project:

- **Wholesale:** You get the property under contract but never actually renovate the property. You find a good deal on a property and sell the contract to another fix-and-flip investor. The new investor will do the work and likely take the most profit. You take a small profit and move onto your next deal. In some cases you do actually buy the property and then immediately sell it. This involves more closing costs than just flipping the contract, so if you do it this way, you must have more profit built into your end of the deal.

- **Renovate and Sell:** This is easy and clean. You move the property, cash out, take your profit, and move on to the next one. This is possible and desirable on a single-family home and a small multi-family home, as long as the numbers make sense.

- **Renovate, Refinance, and Rent:** This is a profitable strategy if the cash flow is very strong. I find that small multi-family properties are much better than single-family homes for this. Here, you remove all or most of your cash invested and then hold the property for a little or a long while. It's a great exit strategy if the property cash flows and if you get all or most of your money out on the refinance.

- **Renovate and Rent:** The only way this works is if you already have conventional financing on the property when you buy it, and therefore a manageably low interest rate. My problem with this is that the money you spent on the renovation is left in the property. The point of fixing and flipping is that you want to remove the initial cash invested as soon as possible, so doing a straight rental is against the nature of a fix and flip. However, if there is some sort of unforeseen emergency with the property and it simply isn't possible to refinance and pull out the cash (for example, if value wasn't created, or if the bank won't refinance), then doing a straight rental is the final backup plan. While not the goal of fixing and flipping, a straight rental is at times better than taking a loss on the property.

Having multiple exit strategies is vital. The worst I've ever been stung on a fix-and-flip project was when I didn't have multiple exit strategies. Always cover yourself by knowing there is a way out if your initial plan fails.

Do Property Due Diligence

A successful fix and flip includes a *lot* of property due diligence. People often make the mistake of thinking that any property will do. This couldn't be further from the truth. In fact, there are *not* a lot of properties that work very well for a fix and flip. A strong fix-and-flip candidate doesn't come around every day, although it may come around every month or two (depending on how wide a net you're casting). And the grand slam of a fix and flip doesn't come around every month—my experience is that these properties can be found every six to 12 months, and only then if you're looking intensively.

You'll never find a good flip, and certainly not a grand slam unless you're well-versed in property due diligence. Included in property due diligence are:

- talking to the neighbours about the property (they know things that realtors don't)
- walk-through of the property (will there be too many renovations to make it worthwhile?)
- scope of work
- project budget
- an accurate comparative market analysis (CMA) of the property (what it will sell for when done)

Why I Talk to the Neighbours

On a recent job, my team and I were taking a former marijuana grow operation and turning it into a *legal* cash-producing machine.

As I was doing my due diligence, I first spoke to a realtor about the property. The realtor told me that there were six marijuana plants in the house and that's why it was shut down as a grow op.

Knowing that the neighbours often have better information about a house than the agent does, I asked around and found out that the house actually had about 120 plants in it. There is a huge difference between six and 120 plants, and this information *could* have meant the difference between a total failure and a huge success.

Why? Well, when you take a grow op and turn it into a legal cash-producing machine, one of the steps you have to take is an air-quality test. If I were operating under the false assumption that there were only six plants there, I probably wouldn't have taken any major steps to remediate the air quality, because really, what damage could six plants do?

Well, 120 plants raised under intensive growing conditions can lead to major moisture (and therefore mould) issues. Knowing that the house had had 120 plants, I took the necessary actions, and as a result my property passed the air-quality test. Property due diligence saved my bacon, as it always does. Passing that air-quality test allowed me to avoid a great deal of red tape and bureaucratic holdups.

Do Regional and Neighbourhood Due Diligence

You could flip a house anywhere, but in order to do it right you need to know what to reasonably expect from the property in the area you're in.

Regional due diligence is about understanding all the larger economic factors of the region you're fixing and flipping in. If you live in a lumber town where the saw-mill is about to be closed down, or an automotive town where the plant is about to be shuttered, then it might not matter how well you do the rest of the fix and flip. When people leave an area in droves, you likely won't be able to profit from a fix and flip at that time.

Conversely, if a large source of employment is coming into a town, you will be in a better position to profit from the increased population numbers and the increased demand for good housing. No matter what, you can't be smarter than the market, so it's best to understand the market.

Neighbourhood due diligence takes a more microscopic view of the factors affecting the specific area you're fixing and flipping in. Are you doing it in a total dump of a neighbourhood where even the nicest house won't sell or rent? If so, you need to reconsider. On the flip side, are you fixing and flipping in the most sought-after neighbourhood in town? Will there be a lineup of wonderful buyers and tenants with money looking to get in when you're done your work?

Regional and neighbourhood due diligence are absolutely essential. Knowing, understanding, and applying the rules of proper due diligence constitute a topic of conversation unto itself. Its application is a skill that crosses beyond the borders of fixing and flipping into the realm of general real estate investing. (Don R. Campbell's book *Real Estate Investing in Canada 2.0* is the bible of the real estate investing basics. It helped me, Mark, and thousands of other successful investors get into the real estate game.)

Consult Experts

As much as I know my business and how to make the numbers work properly, I still always check myself in with an expert.

I have wise advisors in my life who, when they walk through a property, might find something that I would have missed. I have other advisors who might look at the property as it's situated in the neighbourhood and make me aware of any possible problems with the property or the neighbourhood that would make this property difficult to sell or rent. Still others might tell me that the deal I'm looking at is not as strong as some of my other deals, and perhaps I should continue looking elsewhere.

Don't ever get too cocky thinking that you know everything. At the same time, don't take advice from the wrong people. Make sure that the people you rely on the most have a perspective that is valuable, and that they will always be honest with you.

Speculators will listen to other speculators or people who don't really know what they're talking about. Speculators might not have any trusted advisors at all.

Be Prepared for Preparation

A speculator will never be prepared, but a real house flipper puts many, many hours of preparation into each and every flip project that he or she does.

Part of the preparation is the property and regional due diligence that we've already spoken about. Another part is the project management–related issues.

A flipper will have all his or her contractors, sub-contractors, tradespeople, and service providers in place prior to the start of the job. A speculator will not take this necessary step. Instead, he'll fly by the seat of his pants and *hope* it will fall into place as things move forward.

A flipper will have his total scope of work ready before he starts the job. A speculator won't even know what a scope of work is. A flipper will have architectural drawings and permits in place prior to taking possession of the home. A speculator won't even know what these things are. A flipper will find out the cost of insurance and determine which insurance providers will insure them properly, and will have insurance in place on the property.

A flipper will also have all the pieces in place to execute each of his or her possible exit strategies. If wholesaling the property is one of the exit strategies, the flipper will have a list of potential wholesale buyers. If selling the property is one of the exit strategies, the flipper will have knowledge of the market and will have a realtor ready to help sell the property.

Get Good Financing

A flipper will have a good source of money ready to make the deal happen when it needs to happen.

I say a *good* source because not all money is the right kind of money. If the money comes with an interest rate that will completely destroy your profitability, then the money is no good. If the money comes attached to a money partner whose interventions might make your life a living hell, then the money is no good.

A speculator won't have access to the correct financing. He or she will always have to scramble just to get the money, and perhaps even tell lies in order to get it. A flipper can always be above board because the deal is good, and money always finds a good deal.

A flipper will build a presentation in order to show potential sources of money exactly how good the deal is. This presentation will result in the flipper finding the money, and if it doesn't now, it will eventually. But if it doesn't now, the flipper doesn't mind, because he or she can still wholesale the property.

Flippers don't lose a deal over financing. If the money isn't in place, the flipper simply wholesales the deal and moves on. Flippers have a list of buyers they can go to if they need to wholesale the property.

Private Money vs. Hard Money

My friend and real estate educator Julie Broad has an excellent description of the difference between private money and hard money. Since we'll be using both terms in this book, I thought I'd share it with you. Julie's a great real estate educator, and along with her husband, Dave Peniuk, they are active and successful real estate investors. You can get a ton of wonderful free content over at their website http://revnyou.com. Julie's distinction between private money and hard money is below:

> **Private money is simply money from an individual (instead of a bank or credit union).** It's different than hard money. Hard money lenders finance deals for real estate investors as a business. They are more sophisticated in their investment terms and will typically seek quick repayment at high interest rates. With private money you can have more control over the terms of the loan. You can offer terms that suit your needs and offer a good return for your private lender.
>
> The easiest way to find private money is to call your favourite mortgage broker and ask if they have any private lenders. Most mortgage

brokers work with a few wealthy folks that have money to lend or they will refer you to a mortgage broker with private money connections. If you have decent credit and the property generates a solid cash flow you should be able to find money this way, but that money is expensive.

The upfront fees on those funds alone are usually 1-3% of your mortgage amount. On a $250,000 mortgage that means up front you can start off with a $7,500 fee plus pay at least 7% interest on the loan. That's ok if you're in a pinch with a strong cash flowing property, but there are much better alternatives and the best part is that **most of the alternatives involve giving your friends, family and fellow investors the opportunity to make a great return on their money backed by a great real estate asset!**

Tom's Big Mistake

I know a guy, Tom (not his real name), who got into flipping in a big way. He had the blessing (and the curse) of going into the business with a fair amount of money in his pocket.

He went ahead and bought a couple of properties, but the problem was that he wasn't a true house flipper in the way that I've been telling you about here. Instead, he was a speculator, and he went about things as a speculator does. Rather than doing his regional and neighbourhood due diligence, he just bought in a neighbourhood he liked.

This turned out to be quite an expensive neighbourhood. On top of that, he didn't have a true understanding of his costs and he didn't consult with anyone who might. What eventually happened was that he ended up with two houses that he'd bought for too much money, in neighbourhoods where there was only one exit strategy.

He *had* to sell them because there was no way the properties would cash flow if he rented them. The problem was that he couldn't recoup his cost from selling them, so he bit the bullet and rented the places out *at a loss* each and every month. He's back at his job, paying out of pocket every month to maintain his flips gone badly. I wish the TV flipping shows would show the reality that for every successful flipper there are probably five like Tom (many of whom probably got into that situation in the first place because they watched shows like that).

Tom made a lot of mistakes that speculators make. He

- had only one exit strategy;
- wasn't prepared;
- didn't do enough property due diligence; and
- didn't do enough neighbourhood due diligence.

Tom was a speculator. Don't be like Tom!

Stay in It for the Long Haul

As you've seen from the brief treatment we've given them thus far, speculating and flipping are very different. The reality is that flipping—if it's done right—is a sustainable business. If you strive to continually improve each of the areas that we've discussed (and a bunch more) you can improve and improve until you get yourself to a place where the business operates very smoothly, and you can actually make a very good living from it, both in terms of lifestyle and income.

That's the problem I find with speculators—they get in the game because they think it will be easy. This is a misconception that couldn't be further from the truth. It takes real work and real commitment to be able to properly fix and flip houses.

There was a time when my own actions more closely resembled those of a speculator than a flipper. During my first couple of flips, I went charging in without a proper plan. I bought the wrong house in the wrong neighbourhood for too much money. I falsely believed that if I just made my houses into the Taj Mahal, they'd sell for so much money that all my sins could be covered up.

I was dead wrong about all those things, and my first few flips were miserable failures. The only difference between me and a speculator at that point was that I was in the game to be a flipper, and I didn't plan on going away any time soon. So I learned from every little failure and from a few people who had knowledge that I didn't. Slowly, I turned into a flipper, and things got better with each passing job. To this day, my flips are becoming smoother and more profitable with each successive one.

Yours will too if you apply the rules of a fix and flipper: get better each time you flip a house; treat it like the business that it is; and stick around for the long haul.

The last one is no less important than the other attributes of a successful fix-and-flip investor. Be committed to sticking it out for the long haul. If you are, you're already over halfway to success.

The Flipper's Checklist

- Have multiple exit strategies.
- Do property due diligence.
- Do regional and neighbourhood due diligence.
- Consult experts.
- Be prepared for preparation.
- Get good financing.
- Stay in it for the long haul.

3

How Much Profit Can I Expect?

In this chapter, Ian answers a complex question—but one that gets less complicated with time and experience.

The short answer to the question posed in the chapter title is that you can reasonably expect anywhere from $5,000 to more than $100,000.

Yes, that is an incredibly broad range, I know, but that is the reality of this business. To be even more brutally honest: there is a good chance that you won't make any money at all on your first flip. Personally, I believe at least 80 per cent of people lose money on their first one.

The reality is that if you're expecting to make $50,000 or more on your first flip, then you might be unpleasantly surprised by the actual result.

Do I tell you this to discourage you? No! Exactly the opposite. In my opinion there are way too many people out there who believe that "positive thinking" is *all* it takes to be successful in this or any business. Don't get me wrong—I believe in mindset 100 per cent, but I believe that reality is where you have to start from. It's better to know what strengths and weaknesses you have from the very start rather than be armed only with the false and dangerous belief that a positive mindset will overcome all.

However, that shouldn't stop you from trying to create an excellent profit. All I'm saying is that $5,000 to $20,000 of profit should be considered a huge success on your first deal.

The Beauty of Wholesaling

I'm a firm believer in wholesaling fix-and-flip properties, especially in the early days when you're getting started in the business. Wholesaling is the process of finding a good flip type of property, getting it under contract, and immediately unloading it on another fix-and-flip investor. Wholesaling is a wonderful process for the fix and flipper, but how do you find these wholesale buyers? It might seem a little bit impossible if you're a newbie, but the truth is that there will never be a shortage of buyers for a great deal. So, your first concern should be finding a great deal.

But finding buyers is a serious concern. You don't want to be stuck with a property under contract and no buyers to take it off your hands when you're wholesaling a property.

The best way to ensure that never happens is to develop a list of potential buyers. So just go to the Yellow Pages and start copying out the names of reputable wholesale buyers. I'm just kidding, of course. No such list exists!

To find wholesale buyers, you need to be networked. Networking is one of the most important soft skills you need to develop as a fix-and-flip specialist. Being well networked will help you find great deals in addition to buyers for the deals you're trying to wholesale.

The Real Estate Investment Network (REIN), is the biggest and most famous place to learn from and network with other investors, some of whom are fix-and-flip investors. In addition to REIN, there are smaller, local real estate networking events that you can attend. You will have to do a little bit of research to find them, but they are a great source of local knowledge in addition to a great place to find wholesale buyers.

In addition, you will meet potential wholesale buyers through your professional team and in the course of doing business. Just as with finding deals, you always want to be alert to other people who may want to purchase a wholesale deal from you.

Wholesaling at the beginning (especially at the beginning) is a great idea for a couple of reasons:

Feedback

When you don't know what a good flip type of property is, you'll be so full of uncertainty that it will be difficult to ever get beyond analysis paralysis. So how do you learn? Well, you could employ a successful flipper to come along with you and go through the analysis with you. If you can find such a person to help you out, I recommend that you do it. The price that you pay him or her will be well worth it.

However, there is another way that can actually *make* you a profit rather than cost you. You can wholesale your deal to a successful house flipper. Since they know what kind of property works at what price, you will receive instant feedback from these experienced fix and flippers.

If you have a substantial list of potential buyers for your wholesale deals, you will know for certain how good a deal you have because if it's a hot deal, every flipper within a 100-kilometre radius will jump on it.

On the other hand, if none of the flippers with a track record want to buy the property, then you know your deal is no good. You've just received instant feedback, and it's the best kind of feedback because you know these businesspeople will be truthful. They won't buy it if they know it's a bad deal.

If you do happen to get a wholesale deal that the best flippers won't buy, then it's time to take it a step further. Ask them for further feedback. Ask them to share their reasoning and their numbers with you. Why is this property not a good opportunity?

There are gurus out there who will tell you that there are thousands upon thousands of excellent deals in any town on any given day. The reality is that there are more people out there looking for a good deal than there are good deals. That's not to say there aren't enough deals for everyone. There are. But finding the deals is one of the biggest skills you will need. Wholesaling gives you a brilliant opportunity to learn how to find deals.

Track Record

Before people are willing to write big cheques to you, they are going to ask a lot of questions. The first cheque for private money or for a joint venture will always be the most difficult one to get someone else to write.

The above statement is true *unless* you lose your investor's money on the first one. Word might travel fast in your circle if this happens. In such a case, the second cheque might be harder to get than the first.

But in most cases, the first is the hardest because you don't yet have a track record of success.

Remember when I told you that there is always more money out there looking for a good deal than there are good deals looking for money? Well, once you've experienced success at flipping, you'll find this to be true.

For me, I vastly prefer private money over joint ventures. I give my investors 10 per cent on their money for the duration of my flip projects (usually three months or less).

Their only problem with our arrangement now is that I'm not always putting their money to work—they don't like the down time between the completion of one fix and flip and the beginning of the next. They've gotten used to a 10 per cent return and they quite like it. They don't like putting their money back in the bank and earning less than inflation takes from them.

But it wasn't always this way. It took me a couple of years of massaging these relationships in order to get to where I am now.

So what's the difference between now and back then? It's the track record! My track record with my private money lenders is perfect. Every time they've lent me money, they've received their money back with 10 per cent interest, like clockwork.

The track record is part of the reason I like wholesaling so much. You see, when you're doing all the necessary steps of a fix and flipper on a given property, you're building a case at the same time. When your case is complete and solid, you can then take that case to an investor or private lender to show them how good the deal is.

But prior to having a track record, the case is nothing more than a projection. A projection is worthless in the eyes of many (unless they've seen it happen). That's what the track record brings you; it shows people exactly what *did* happen, not just what *could* happen if things go according to plan.

So when you wholesale a property, I recommend that you don't just take the money and run. Retain a vested interest in what happens with the property. Get to know the person who flips the house. Get to know him or her *really* well and find out the numbers. See where they succeed and where they fail.

Complete your entire case study on the property. Put it into a presentation and take that presentation to whoever will listen, especially potential money partners.

They will see how serious you are, and they will see that if they had loaned you the money, they would have profited nicely from the deal rather than some other flipper or investor.

This is how wholesaling can help you build a track record.

Risk Mitigation

Wholesaling means you're not spending money on renovation expenses. This reduces your risk at the beginning and gives you time to practise this most difficult aspect of fixing and flipping.

While you can expect much lower profits on a wholesale, you also eliminate the risk of a major loss, which is a legitimate concern at the beginning.

When you "sell" a wholesale deal, you're not actually selling the property, so you can avoid costly land transfer taxes and legal fees. What you're really selling to the wholesale buyer is the contract. Your job as a deal finder is to get a property under contract—a contract which you will then transfer to your wholesale buyer for a fee. This structure enables you to avoid the unnecessary expenses of a real estate sale when you're only looking to take a profit for finding the deal.

Let's put it this way: a profit—even if small—is better than a loss. This might be obvious, but if you're looking to hit a home run on your first one, you might have another thing coming. A small profit is a good aim on the first few because it allows you time to continue learning and growing.

The Reality of Profit Expectations

The reality of how much you can expect to profit (as I've said, between $5,000 and $100,000 on an average house) depends on some key factors:

- How much did you purchase the property for?
- What is the highest possible value or ceiling for the property?
- How much did you spend on the renovations?
- Did you flip it yourself or did you wholesale it?

These questions are very superficial, though. They don't give you the real answers that you need to truly get a handle on how much you can expect to profit. The details of the question as to how much you can expect to profit are what the rest of this book (and a whole pile of your own personal time) is about.

The deeper question of how to calculate the amount spent on renovations will deal with things such as:

- Who is doing the work?
- How much are you spending on materials?
- How good are you at finding deals?
- How good are you at negotiating deals?

For now, let's say that on your first few flips you should be happy with any profit, even if it's only a small one. After that, you can reasonably expect at least $30,000 for every flip that you do. If you're not making at least that much, it might not be worth your time because each flip might take you three months to complete. It's a big risk to put yourself out there flipping houses, so if you're not making at least more than most jobs will pay you, you might as well not do it.

4

How Much Money Do I Need to Get Started?

In this chapter, Mark begins to take a look at the financing aspects of fix and flips.

Do you think you have enough money to buy fix-and-flip properties? If you've never done a deal before, you might answer no. But if you've done one, or a few deals before, then you might understand what we mean when we say that there is more money in search of a good investment than there are good investments in search of money.

Think about it this way: people have a few choices when investing their money. One of the most common is to invest the "normal" way, through RRSPs and mutual funds, which are recommended by a financial planner. The big problem with this is that the returns are abysmal. In fact, in today's low-interest-rate environment, once you remove the fees of the financial planners, the returns are negligible.

One benefit of investing the "normal" way is that the consumer does not need to put a lot of time into researching and understanding a complex market.

A second benefit is that, because the money is invested broadly across a wide variety of sectors, the risk is considered minimal. There's a good chance that consumers won't lose money. They might not make any money, true, but the thinking is that they will at least *preserve* their wealth.

A third benefit is that it's a hands-off investment. Once the consumer puts his or her money in, his or her involvement is essentially limited to looking at a monthly statement (and muttering all the while that there's got to be a way to actually make money).

The fourth major benefit of investing the "normal" way is that the investment is quite liquid. It's fairly easy to convert the investment into cash if the investor should ever need to do so.

But many investors are dissatisfied, to say the least, with the "normal" way. The return just isn't there, and no amount of convenience, security, or liquidity can make up for the fact that many people relying on their investments are not making much money at all—and they're feeling the pinch. By inviting others to provide financing for your fix-and-flip projects, you are providing a solution to the problem of low returns.

If you know how to fix and flip for profit, and can do it in any market, your projects become an attractive alternative to the "normal" way of investing. When investors have proof that you know how to fix and flip for profit, and when they understand that they can have their money back quickly and safely, with a great return, without them lifting a finger or needing to do an ounce of research, you *will* have all the funds available to you that you'll ever need.

It's possible that you will even be able to get investor money on board on your first deal. I know of people who've done this. It is *much* easier, however, to raise investment money when you can show a track record.

By working backwards, it's impossible to ignore one major lesson: focus on how to get your *first* fix and flip successfully done, and the rest will worry about itself. It seems a little unrealistic, but you're just going to have to apply a bit of belief and faith on this one. *It's true* that money follows the deals and that there's an unlimited amount of money available for you to do your deals.

Financing the Purchase

You can look for money on your very first fix and flip, or you can use your own money. As mentioned, it's most likely you'll have to use your own money on your first one, and if you're using your own money, it's a fairly simple formula. You will need one or more of the following to finance the purchase:

1. A 20 per cent down payment
2. The ability to qualify for a mortgage
3. A line of credit
4. Cash

Obviously, the amount of cash is completely dependent on the property, what kind of deal you can negotiate, and where the property is located. Always know the neighbourhood and what a comparable property will sell for. We'll discuss this in much greater detail later in the book. The bottom line is that there is no exact answer for how much money you'll need to purchase a fix-and-flip property. The minimum you'll need, if you don't have a money partner who will bring cash, is 20 per cent of the purchase price.

Financing the Renovation

The same rule applies to renovation expenses as to purchasing the property. You can work with a money partner who would finance the entire value of the renovation. However, there's a good chance that you'll have to fund the renovations yourself on the first one or the first couple.

The amount you'll need to spend on a renovation is completely dependent on the property and the renovations that are needed. It's possible to do a fix and flip spending next to nothing; by the same token, you can easily spend more than $100,000 renovating a property and *still* make a tidy profit.

There are strategies and ways to buy all of your renovation materials on credit, so it's possible to do your renovation with no cash, but for our purposes right now, it's best to think of the renovation expense as a cash expenditure. To answer how much you'll need to get started, you have to consider paying for your renovation with cash. Reno expenses are covered in more detail elsewhere in this book, but a minimum guideline on a cosmetic flip is around $5,000, whereas a maximum guideline on a gut flip is $100,000 or more. Whether or not this fits your financial model will depend 100 per cent on how little you were able to pay for the property, and the property's market potential once renovations are completed.

"Fix and Flipper Makes a Small Fortune without Renovating"

Upon reading this headline, you might be thinking that the fix and flipper in question purchased a property in a hot market and quickly sold it for a substantial profit. While that kind of story is common in a hot market (for example: Alberta in the mid-2000s), it's not the subject of this story.

Fixing and flipping is different from speculation, and if your only plan for fixing and flipping is to sell into a strong market, then you're speculating. Fixing and flipping is about adding value by solving a problem.

I had a client once who figured out that value is added by solving a problem. My client bought in Toronto. The details were as follows:

Purchase price: $260,000

Length of project: 7 weeks

Exit strategy: Sale

Sale price: $335,000

Renovation expense: $1,000 (approximately)

If I were you, the first question I'd be asking is, "How did he manage to add $75,000 of value with only $1,000 of renovations?" The answer is that he didn't renovate, but he did solve a problem. Here was the scope of work:

- Rent eight garbage bins.
- Remove all garbage from the house.
- Remove destroyed drywall.
- Gut kitchen.
- Gut bathroom.

As soon as he'd cleaned the place up and *prepared* it for a renovation, he immediately put it back on the market. It sold in not too much time with a $75,000 lift.

My client could have spent $80,000 renovating the property and then sold it for closer to $470,000, which would have meant he'd have made well over $100,000 on the deal. He could have made more money, and he could have done more work. But at the time, he realized that taking more than $65,000 (after carrying and closing costs) away for seven weeks of work wasn't too bad.

I just love this story, because it perfectly illustrates how solving a problem is the way to add value to a property.

In this case, the lady who was living in the house prior to my client buying it was living like a squatter. There were no locks on the door. A family of racoons was in the attic, and, as a result, water was entering the house. There were holes in the ceiling as a result of the racoons and the water.

Solving the problem and adding value to this place was in finding the deal and in cleaning it up. There was a bunch more value to be added by renovating it, and the person who bought it from my client no doubt earned a tidy profit. My client took the following steps in creating a solution to the problem:

- Found a property that needed to be rehabilitated.

- Cleaned it up and prepared it for rehabilitation.

- Marketed the property to a renovator.

Of those three, finding the deal is probably the most valuable problem solved. No doubt the house ended up with a nice couple or family living there. They likely bought at market value or perhaps slightly above. The end user's problem was solved by my client. The renovator who continued the project and took a tidy profit found great value in what my client did. How else would the eventual renovator have found the property? Toronto is a big city, and the truth is that there are not a ton of deals around like the one he got.

Learn to solve problems and you may find that the amount of money you need to get started isn't as much as you might think.

Financing the Carrying and Closing Costs

The final major expense that you will have to come up with when you're doing a fix and flip is the carrying and closing costs. If you've purchased the property with a mortgage, you'll have to service the debt every month by making mortgage payments. If you're drawing from a line of credit, then you must make your minimum payment each month. If you've purchased the property with your own cash, then you will not have any additional cost while carrying the property.

Obviously, the carrying cost can be significant, but you really have to put it into perspective. If it takes you three months to complete the project, and your monthly mortgage payments are in the $1,500 range (for example), then you'll only be shelling out $4,500 to service the mortgage over the course of the project. Plan for that expense in advance and make sure you have the additional cash to take care of it along with the renovation expense and the purchasing expense.

The closing costs will vary depending on the deal, your lawyer's expense, realtor fees, and the big one: land transfer tax.

Unless you're doing deals in Alberta (the only province without a land transfer tax), you will have to pay a land transfer tax. The rates range from as low as 0.25 per cent to upwards of 2 per cent depending on the province and the city in which you're buying. This means that your deal has to be that much better. Never forget to calculate the land transfer tax into your numbers when you're running the numbers on your deal. It only has to be paid when you purchase a property, so it is not a concern to you as you sell a fix-and-flip deal. Never forget about it when buying, though.

The important thing to note is that it's another expense that you *will* have to come up with the cash for—according to banking regulations, it can't be factored into your mortgage.

Sample Carrying Costs – Three-Month Project

- Lawyer: $1,000 to $1,500

- Realtor (when selling): $10,000+

- Financing service (broad range: line of credit is lowest and private money is the highest): $2,000 to $10,000 (more if fixing and flipping a luxury home)

- Land transfer tax: (range: generally 0.25% to 2% of the sale price, but depending on province and city can exceed 3%)

So, How Much?

The actual amount of money you will need to come up with will be the combination of:

- down payment

- renovation expense

- carrying costs

- closing costs

If you've factored in those four items, then you will be able to make your own calculation based on your own deal. Keeping the costs down is part of the art of successful fixing and flipping.

Fix-and-Flip Profile: Cindy Wennerstrom

"Targeted Design" Yields Above-Market Rent on Slow Flips

How She Got Started

Cindy Wennerstrom didn't plan to have a career in real estate. As a fresh-faced university graduate, she took a corporate position in her home town of Sudbury, Ontario, with McCain Foods before being transferred to Toronto.

Her first position with McCain was in sales, a position that she held for nine years before spending her final two years with the company in marketing. McCain was good to Cindy, and she learned a great deal by working there.

Both her sales and marketing positions required skills that Cindy would need later on when she got into real estate. The corporate world of McCain turned out to be a wonderful proving ground for her. But, Cindy's greatest real estate asset was a little more latent than the practised skills of sales and marketing. She eventually learned that she had a talent for designing a property in such a way as to maximize its perceived value.

Today, she leverages that talent to great advantage (for herself, her investors, and her tenants/buyers). Cindy fetches excellent rental income and sales prices on any property she touches. With a deft touch, Cindy demonstrates the power of design, and why a well-designed fix and flip has many advantages in the marketplace over traditional buy-and-hold rentals.

But this golden touch didn't come immediately; it took Cindy a bit of time to round into her real estate sweet spot. Like most people, she bought homes for herself simply because she needed somewhere to live. Only after seeing the power of real estate ownership did she start to consider purchasing property purely for investment purposes.

It started for her back in her hometown of Sudbury, Ontario. She was only 24 years old when she purchased her first home there. When she agreed to take the transfer to Toronto, she had to sell her Sudbury home. She wanted to take the equity she'd built up and purchase a property in Toronto, but because she was moving from a relatively small market to the big city market, she faced high purchase prices and had to rent for a little over a year before she'd saved enough to buy.

While searching for her rental, she became aghast at how expensive it was to rent places that she thought were—for the most part—ugly and undesirable. She made a mental note of this fact, and moved on with life. After a year of renting, Cindy was able to get back into the ownership market and bought her first Toronto property, a condo. "Condos are usually the first step when people move to the city because they can't fathom spending the amount of money it costs to buy a house," says Cindy. She took the same tack, and at the time, she was happy to get into the market, a move that would prove very fruitful some years later when she was able to plug her accumulated equity back into investment properties.

She held that first condo for five years before selling and moving into her first house, a semi-detached home in a transitional neighbourhood. "I bought in Leslieville, which was an up-and-coming area at the time. Now it's arrived, but back then it was still transitioning," says Cindy, showing a penchant for choosing the right neighbourhood very early in her real estate journey. At that point she hadn't taken any training, but she did have an eye for what was desirable and in the ever-changing landscape of Toronto real estate, an up-and-coming neighbourhood can be a gold mine.

"When I realized that I now owned a $380,000 home, I decided that I'd better put a basement apartment in the property to help with the finances. The first tenant I had is still there today, six years later. It kind of inspired me to think, 'Hey, there are some great tenants out there,'" says Cindy. It was the piece of information that pushed her toward a future in investment real estate. Her great tenant, along with the memory of her own ordeal as a renter, helped the idea of quality rental properties coalesce in her mind.

"I'm single, and had only one income, so the decision was a little bit scary. But I knew I wanted to do it, so I started taking free courses first, and eventually I joined the Real Estate Investment Network (REIN). That decision catapulted me into understanding real estate as a business," says Cindy. By getting educated, her confidence to take action grew, and she was ready to take the first step.

Becoming an Investor

Cindy's grasp of the twin facets of a) adding value and b) transitional neighbourhoods served her well, as the home she bought became the springboard for focused investments. She'd added a basement suite and did attractive landscaping to her home, and in addition, the Toronto market was appreciating rapidly at the time. The sum effect of adding value, along with market appreciation (both in the region and in the neighbourhood), was that she was able to pull $150,000 of equity out of her home after the first year.

She used that money to purchase her first rental properties, and again two years after that her home had appreciated again and she purchased another one. She was off and running as a real estate investor. With the springboard of her personal residence providing the initial capital, and with her education through real-world experiences and REIN, Cindy's investment projects started to attract the attention of others who wanted to take part in the success she was creating.

She got more sophisticated as an investor. Before long Cindy was renovating, refinancing, and doing "slow flips." Through the combined experience of her previous properties and the real-world experience of being a tenant when she first moved to Toronto, Cindy developed what would be her bread-and-butter strategy, which can be described this way:

- She buys C properties in B neighbourhoods that are on their way to becoming A neighbourhoods.

- She adds a second suite and renovates to attract high-end tenants.

- She refinances, pulling most of the initial investment out.
- She holds the property for a period of time, capitalizing on strong cash flow (minimum $1,000) during the holding period and on above-market appreciation (due to gentrification).

Please note that nowhere in the above description does it say that she sells her properties immediately. The core attribute of a fix and flip is to remove cash soon, not sell the property (although selling may be part of it).

Key Design Elements to Create Demand

Cindy's unique gift in the fix-and-flip world is her ability to create incredible demand for her properties. How she does it might surprise you. She doesn't believe in expensive renovations, but she does believe in the right renovations. As previously mentioned, she seeks out transitional neighbourhoods, and by the time they're ready for the market, whether it be the rental market or the sale market, she is the proud owner of a highly sought-after property.

Choosing properties on this basis also has another result. The transitional neighbourhoods that Cindy is dealing in are often magnets for the professional crowd. "When I was renting a few years back, I realized that it would not take much to provide a higher quality of housing. I like clients who expect more but are also willing to pay more in return," says Cindy.

So she focuses her efforts on the high-demand transitional neighbourhoods that not only have a great appreciation upside, but also emotional significance for trendy city professionals. Cindy's mantra is: "If I wouldn't live in it, I won't rent it." Along with her philosophy of making her rentals highly attractive comes a simple renovation philosophy. "I am not someone who thinks renovations have to be super expensive to be powerful. I always operate on a budget and stick to the budget," says Cindy.

The Features

"The features I provide are ridiculously simple. I base my design philosophy on personal experience. I simply remembered what it was like to be a renter looking for an attractive home, and I provide what I wanted when I was a renter," says Cindy.

Cindy's strategy depends on the professional crowd. She likes to rent to professionals in the nicer up-and-coming areas of the city because she wants to capitalize on neighbourhood gentrification. Cindy becomes not just a bystander in the neighbourhood gentrification but also an active participant. Not only does she do her part to improve the neighbourhood, but at the same time she gives the professionals (who also want to participate) exactly what they want: a feeling that they're part of the cool and cutting-edge scene in the newly minted neighbourhood.

So what features does Cindy focus on to appeal to her target demographic?

Private Laundry

"When I do my laundry, I don't want to have to leave my place. I don't want to have to go down to the basement, and I definitely don't want to have to go to a laundromat," says Cindy. It's simple, really: if you want to attract a higher-end client, you have to provide what higher-end clients are looking for. Private laundry is a no-brainer. "How often do you see a man or woman in business attire at a laundromat? You just don't see it," says Cindy. "They want private laundry, so I provide it."

Separate Entrance

Cindy buys properties that she will be able to design in such a way that each suite has a separate entrance. "If there is a shared entrance, it immediately raises the question of who is going to clean and take care of the shared entrance. Also, when you have to share an entrance, it just doesn't feel like you have your own private place," says Cindy.

Lacking privacy diminishes the upscale feel of a property. It's especially a problem for professional women. A shared entrance just doesn't feel safe to many female renters. Not only is there the question of cleanliness, there's also the question of whether or not the other renter has guests, and who has a key to the shared entrance. A private entrance allows the tenant a level of security, knowing she or he has total control over the entrance.

One-Bedroom Basement Suites

In the more central, higher-density neighbourhoods of Toronto, where Cindy focuses her attention, space is often at a premium. As such, many basement units are configured as bachelor suites. Not Cindy's. "Typically, there is very little difference in the size of a bachelor and a one-bedroom. Almost every bachelor can be made into a one-bedroom," says Cindy.

The advantage of converting a bachelor basement suite into a one-bedroom is in desirability and rental income. In her target neighbourhoods, bachelor suites rent between $700 and $800 per month, but a one-bedroom basement suite can fetch $1,000. The difference is significant enough for Cindy to add the bedroom wherever possible.

"A lot of my basement suite tenants are older professionals who live in the distant suburbs or in cottage country. They stay in the city during the week and go back home for the weekends. They want an affordable suite, but they don't want to feel like they're living in a dingy basement while they're in the city," says Cindy. She makes her basements nice by adding a bedroom along with the other features mentioned.

Appliances

"A lot of my competition comes from the new condos that are going up everywhere, so I need to provide a modern and clean look. That's why I use stainless steel appliances in most of my units," says Cindy. By keeping a membership at Direct Buy, Cindy can purchase stainless steel appliances for a similar price that white appliances normally sell for.

The sleek and modern look of the stainless steel appliances adds another touch that Cindy's target clientele are looking for.

Dishwasher

"I try to put a dishwasher in every suite, no matter how small. All of my units have dishwashers. Some of them are small 18-inch dishwashers, but they all have one," says Cindy. Dishwashers are another comfort feature that people love to have and Cindy's target client demands.

Kitchen

As a rule, Cindy doesn't do custom features such as granite countertops, but from time to time she will if the property fits certain criteria. "If the neighbourhood is a B, but we're trying to attract an A-type client, we will sometimes put in granite countertops to pull them into the neighbourhood. It's a way to lure a high-end tenant into the neighbourhood even though they thought they didn't want to live there," says Cindy.

If she's trying to lure high-end tenants into a B neighbourhood, she'll also install a tile backsplash in the kitchen. Between the backsplash and the granite, she significantly elevates the desirability of her rental units.

Other than circumstances like that, Cindy doesn't install overly expensive kitchens. She is always cognizant that her renovations have to be done on a budget and still produce a positive cash flow when: 1) the renovation phase is complete; 2) the property has been refinanced; and 3) the property has been rented.

Range Hood/Fan plus Microwave

When tenants are walking through their future home, they like to see clean and uncluttered spaces. Most apartments in Cindy's target neighbourhoods are rather small, so a microwave on the counter tends to make the place look small and cluttered. Removing the microwave from the counter and putting it above the stove takes care of that problem. It's also nice to have some form of hood fan to keep the place free of cooking smells and smoke. This makes it easier to keep the place clean for the next tenant, should there be a turnover.

Lessons Learned from Cindy's Example

When employing a refinance-and-hold exit strategy, we have to consider the rentability of the long-term property. Cindy is a wonderful example of a real estate investor who focuses on her target with laser-like intensity. From the beginning of any fix-and-flip project, through the process of tenanting the property and then eventually selling it, Cindy keeps her end objective in mind. Cindy focuses—as you should—on the following:

- **Cash Flow**: Cindy's average cash flow on any property she owns is $1,000 plus per month. Since she's putting low-maintenance tenants (they're low maintenance because they don't damage the property and they very rarely miss rent day) in highly maintained properties, Cindy doesn't have to plug much of her cash flow back into ongoing maintenance. Over a 5-year (60-month) hold on a property, she will earn around $60,000 in cash flow alone.

- **Gentrification**: Cindy buys, renovates, and holds properties in specific neighbourhoods, in specific parts of Toronto. In an ever-growing and ever-changing city such as Toronto, there are new neighbourhoods gentrifying all the time. Cindy strategically buys in these neighbourhoods in order to profit from local market appreciation.

- **Tenants**: Cindy knows that she wants a certain kind of tenant for her certain kind of property in her certain neighbourhood.

- **Design**: Cindy knows that to attract strong rents and strong tenants, and in effect to play her part in gentrifying a neighbourhood, she has to add certain design features. She focuses on providing these features with minimal cost to herself, and in the end she walks away with all her objectives met.

We can all learn from Cindy about being focused. She knows her target clientele and keeps up to date on gentrifying neighbourhoods. In addition, she remains true to her targeted strategy.

Having this specific focus allows her to ignore all the noise, and deliver results.

5

How Long Does It Take to Put a Property on the Market?

In this chapter, Ian talks about the time commitment relative to the strategy.

How long does it take? The short answer is that a flip could take anywhere from one to four months. Of course, it's possible that a flip could take much longer than that, but your goal should be to keep it to a reasonable time frame. With such a broad range, it's difficult to accurately answer the question of how much time it might take. What we can say with certainty is that the amount of time it will take depends on the *number of renovations* that need to be done. The renovations themselves are the biggest factor, but there are other factors involved as well, most of which depend upon the fix and flipper's ability to organize and prepare.

Other major factors include *sub-trades*, *plans and permits*, and *execution of exit strategy*. While the *number of renovations* may be somewhat out of your control, the three secondary factors are largely within your control. More than anything else, your ability to manage the job and the plan is paramount to controlling the length of the project.

Regarding the *number of renovations* required, by preparing in advance, you will have figured this out before buying the property, so you should have a stable grasp of approximately how long your project will last.

The art of knowing how long a fix-and-flip project is going to take is something that a fix and flipper develops over time. Whenever I start a project, I can predict within a week how long the project will last, and I can't stress enough how valuable this ability is. You will get better at it over time, but I want to provide you with a basic framework that you can build upon.

There is a simple way to differentiate between two types of fix-and-flip projects, and while this line is often blurry, it is a useful distinction when speaking about flips and estimating the time from purchase to market. The two major types of flips are *cosmetic flips* and *gut flips*.

Cosmetic Flips

A cosmetic flip is a lot like it sounds. The fix-and-flip investor takes a property that is generally sound. By only needing to fix the things that give a property its character and look, the fix and flipper turns a property relatively soon, and gets it on the market with minimal carrying cost.

It's as though the fix and flipper is a makeup artist and/or fashion designer rather than a surgeon replacing vital organs. You're putting the renovation equivalent of lipstick, makeup, a pretty dress, and a nice pair of high heels on a property. What you're *not* doing on a cosmetic renovation is operating on the property. You're not opening the property up and making alterations to the internal organs (electrical/mechanical/plumbing/structural).

The typical renovations on a cosmetic job are basic paint, trim, flooring, kitchen, bathroom, fixtures, and some minor landscaping. None of these takes too much time in and of themselves, nor do they cost very much. And when you put them together, they still don't add up to too much money invested in renovations. Of course, cost is relative, and if you don't get a great "bang for your buck," the cost of renovating could be a total waste, even on a relatively cheap cosmetic flip. This goes back to the most important rule of fix and flips. You have to buy well.

Doing a small cosmetic flip is a valuable strategy to many, especially people just starting out, or people who are concerned that they don't have the experience or knowledge to do a bigger flip. In addition, cosmetic flips appeal to many because of the shorter time frame and more manageable financing possibilities (both of which we'll discuss in more detail later). I recommend doing cosmetic flips as a way to start out fixing and flipping properties. I did quite a few when I was new to the business, and I still do the odd one. It's simply less risky in terms of both time and money.

When you're searching out a cosmetic flip, the recipe looks like this:

- You are looking for a standard house in a standard neighbourhood (in my hometown and focus area, a standard house is worth about $300,000 after it's renovated).

- You will find it for about $40,000 to $50,000 below the after-repaired value (ARV). (Every dollar discount you get beyond that price is money in your pocket.)

- The house will need between $10,000 and $25,000 in renovations.

- When you sell it, you'll pay around $10,000 to $20,000 in agent and legal fees if you sell with an agent.

- Your net profit is between $5,000 and $15,000.

Again, the profits may not be mind-blowing on these types of properties, but what they lack in income, they make up for in simplicity and low risk. There is also less need for advanced project management skills when you're doing a cosmetic flip because you have to coordinate fewer sub-trades, submit fewer permits and plans, and the exit strategies are simpler.

Profit may also go up dramatically if you're a do-it-yourself fix and flipper. Whereas you may spend $15,000 to $25,000 by hiring trades and sub-trades, you may only spend $5,000 by doing all the work yourself. When doing it yourself, you're essentially investing more time for more profit. This is often looked down upon, but in certain circumstances it's not a bad idea. Trading time for money is exactly what people do when working in a job, so this concept might be a logical fit. I'm not saying you have to continue to do it the same way, but what I am saying is that you shouldn't discount the do-it-yourself method if you're suited to that style—and have the necessary skills, of course.

Sub-trade Management

On a cosmetic fix and flip, you'll only have to deal with a handful (at most) of *sub-trades*. This is why a cosmetic flip takes a lot less time. The orderly progression of sub-trades is one of the most important secondary factors to keeping your timeline in order, and when you're doing a cosmetic flip, there aren't too many to juggle.

The exact number of sub-trades needed will depend on how many individual jobs need to be done on that particular flip, and it also depends on how much work you're doing with your own hands. For good reason, a lot of people like to start off by doing much of the work themselves. Still, even if you're doing a good chunk of it yourself, there will likely be a need for sub-trades. These are the ones you might need when doing a cosmetic flip:

- painter
- finishing carpenter (trim, etc.)

- plumber (minor plumbing in kitchen and bathroom)

- flooring installer

- landscaper

- electrician (minor fixture installations and perhaps a bit of wiring in kitchen and bathrooms)

If you're doing much of the work yourself, you can pick and choose what jobs you want to use sub-trades for. The other option is you can hire a small general contractor. These are the guys who focus on the smaller jobs and are capable of handling the easier aspects of most of the different trades, but you wouldn't want to ask them to do the more difficult stuff on some renovations. A cosmetic renovation is tailor-made for this kind of contractor.

On a cosmetic job, you will never have the stampede of different specialists through the property that you will have on a *gut flip*. So not only do your project management skills not have to be as developed, but your timeframe can also be kept tight.

From the day you take possession of the property, it should take you between three and five weeks to renovate the property so it's ready to exit. An efficient crew of two or three should take approximately:

4–6 days to paint

1–3 days to landscape

4–6 days to install bathroom

4–6 days to install kitchen

2–4 days to do flooring

1–2 days to install fixtures

16–27 days total

Plans and Permits

Cosmetic flips also offer simplicity in the *plans and permits* process. In many cases, you can even do an entire cosmetic flip without needing *any* permits at all! This is true as long as you don't tear out certain items, such as the bathtub.

However, if you're doing any demolition or replacing key items such as the bathtub, you will need a couple of minor permits for plumbing and potentially electrical, if you're wiring in some new lighting. In any case, it does not take excessive planning to get the permits in place. Again, this is a benefit to the beginner.

Exit Strategy

One potential risk of the cosmetic flip comes during the *execution of the exit strategy*. Because the margins are not very large, a cosmetic flipper does not have much room to drop his or her price if the property doesn't sell quickly. This makes the timing of the flip important because small market factors can really affect your ability to exit the property via a sale, which is likely to be your preferred exit strategy.

When you're servicing a debt, the longer you hold a vacant property the more your profit is eroded. This means that holding a standard house for only two or three months could erase the cosmetic flipper's profit if the difference between input and sale price was small to begin with.

Multiple exit strategies are essential for the fix and flipper on the cosmetic flip because if you can't sell it with profit immediately, then you need to be able to quickly execute a strategy for loss minimization. This is an essential component of risk mitigation.

Buying right is also beyond compare in its importance to any deal. On a cosmetic flip, buying right is even more important than normal because if by chance the property doesn't sell at the price you thought it would to begin with, it's essential that you have the flexibility to drop the list price in order to sell quickly. Hanging on to a money pit will quickly drag you down, so having the flexibility to sell quickly through a price reduction is essential.

Conventional Financing

Cosmetic fix and flippers can often purchase a property with conventional financing. This means that they won't be servicing a high interest rate (as they would with private money), which is good. But, due to the typical numbers involved, it also means that they won't be able to refinance the property (due to lack of equity; with a small value lift, there is a small equity upside). If this is the case, your cash invested to renovate will remain sunk into the property while you hold.

Sometimes, if the cosmetic flip is outstanding, the property can be appraised by a professional appraiser and that newly appraised value can show that there's enough equity in the property to allow you to refinance with a higher mortgage but a low interest rate; you pull out the renovation cost from the new mortgage and pay off your suppliers and creditors, then keep the property as a rental. If this is possible it's an excellent strategy; it also means that the deal was likely outstanding (i.e., better than the "typical" guidelines I laid out above).

There are usually two, and sometimes three, possible exit strategies on a cosmetic flip. The flipper can: 1) sell; 2) refinance and rent; or 3) hold the property with the same financing used to purchase the property (and then rent it out). If the rental numbers work, this is not such a bad thing, especially if holding properties long term is already part of your goal. The downside is that much of your working capital (the cash used to renovate) will be tied up in the property.

Again, the amount of cash used to renovate is variable, and if you do most or all of the work yourself, you might not mind leaving that small amount in the property for the duration of the hold.

Cosmetic Flip – A Case Study

The truth is that I haven't done a lot of cosmetic flips lately. I did more when I was just starting out as a fix and flipper. Perhaps I'm a glutton for punishment, or perhaps I love the challenge of tearing things apart and rebuilding them, but I've done more gut flips lately. Certainly it has something to do with my contractor background too, as it feels natural to make a very large change to a property. I'm going back a little in time now to tell you about the best cosmetic flip I've ever done. Check out the details:

Property type: Semi-detached home

Renovations needed: Reconfigure kitchen, two bathrooms, repaint, fix holes in the walls, and do some minor electrical

Purchase price: $178,000 (using all private money at 10%)

Exit strategy: Refinance and rent

Timeline: Four weeks to complete renovation and refinance

Renovation cost: $30,000 (private money at 10%)

Appraised value: $248,000

Refinanced at 80% appraised value: $198,400

My costs after refinance: $9,600

Cash flow/month: $500

All in all, it was a good deal. I had to leave some cash in the property ($9,600), but the property generated significant cash flow and built strong equity quickly. It was financed at a good rate and in a neighbourhood with above-average rental properties and tenants.

Everything about it made sense, so I did it. The exit was better in my mind than a sale because the cash flow was strong on an excellent property. This is a very good cosmetic flip, and if you can do this type of property, I recommend you do it all day long.

Gut Flips

A *gut flip* is a more advanced proposition than a cosmetic flip. A gut flip takes a lot more time, there is a more aggressive capital outlay, there is more risk, there are more moving parts, and there is just a lot more of pretty much everything that is involved in a cosmetic flip. For these reasons, a gut flip will take a lot more time than a cosmetic flip. See the chart below for a breakdown of the main and secondary factors that make a gut flip longer than a cosmetic flip.

As with the example of the cosmetic flip, I'll use the model of the standard house in the standard neighbourhood. In my main flipping town of Whitby, Ontario, that "standard" property is an (approximately) $300,000 house and it's likely a 1,200-square-foot bungalow.

For a gut flip on this type of property, you can expect it to take anywhere between two and four months to complete and exit the property. Again, it is more than possible to go well longer than four months, but it is our job to try to keep the timeframe tight.

On a gut flip the *number of renovations* required will still be the largest factor in determining how long your project will take. The range here is incredibly broad. On any given job, you could be doing such things as adding a suite (if and only if it makes sense in the market you're in), redesigning the layout of one or more floors, adding bathrooms, restructuring kitchens, or any number of other renovations.

You may also be adding specialty features beyond just a standard renovation (again, if and only if they make sense).

At bare minimum, though, you'll be demolishing and rebuilding certain components of the property. What this likely means is that on our 1,200-square-foot bungalow, instead of buying $40,000 or so below the after-repaired value, you'll now be buying for close to lot value. (In my town of Whitby, that's around $200,000 or less.)

Where you might put $15,000 to $25,000 into renovating a cosmetic flip, you'll now have to put in somewhere between $40,000 and $60,000. Obviously more questions arise when we're speaking of this kind of property, questions such as "How am I going to finance that kind of flip?" and "What kind of property will I be looking for and where can I find it?" (These and many others are legitimate questions that we'll deal with in other sections of this book.)

For now, though, I just want to give you an idea of what a gut flip is and some of the numbers that might be associated with it.

The number of renovations required on a gut flip varies greatly from project to project, but they can be broken down into these approximate timeframes:

5–7 days for demolition

5–7 days for the roof

2–3 days for the windows

2–3 days for reconstructive framing/beams/drywall backing

3–5 days for electrical and plumbing (both trades in house at the same time)

3–4 days for insulation

2–4 days for drywalling

3–4 days for taping

3–5 days for trim/casing/quarter-round/door installation

4–6 days for all your flooring (including ceramics and shower surround)

2–4 days to paint the whole house

2–3 days for landscaping

4–5 days for touch-ups and general repairs

40–60 days total

Forty to 60 days is about two to three months. However, if the job has some special need, there is a good chance any number on the list above could end up taking longer than the timeframe listed here. What you see here is a standard example, though, and most of my gut flips fit into this framework.

You may also notice that certain jobs aren't in the list above. That's because some jobs are done alongside other jobs. This means that while it's an extra job and extra work, it doesn't actually take any extra time. The fix and flipper's ability (on any given job) to complete multiple jobs at the same time will play into how long each flip will take. I'm not asking you to multi-task, I'm asking to you stack tasks whenever possible. Wherever possible, whenever it makes sense, you'll have two different sub-trades working at the same time. This is only practical when the sub-trades are far away from each other and won't bump into each other.

As with the cosmetic flip, the *number of renovations* required is the largest determinant of time needed for a fix and flip. If any of the jobs above are unnecessary, the timeframe will be shorter, and if any of them are expanded, the timeframe will lengthen. It's a simple and predictable formula.

Sub-trade Management

The biggest of the secondary factors that will affect the length of a gut flip are *sub-trades*. As evidenced by the sample timeline above, there are often many different types of workers moving in and out of a property on a gut flip. Having them all work in an orderly progression and getting them all to do what you need, at the right time, is truly the art of house flipping. It takes a lot of effective relationship building with a great number of people to master this art.

The biggest risk factor with respect to sub-trades has to do with primary school math. It's called multiplication. If one of the sub-trades is late, then the next trade in the sequence will also be late. When jobsite organization is weak, it leads to multiple trades being just a little bit late, and when you multiply a little by a little, then do it a few times, the result is actually quite a lot. So $2 \times 2 = 4$. But when you multiply 4×2, you're up to 8, and $2 \times 8 = 16$. Like I said, it's a matter of simple math. The multiplication of "a little bit late" sub-trades quickly results in a very late project, and very late projects result in higher carrying costs, which is not a desired outcome.

Consider the same sample timeline from above when each of the sub-trades are "only" a couple of days late. Rather than 40 to 60 days, the project will take 66 to 84 days. This is a big change, and is potentially enough to ruin the profitability of the project. This may seem extreme, but many projects run exactly like this.

Take some time to think through the above example, adding two days to each sub-trade. It might not seem like that big a deal to you at first, but in reality, this is what happens to many fix and flippers on their first go-round. Whereas 60 days was your *maximum* time needed when sub-trades are well organized, now 66 days is your *minimum* timeframe.

This *does not* account for a major problem (for example: discovering a faulty sewage line), which happens from time to time. The example given only deals with time added to a project due to poor organization of the sub-trades. This is very tricky to do well, and it's the reason many people fail at fixing and flipping.

The other cost is in the relationships you have with your team. If you've scheduled a sub-trade two weeks in advance and then you have to call them a couple of days before they were supposed to start to tell them you're not ready, it will inevitably make them angry—and rightly so. You only have a few chances with the good ones. They will walk out on you or find a way to penalize you. Your job will be at the bottom of their list of priorities if you make them wait more than once.

Plans and Permits

Many plans and permits are required when doing gut flips. Along with your ability to organize and lead all the various sub-trades, this will be the other big test of your project management abilities. To do it well, you'll have to do advanced planning, have a solid relationship with your professional draftsman or designer, and have a solid relationship with the permit department at your local government.

After you've seen the property you are going to buy, you must envision what you ultimately want it to look like. I like to create my own plan on-site and then bring a draftsman to the site and explain my vision to him or her. From our discussion and the measurements we take together, my draftsman is able to create the drawings I need to take to the permit department when I apply for permits. The other option is to hire a designer to help you draw up a plan, and from that plan, you get the draftsman to make drawings.

In addition to the typical architectural drawings, you might also need to get an audit for heating and cooling loss, and you might need to hire an electrical engineer, depending on your particular project. Typically the drawings are first and foremost of the fix and flipper's concerns, and the permit department is second.

In my experience, it usually takes about two weeks from the day you give the draftsman the plans until the day you receive your drawings back. Once you receive your drawings, the process of getting permits is typically another two weeks, which means that you'll likely be waiting four weeks until you're allowed to start demolition on a gut flip.

Now, here's where your advance planning and negotiating skills come into play. I always push the seller very hard for access to the property prior to taking possession so that I can get all my permits *in place* on the exact day that I take possession of the property. I recommend that you do the same. This is an advanced step that will make a big difference to your timeline.

The day that I take possession of a property, I show up there at 7 a.m. with my crew. We put our garbage bin on the property, we set up our safety equipment, and we move in for demolition. There is no lag between possession and demolition. This may seem obvious, but many fix and flippers fail to prepare this way, and they end up waiting for demolition permits!

If you wait until you have possession of the property to start applying for permits, your project is immediately *four weeks* behind schedule. It takes two weeks to get your drawings and two weeks for the permits to arrive once the drawings have been submitted. This is too much time to wait for demolition when you're speaking about an eight- to 16-week project. Waiting an additional month is simply too significant a period of time for a fix and flipper.

It's unacceptable for another reason as well: I use private money for most of my deals, and I pay 10 per cent interest on the money I borrow. A little bit of math in my head is enough to realize that if I've borrowed $200,000, for instance, I've just wasted $1,667 on interest alone by not having my drawings and permits in place prior to possession day. Disorganization on this aspect of the project is a costly nuisance that I simply can't accept.

After you have your plans in place and you've received your permits, there is really only one way you can be held up by this process. That's if you change your plan and therefore need to get new permits. The odd time, you'll have to wait for inspectors, which is frustrating. Fix and flippers don't want their projects held up for anything, let alone red tape. But for the most part, inspectors get their job done when they need to. The most important thing you need to focus on as a fix and flipper is to have your preparation in place. If you're well organized, it drastically increases the chances that your inspectors will arrive when they're supposed to. Focus on your preparation and the inspectors usually fall into place.

Advance planning and sticking to your plan will enable you to go smoothly through the plans and permits phase of your project. So the onus is on you to stick with your plan, and call your inspector when he or she needs to be called. If you struggle with this, there's a chance that you will be held back by days, weeks, or months.

Execution of Exit Strategy

This is the final secondary factor (that we'll deal with) of doing a gut flip. It also can have an impact on how long a fix and flip will take.

One of the reasons I like gut flips over cosmetic flips is that I have more options when exiting the property. Typically, I use one of three exit strategies at the end of a gut flip:

1. Sell

2. Bring in a money partner and rent the property

3. Refinance and rent

Each of these has a similar element, namely, that I recoup all the money I initially invested. This is the essence of flipping—the fast return. When you buy and hold, your money is tied up at the beginning, and you might not be able to retrieve it for a while. Fixing and flipping is powerful because you're able to pull all or most of your money out very early in the project. This is true whether you sell, refinance, or bring in a money partner. Keep in mind that if you bring in a money partner, his or her money will be tied up for the duration of the hold.

I like to know my exit strategy about four weeks prior to the end of the renovation process. This is where your relationship with your real estate agent is all important. A good agent will be able to tell you the likelihood of moving (selling) the property and the price that you can expect to move it for in advance of your exit. You may determine that you don't want to sell the property, depending upon what your agent tells you. My most common exit strategy is to sell the property, but sometimes if the property is a slam-dunk big cash-flowing rental property, I will utilize one of the other strategies and keep the property as a rental.

Most of my gut flips sell immediately, often on the very first day, and almost always in the first week from the day the renovations are complete, and often in a multiple-offer scenario. The reason for this is simple: I buy the property at the right price, then I renovate with as little cash as humanly possible. The combination of buying right and renovating right means that I don't need to squeeze top dollar out of the property when it comes time to sell it. Think about it like this: you've just totally overhauled the property, and it's in a neighbourhood of similar properties for sale where none of the other ones are in the same kind of shape as the one you've just renovated. Assuming that each of the properties has similar exposure to buyers, the nicest one at the best price will always be the first one to go.

Not being too greedy is a key element here. I typically list my properties for sale at a reasonable price. I'm not one who tries to get well above market because I know there is a ceiling on what a certain type of property will fetch, in a certain market, in a certain neighbourhood. So, given that there's a strong demand for the type of property that I'm trying to sell (and I know there is because I've done neighbourhood due diligence), and given that I'm likely selling the very best property available at that time, and given that I'm not asking an unreasonable price, I know I'm likely to move my property immediately. As I've said, my properties usually sell very quickly.

If you do your renovations right, with the right pricing in place, you should not be held up on the execution of the selling exit strategy. But there will be those times when selling is not the best option and you have to employ another exit strategy.

If the cash flow numbers on the property are strong, it might make sense to hold it and rent it for a while. After all of the property expenses are paid, I like to have at least $500 left over. This is what I consider to be strong cash flow.

When holding a property after renovations, you can consider a couple of different ways to execute: a) you refinance and hold; or b) you bring in a money partner and hold.

Money Partner

If you choose to bring in an investor, you can be held up waiting if you haven't set up an investor in advance. It's paramount to have a money partner ready if this is your strategy. Luckily, there are more people with money looking for a really good deal than there are deals looking for money. But if you don't already have a network of potential investors, then you are at risk of getting stuck without a money partner.

More on Joint Ventures

Raising money for this type of joint venture is a big discussion. For additional discussion of raising money for your real estate investments, I recommend checking out the following website: http://revnyou.com, or another great book by Don R. Campbell and Russell Westcott: *Real Estate Joint Ventures: The Canadian Investor's Guide to Raising Money and Getting Deals Done* (John Wiley & Sons Canada, Ltd., 2011).

The way I get around this issue is by having a discussion with my private lenders in advance. Remember that I typically purchase and renovate a property with private money at a 10 per cent interest rate. Clearly, I can't afford to hold the property for a long time at that interest rate, so whatever my exit strategy is, I have to find a way to stop paying that 10 per cent.

Often, it's most intuitive to invite the private lender in as a long-term investor on the project. When private lenders lend me the money for the purchase and renovation of the property, they're already getting a good return on the money they lent me, and I make it clear that my intention is to sell and pay them back with interest, but we discuss in advance that there is also money to be made by holding and renting a property. In such a case, we can refinance the property, and my lender (who becomes my partner) will qualify for a mortgage. The money we draw out is 80 per cent of the appraised value of the property.

I don't employ this strategy unless I know that the mortgage amount will completely pay back my investors for their money invested.

On top of that, I'd never employ this strategy unless the cash flow was very strong (minimum $500 per month after all expenses) on the property in question. This is a very important point because the strong cash flow is the feature that sells my lender on becoming my partner.

Even after we put a mortgage on the property, the money partners will typically receive such strong cash flow that it's a better deal for them than any other investment they could make, so they're often more than happy to continue in partnership with me. Typically, I structure my continuing partnerships so that I take care of the management of the property and all profits and losses are split 50/50. But, partnerships can be structured in many different ways. We will discuss partnerships in greater depth later in the book.

Refinance and Hold

Sometimes I keep the property under my own name. In these circumstances I refinance and pull out 80 per cent of the appraised value of the property. Again, I always seek to have the mortgage completely pay out my private loan, and typically it will put some money in my pocket on top of what I have to pay back to my private lender.

The icing on the cake is the strong cash flow I receive while holding the property. This exit strategy works for a few reasons. First of all, it has to be a property that cash flows well, and in my area, which usually means it's a small multi-family building like a duplex or a triplex. If I'm flipping a straight-up single-family home, it usually doesn't make sense to refinance and hold, although in a pinch I can do it. I just don't expect much cash flow from a single-family refinance-and-hold situation. This strategy is more of an emergency measure with respect to a single-family home. The risk is that the property won't cash flow very well once the refinance is complete. But putting a low-interest-rate mortgage on the property and renting it is superior to keeping the private loan in place and losing my shirt every month.

Refinancing the property and holding it in my own name only works because I'm lucky enough that I'm able to qualify for financing on a typical property. This is because I've been able to pay my home mortgage down to almost nothing and my wife has an income. In between projects, we often juggle who is on title of our hold properties and sometimes we hold a property for only a little while before selling it. This gives us a greater chance to qualify quickly for a new mortgage if need be. As with most investors in residential real estate, there is a limit to how many mortgages my wife and I can carry at a time. I try to keep my portfolio in a position where I can qualify for a mortgage if I have to refinance and hold a flip instead of selling it.

If you aren't able to qualify for a mortgage on your own or with your spouse, then this strategy is out of bounds for you. What this means is that you have to ensure that one of the other strategies (or another solution) is available to you.

Have your exit strategies planned out and ready in advance. If this means having partners, then ensure you have partners in advance. If it means selling, then make sure you have enough of a spread that you can sell at a reasonable price for quick sale if needed. If it means refinancing and keeping the property, then make sure you have the wherewithal to qualify for financing on the property.

If you're buying the property with cash, then all the pressure is off, but you still don't want to keep your money tied up in the property. Therefore, exiting the property is still very important. If you're purchasing fix and flips with private money, the exit strategy is all important. Nothing will cause you more stress than holding a property while paying a high interest rate.

Not executing your exit strategy well can lengthen the amount of time you need for your fix and flip, and on top of that it can cause you a lot more grief, so don't get stuck holding the house. The purpose of fixing and flipping is to remove your money and move on to the next deal. This is true whether you continue to hold the property or not.

Gut Flip – A Case Study

I recently (spring 2011) fixed and flipped a house that illustrates what a gut flip is and what is required. It was a brand new house when we finished. Let's take a look at the details:

Neighbourhood: The Beach neighbourhood in Toronto

Property type: Two-storey single-family home

Purchase price: $220,000

Renovation expense: $100,000 (debt service, labour, materials, insurance)

Financing: Private money at 10% (purchase and renovation)

Timeframe: Three months

Major renovations: Complete gut, complete structural rebuild on rear of house, relocating staircase, all-new plumbing, heating, drywall, electrical, and insulation

Sale price: $433,000

Exit strategy execution: Sold with competing offers in one week (it only took that long because we didn't accept offers for the first week)

This was a stellar flip. My exit strategy on this one was limited to selling the property. I did have the backup exit strategy of holding and renting if I absolutely had to, but I knew there was no possible way that was going to happen. I knew it because I did my neighbourhood due diligence and my property due diligence. I knew that the Beach area in Toronto is one of the most sought-after neighbourhoods in the whole city.

There is a major shortage of nicely renovated properties in this neighbourhood, and no matter what the economy is doing, the demand from purchasers is high. The kind of people who buy in the Beach are people with stable, well-paying jobs, so I knew I could sell it.

If, on an outside chance, the property hadn't sold, it would have just carried as a rental (just). I didn't like my secondary exit strategy, but it would have sufficed in a pinch.

This gut flip was one of the biggest junkers I'd ever seen. There was literally a hole in the floor from many years' accumulation of dog urine. The stench was unbearable in the house, and we dealt with a picky neighbour when we were renovating. She gave us grief about everything (though you'd have thought she'd be happy we were cleaning up her neighbourhood).

I had to put my back into this flip, and in the end it paid off well. Gut flips like this don't come along very often, and I don't want you to get the idea that they're common. But if you stick to the process of searching, you'll find the odd one like this. When that day comes, relish it and be proud that you found a good deal and executed it well.

So, How Much Time?

I think you've seen from this chapter that there is no easy answer to that question, although within a broad range we can say that it will take anywhere between one and four months to complete a fix and flip.

On the negative side, it can take much longer if things are not organized or ready, but with practice, planning, and education, you can keep your timelines tight and finish your flip quickly, in an orderly way, and without too much drama.

6

What Skills Do I Need to Bring on Board for Fixing and Flipping?

In this chapter, Ian describes the skill sets required to undertake a fix and flip.

There is a common misconception about the skills required to do fix and flips. Prospective fix and flippers routinely limit themselves because they think they need to come into fixing and flipping with a certain background. Contractors think they can't do it because they're not sales experts. Sales experts think they can't do it because they don't have a contractor's level of expertise in renovations. Managers don't see how strongly their management experience will correlate to fixing and flipping. The truth is that whatever you bring into fixing and flipping can be a major advantage or a detriment. How you apply your talents is up to you. The key is to know your talents and use them to your advantage, while finding ways to outsource or work through your weaknesses.

When I was getting started in fix and flips, I had a strong background as a contractor. I was the "fix guy" in the fix-and-flip world.

As I will explain below, my co-author Mark was one of the biggest influences in helping me understand the financing aspect of fix and flips. To this day, I'm strong on the renovation end of a fix-and-flip project, but I'm now also very proficient at financing. Perhaps I'm not the most skilful financier in real estate, but I've found a system of private lenders and refinancing that works well for me.

I don't want you to be discouraged if you feel like you're missing a key piece of knowledge. There are people out there like Mark who can help you understand parts of the project that you aren't confident with, and you *will* get better.

Below, I will talk about some of the skill sets and professional backgrounds that people bring into fixing and flipping, and how they may be an advantage or disadvantage to you.

Skill Sets and Backgrounds

Contractors

A lot of contractors think that because they are contractors, they possess most of the necessary skills to do the business well, while others believe they "only" know how to renovate houses. I am a firm believer that contractors *do* come readily equipped with many of the necessary skills. In fact, I think it might be one of the best backgrounds to come from in order to do well at flipping.

But often the core skill set of contractors can also be a detriment, and here's why: many contractors have become excellent at selling themselves to clients, homeowners and other end users of the building and renovating jobs that contractors do. This can often involve expensive upselling and an emphasis on the most expensive materials and processes.

So the contractor skill set is an excellent one *if* the contractor who is doing flips can let go of this mentality and learn that every aspect of the fix portion of the project is subject to their own self-imposed budget. When you use expensive materials on your own fix-and-flip projects, there is no opportunity to charge a spread to anyone.

Contractors can be the best suited to fixing and flipping if they can resist the urge to over-renovate.

Managers

Just like contractors, I think people with strong management skills have a wonderful background to do fix and flips. However, many times people who come from a management background in a large company are not accustomed to all the on-the-fly changes that have to be made while fixing and flipping a house.

And if the manager in question has a weak background in the trades, it can be difficult to truly manage the trades he or she is employing.

If, as a good manager, you don't know that a $10,000 job can actually be done for $5,000, then all the skills or organization and tracking processes in the world can't help you.

You need the specific ability to make sure your trades are doing the job you need them to do.

This can be learned, but before learning comes awareness. So, if you have a strong management background, just be aware of where you might be a little bit lacking, specifically in renovation-specific management knowledge. Strengthen your knowledge of renovations costs and be ruthless in your application of budgets, and you will be able to maximize your management skill.

Sales/Deal-Making

As with contractors and managers, people with the sales gift have a huge advantage when they come into this business. A *large* part of the fix-and-flip business is finding and negotiating excellent deals, so having that ability going in is a wonderful asset.

There can also be a shadow side to the sales/deal-making ability. If sales is your strength and you only see the world of business through this lens, you might not be detail-oriented enough to be a true on-site taskmaster. You might also not be tight enough on your expenses and end up spending too much money. Both of these can sink your ship.

The same rule about awareness applies to salespeople. If your core skill set is sales and you lack detail orientation, you'll have to pay special attention to learning this skill or you'll need to take the advice and direction of others who do have that skill set.

Other Backgrounds

These examples are not exhaustive, but I wanted to give you a sense that your core skill set might be an advantage and it might be a detriment. Use this knowledge of yourself to your advantage and you will be further ahead as a fix and flipper.

If there is an aspect of fixing and flipping that makes you feel like a fish climbing a tree, then you would be well advised to find a way to partner with someone who has that skill, or outsource the tasks of that skill set. What you can never outsource, though, is the sense of direction that you, as the boss, must give the project. You must find the balance between utilizing the core skills of others and retaining the strategic direction of the project.

What Makes a Successful Flipper?

There are two kinds of skill sets: the first kind is hard skills, the skills you develop in a certain profession or education program; the second kind is soft skills, the attributes that allow you to adapt, learn, and grow. Let's call a spade a spade: starting anything new is difficult. There is an inevitable learning curve that the learner must navigate. Having the soft skills to change and adapt is highly valuable.

I've spent a *lot* of time asking myself the question: What makes a successful flipper? I ask myself this for many reasons.

First of all, I'm always trying to improve myself. If I see an area where I'm strong, I know that it will be a good idea to emphasize that skill in my daily work. If I see an area where I'm weak, I seek to either a) improve, or b) develop a relationship with someone who will strengthen me and my team where I'm weak.

Second, I have members of my team who are emerging flippers themselves. They started with me from square one, and with each passing year they get better and better at the game. Their goal is to be able to do their own flips one day, so we're always talking about how to improve at the various aspects of the business. I'm doing my best to teach them, so I think about the subject often.

I've narrowed it down to some key skills that I think are necessary in a house flipper.

The softer skills might take some time to grasp, and you might have to take some action in order to really see them at play.

Taking Advice (a.k.a. checking your ego at the door)

In some sense, this could be thought of as the master skill because it's a simple fact that you will never be a master at *every skill* needed to succeed at fixing and flipping.

Since you can't be an all-knowing master of everything, you're going to have to be able to take the advice and expertise of others, and you'll have to use that advice and expertise toward the tangible aspects of your project.

I wrote earlier about the image of the flipper as the independent man or woman. Well, in some respects this is true because (as I'll discuss below) you need to be self-directed in order to succeed. At the same time, you can't be bullheaded about your flip projects. You *will* need to accept and implement the advice of people who know things you do not, and who are experts in areas that you are not.

Here's the important thing about accepting advice, though: make sure the people you are accepting advice from have the *same interest* as you do. In other words, their interest has to be your profitability or your success. If an expert has a vested interest in your spending too much money, or in your job taking longer than you need it to, then you are seeking advice from the wrong expert. (See section on being self-directed below.)

How Taking Advice Helped My Business Grow

Sometimes I'm a pigheaded fool (just ask my wife). And I think sometimes that trait can actually help you in this business, especially if you apply it to the right things. For me it manifests itself in the fact that I don't take no for an answer. If someone tells me I can't do something, I dig in deeper and find a way to do it.

However, there is another side where being pigheaded is just foolish. When it comes to working within your skill set, you have to be able to accept the fact that someone else will often know better.

As I developed in the fix-and-flip business, I knew that I was good at finding deals, negotiation, and the renovations aspect. Likewise, I was excellent at systematizing processes from my days as a chef, and from the same training I was a capable taskmaster: I knew how to keep my guys working on the right things.

But I was horrible at the financing aspect, getting the money, and presenting deals to potential money partners. Without the addition of private money into my business, I'd probably be doing one flip every three years rather than three to six per year as I'm doing now.

So I found my friend, business partner, and co-author Mark. He is a master at selling a deal to a potential money partner, and he's a master at finding finance. He's a genuine numbers guru.

Mark truly taught me how to do all these things and many more. He taught me the power of teaming up with those who have different skill sets, and I've benefitted enormously from it.

But the only reason I was able to benefit from that relationship is because I was able to take advice. The truth is that it was pretty tough at the beginning, but I checked my ego at the door and I learned from a master.

Please do as I was able to do in this case. Take advice from others who know better than you—and watch your business thrive.

Practise Self-Reflection

This one ties in very closely with the one above (taking advice) because before you know who you should ask for advice, you have to be clear on what you're not good at and what you don't understand.

It's *very* important that you know what you *are* good at, and this takes self-reflection as well. However, it might be even *more* important to know what you are *not* good at because if you're good at something and you don't know it, you'll at least be doing it well, even if you're not aware of it.

However, if you're poor at something and you don't know you're bad at it, you will really be causing havoc because you'll continue to apply yourself to it in the delusion that it's a skill of yours. If you're aware that you're bad at it, you can find someone to take advice from or maybe even outsource it completely.

A great example is the above story, about how Mark helped teach me to finance deals. Before that, I was banging my head against the wall somewhat. Though I had all the desire in the world to do deals, I was limited by my lack of financing options. Luckily, I was aware through self-reflection that I was missing something, and I managed to swallow my pride and allow myself to learn from Mark. I didn't completely outsource this portion of the fix and flip, but I did manage to learn it well enough to become proficient at it.

I just said that it's more important to know what you're bad at than what you're good at. I believe this to be true, but it is still very important to know what you're good at because when you do know, you can apply yourself to your genius skill set more often. When you do this and at the same time outsource your weaknesses, you will truly see results in your business.

Self-reflection is the way to figure out honestly what you're good at; sadly, many people don't know. People are not always correct in their own assessments of themselves and their skill sets, and if you have a really difficult time figuring this out, I recommend you do some kind of skills assessment and then really reflect on it. Figure out how that skills assessment might relate to fixing and flipping.[1]

---

[1] There are many such skills assessment programs available. Personality profiling such as Myers-Briggs can also be very useful. Practising meditation is another way to develop self-reflective capabilities, and group or individual mentoring may help you gain the skills of self-reflection. This is a fix-and-flip book so I can't go into too much detail on this topic, but it's worth mentioning that improving oneself from the inside helps to improve one's external circumstances. Develop the ability to self-reflect, and above all know yourself.

At the very least, you will gain some awareness of what your strengths are and you can apply this knowledge toward your flips.

Although the skill we're discussing here is self-reflection, there is nothing wrong with using the help of professionals to boost your ability to reflect on your skills.

Develop People and Project Management Skills

One of the biggest misconceptions people seem to have about flipping is that it's somehow different than any other business. They think of it as a fun and informal game where anything goes.

The reality is that your project sites have to be very well organized. This doesn't mean you can't have fun. My guys and I have fun every day on the jobsite. But I do not sacrifice organization and project management in favour of fun.

What this all means is that your on-site organization and management will be one of your keys to success or failure.

In what you read below, I will be talking all about team and the importance of keeping team morale high. If you're planning on doing the entire project on your own, just pretend that I'm talking about keeping your own morale high. Whatever I recommend that you do for your team, you should also do for yourself.

First and foremost you (or someone you partner with or hire) *must* be an outstanding project manager. I'll flat out say it on this one: if you or someone you're working with isn't excellent at this, you will not be able to succeed.

Project management—in my eyes—is largely the implementation of people skills. For example, when I walk onto a jobsite, and I look around at all the people who may be working there that day, I can tell how the morale on the jobsite is at that moment.

Without a high level of morale on the site, every project will suffer. Without morale, there is no production. On all the jobs I've run, I find that this one aspect is of the utmost importance. So, as the project manager, it is my job to ensure morale is high. Now don't misunderstand me here, I'm not talking about cheerleading. Being a cheerleader is only a short-term solution at best; it will not carry the team forward in terms of morale.

The job of keeping morale high is more a matter of understanding what the crew is going through. In other words, to be able to truly keep morale high on your project sites, you have to be able to have empathy for the workers. You have to understand that they're more than just workers. They are people who have higher dreams and aspirations than to just do your bidding. In my opinion, the way of treating employees like machines or robots is fading quickly into the past, if it hasn't done so already.

If you have compassion for what your team is going through, then you're more likely to do certain things for them. First, you'll show them appreciation. Here's the trick to this one: there is no trick. If you truly feel appreciation for them, then you'll show appreciation to them.

They're intelligent people, and they'll know if you're buttering them up, which is the kind of false appreciation that—I believe—too many people show. What I mean is that too many managers have heard somewhere that they should do something for workers in order to show appreciation, so they do it.

And then there's true appreciation. That's when you truly feel compassion for what other people are going through, and you realize that they're working on your behalf. This arouses a genuine feeling of appreciation, so you show that appreciation. The team will know if it's real by your eyes and by the expression on your face, so don't try to fake it.

Showing appreciation is an important way to boost morale. To show my appreciation, I always try to do something for my team that I know they like and appreciate. My team likes having barbecues and beer on Friday afternoons, so from time to time we'll do that. There are a million ways you can show appreciation, and I encourage you to find your own ways, but please only do it if you feel genuine appreciation.

Another thing you might do if you truly understand what your team is going through (and you want to keep morale high) is that you will do everything in your power to put your team in a winning situation.

Let's be honest here: when you ask a crew of men and women to help you complete a fix and flip, there is a lot at stake. It's not quite the same as a typical nine-to-five job that each member of your team might have had before they started with you. Although time and budget constraints are very important on each type of worksite, I would say both considerations are more important on a flip site than on others. The reason for this is simple: flips are never consistent from one to the next, so you're often faced with finding creative solutions to complex problems.

Imagine that a worker on your fix-and-flip project was a framer for a large homebuilder before he or she joined your team. Every day was basically the same for the worker before. He or she had to frame up houses with the same materials and typically the same designs every day.

Now the worker shows up working for you, and you're asking him or her to do different tasks with different materials every day, and often the worker has to be creative about how he or she does it. Your team members can't spend too much time or money on anything they do for you, and they still have to adhere to the highest quality standards.

So, as a fix and flipper, you are asking your people to be super-employees. In fact, this line of work is so different from a typical job that I hesitate to call them employees at all.

Since you ask that much of these people, you have to set them up for success in order to keep their morale high. You have to show them every day that you're there to support them. They need to know that you will have what they need there for them *when they need it* and that your plans and preparations will enable them to perform what you ask of them.

There is another thing you might do to keep morale high. If you truly understand what your team is going through, you might consider their future in a positive light. What this means is that not only are you looking to get the immediate result of completing your project out of your team, but you also understand that your position is perfectly suited to help your team grow into their future dreams.

Some of your team members might want to actually learn special skills and strategies from you. Fixing and flipping a house is a special thing, and the fact that you're doing it will impress the people on your team.

Doing whatever you can to help them learn about something that will be beneficial to them down the road is one of the most important actions you can take to keep morale high on your jobsites.

Your people skills and project management skills (or those of a partner or employee) will be some of your most necessary skills in order to be successful at this business.

Pit-Bull Detective (Building a Case Like a Dog with a Bone)

On a recent flip project I had the opportunity to turn an illegal duplex into a legal triplex. (See the rest of the story below under the section "Being Flexible.") I went ahead with the necessary renovations in spite of the fact that I don't know at the time of this writing whether I'll actually get the approval to make it a legal triplex.

> But I'm very confident that I will get the approval because—like a dog with a bone—I've been all over this one. I've learned the rules that the city has for the legalities of suites, and I know how to pass inspections.
>
> There's a chance they'll give me grief on this triplex idea, so I've gone ahead and taken some proactive steps to ensure that I get my approval. Here's what I did:
>
> - I printed off a map of the area, and I went around looking at each building to see if they were being used as triplexes or duplexes or singles.
> - When I had that information, I called the city and checked on the status of each building to see what it was zoned as.
> - Then I highlighted and made notes of each property, the lot size, the zoning, and how they were being used.
> - I took the map to a local Staples store and got them to blow up the map and laminate it.
>
> Now, if I have any difficulties in getting my third suite approved, I've built a very solid case. I can go before town council if I have to, armed with direct knowledge of all the illegal suites in the area. I can show them that I have brought my property up to their standard, and I have the inspections to prove it (see rest of story below).
>
> I've used all the city's rules to make a legal suite, and they can't possibly say no to it, but it's only because I'm the pit-bull detective, and I built up a case like a dog with a bone.

Multi-tasking, Being a Taskmaster, Dissecting Problems into Parts, and Being Practical

Okay, this category is a hodgepodge of skills that could potentially all be thrown under the previous skill set of *project management and people skills*. But they're worth mentioning separately because they're critical skill sets when you start working with a team.

The same disclaimer stands here as well, though: even if you don't have a team, understand that you'll have to apply these skills to yourself.

Multi-tasking

I know multi-tasking is considered inefficient by many because multi-tasking can reduce your effectiveness at any one task. So perhaps you want to call it juggling many tasks, knowing that you'll be giving each task your complete focus during the time that you spend on it.

It doesn't really matter what we call it, because the truth is out there: go ahead and ask any fix and flipper if they have a lot on their plate for the duration of their flips. The point here is that a necessary skill for flippers is to be able to handle the fact that many things are going on at once for the duration of the project. You'll have to figure out some system for keeping everything running smoothly.

As a job is ongoing, I'm always considering the entire job. I'm better at this now than I was before. I used to work *in* the project, and now I work *on* the project. But the thing to remember is that you have to keep your eye on the bigger picture. Even if it's you alone doing the work, you can't let small problems pile up.

A good example is that whenever there is a project ongoing, I always keep a roll of green painter's tape and a felt pen on me. When I bring in a sub-contractor to do a job, and I find that there are deficiencies in his or her work, I know that I'm better off to tag it with the green tape and label the sub-contractor's instructions on it immediately. It's always wise to have sub-contractors repair their deficiencies on the spot. This works better than trying to get them to come back.

I utilize the green tape trick as common practice and I estimate that it saves me at least $1,000 and one work day per project. It saves me because my own in-house crew doesn't have to spend their hours on the repairs, and we aren't held up waiting for sub-contractors to return.

This is the kind of multi-tasking I recommend; it's as though you're keeping your eye on the bigger picture, and the small tasks that make up that bigger picture, all at the same time.

Being a Taskmaster

The idea of being a taskmaster might sound kind of like being a schoolmarm to you, but if you look at it in perspective with the previous conversation about keeping morale high on your jobsites, then you know the connection I'm trying to make. In other words, yes, you need to use those essential skills to keep your morale (and everyone else's) high on a project site, but you can never do this at the expense of keeping everyone on task.

It's true that the more holistic your strategy for managing and leading your project, the more likely you and your team will be self-motivated. But if there is ever a lull or a lack of direction on a jobsite, you have to think about the immediate goal of getting the darn job done!

So being a taskmaster is important.

Breaking Problems into Parts

If you can't segment problems into parts you'll likely be overwhelmed on a fix-and-flip project. As mentioned above, there are a lot of moving parts when the project gets going. Trying to attack everything all at once is a certain recipe for failure. Learn to break it down into many small chunks.

Being Practical

Being practical means having a real-world understanding of what is needed in a flip project. I have a favourite saying. It goes like this: "I used to be a perfectionist, but now I only do what makes perfect sense."

This was critical for me in shifting my mindset from the idea that my jobs had to be the "best," to the understanding that they had to be the best fix and flips. It's not always practical on a fix and flip to try making your project the "best."

It makes sense to be a perfectionist seeking the "best" in certain realms, but as a flipper, you have to do what is most practical, and it's definitely not always going to be the same thing as what you once thought it was.

Practise thinking about and developing your skill of practicality, because it will enable your ability to be self-directed (see below) in the business of fixing and flipping houses. Without first knowing what is practical, it will be a struggle to know where to apply your best efforts and it will be all too easy to overspend money and time.

Being Self-Directed

What does it mean to be self-directed? Well, it could mean a million different things to a million different people. But in this circumstance, it means not being easily swayed by the opinions of others.

Let's face it: we're bombarded by a million images every day in advertising. Beyond that, everyone we know (the most influential people to us) has their own opinions. On top of that, when we're flipping houses, we spend a lot of time dealing with professional tradespeople. These are people—often with years and decades of experience—whose willpower is strong and whose personalities are forceful.

When it comes to the *advertising industry*, and by extension the reality TV show industry, we must remain steadfast in the face of their influence. Everywhere you look, you will be bombarded by messages telling you to spend money where it's not necessary for a flip. And the extension of that is in all of the salespeople, contractors in your circle, and friends and family who consume the information they're fed by the twin industries of advertising and reality TV.

Being self-directed in this case means you're not going to demolish your own plan and your own chance at profitability for what is fashionable in the public eye.

When we're speaking about *friends and family* as a separate group, you have to consider how influential they are on you. It is truly remarkable what people will do to remain "normal" in the eyes of their current peers. Changing your group is difficult, and no matter what we want to believe, each and every group that we're a part of has its own standards and what it considers normal.

Chances are, if you've been at the same profession for the past many years and everyone you know thinks of you as *that* profession, then your friends and family are going to be a little bit shocked when you start telling them that you're spending your weekends learning about flips and your downtime after work running materials to the jobsite.

There are thousands of reasons for this, and I honestly could write a whole other book about how this has happened in my own life. The cool thing is that there are going to be those friends and family members who will support you no matter what. Cherish those people, because they are the real supporters you have.

There are a million ways in which being self-directed is necessary to do well at this business, but the last major one I want to mention here is the skill of being self-directed in the face of *professional tradespeople*. This can be the most difficult of the three I'm mentioning here, because you will sometimes have to disagree with their view and stand firm.

They truly do know what they're doing, and I'm not trying to argue otherwise. But what they don't always understand is that their suggestion for how to do a certain job is not necessarily the best solution for your particular situation on the particular fix and flip that you're working on.

On a recent flip, I was faced squarely with this problem. I brought in my electrical team to go over the electrical work that needed to be done. Things got a little bit heated when we disagreed about what needed to be done. In fact, my regular day-to-day crew was getting a little bit concerned with how intense the conversation was getting.

What it boiled down to, though, was that my electricians were trying to dictate to me the way in which the job was to be done. They claimed that a whole section of the house had to be rewired in order for the entire electrical system in the house to work properly.

Now, I don't doubt that on most jobs the customer would agree with them and do the extra work "just in case." But I had done a good job of inspecting and scoping the electrical system out, and in my heart and in my mind, I knew that it did not have to be done the way they were telling me.

What it eventually came down to was that I had to challenge the electricians by telling them that I'd give each of them $20 if I was wrong. So we hooked up a generator to test whether the other section of the house was properly wired or not.

A huge smile crossed my face when we tested the outlets and lights in the section of the house under question and (unsurprisingly to me) found that they worked.

Now, you may think this was just a case of chest-puffing by a bunch of guys around a jobsite, but the reality is that the stakes were high: if I had been swayed by these highly professional tradespeople, I would have ended up spending $5,000 more than I needed to. That five grand was a major portion of my profit, and there are dozens of chances to spend that extra unnecessary money or save it on each and every fix and flip.

If you're self-directed in the face of these multiple voices, you will have a much better chance of success on your flip projects.

When it comes to fixing and flipping, this means that we don't do renovations that the advertising and reality TV industry tell us we have to do. It means that we know for ourselves what renovations need to be done to make a fix and flip successful.

Being self-directed means that just because our friends tell us that we should get a "real" job, we don't have to quit. It means that when Joe Blow from down the street tells you that adding a granite countertop to your fix and flip will add value, you don't need to listen to him.

And being self-directed means that when standing before intelligent and forceful professional tradespeople, we will have the fortitude to stick to our guns when we need to.

By fixing and flipping, you'll be going against the grain. You won't find many friends who will understand and support what you do, especially in the beginning, so practise the art of being self-directed when you need to.

The Wisdom to Know the Difference

I've spoken about being self-directed and I've also spoken about being able to take advice.

While it would seem that these two skill sets are at odds with each other in some circumstances, the reality is that you must know the difference and when to apply one or the other.

Knowing when to take advice and when to be self-directed will depend greatly on *who* is giving you the advice. If the advice giver is someone whose end goal is in line with yours and if you trust them, and if they're better informed than you in a specific area, then you would be wise to take the advice.

On the other hand, if it's someone whose goal is different, or who can still benefit even if you lose, then you'd be wise to practise self-direction.

In the case of the hard-headed electricians, I knew that their business interest was to upsell me on a much more expensive job. I don't hold it against them. This is simply business. Every professional worth his or her salt is trying to apply the highest standard in his or her industry and profit from it. I knew that and had to stick to my guns in order to avoid spending an unnecessary $5,000.

Dealing with Rejection

This one might be considered a relative of *being self-directed*. It's a simple fact that as you move forward in this business, you will have to deal with rejection on many fronts. Nowhere is this more obvious than in your search for a suitable property, though.

I always say that a good test is to go knock on 50 doors of ugly houses and tell people that you want to buy their house. Ask if you can see each one of them and tell the owner you will write an offer if you like what you see.

If, after doing this 50 times, you still feel like being a house flipper, then you might be well on your way. The reason I say this is because you will experience some serious rejection during those 50 house visits! People will often not trust your motives. Let's be honest, this is like a cold call. Often people have no intention of selling, and they let you know in no uncertain terms. When a house looks ugly enough that you might think it's a fix-and-flip candidate by seeing it from the street, you know it's a truly ugly house. Ask yourself this: what kind of person lets their house go that far? Often it's people who are dealing with other personal issues. They might be reclusive, shy, or untrusting of anyone. On the other hand, when they're ready to sell, you'll be like a beacon of shining light for them. They will be very receptive if you can solve their problem for them.

Looking for properties might be the most obvious way in which you'll have to deal with rejection, but it will not be the only way.

In many ways you're standing on an island alone when you're a house flipper. At times it's a lonely feeling. There are a few reasons for this: as mentioned before, your friends and relatives will have a hard time understanding you. When you first start, they will think you're crazy, but when you keep doing it they will assume you're some kind of multi-millionaire.

They will not necessarily understand that you're out there working your butt off like anyone else. This is true at the beginning when you start, and remains true further down the road when you've met with some success.

So you will have to become accustomed to feeling rejected by your friends and family as well as by potential house sellers. Please note that I'm not lumping all friends and family into one pile. No doubt you will meet with some supporters, and that's fantastic. But my experience is that there are more than a few disbelievers among the family and friend circles of fix and flippers.

Rejection is not for the faint of heart; it can be very difficult to deal with, not only when you're starting out, but every time you have to deal with it, even as an experienced fix and flipper.

Rejection is a fact of life, but it serves a very important function. If you use it correctly, it can steel your resolve and help make you better at what you're aiming to accomplish in the fixing-and-flipping business.

Being Flexible

Now, this one is a bit tricky, so I want you to treat this with great caution. First of all, let me state that I am a firm believer in having a strict job plan and a very detailed scope of work. Whenever possible, I stick to my plan in spite of any distractions—and there are a lot of distractions. But there will be times when you can profit greatly by being flexible. Let me give you an example.

As I'm writing this, I'm also working on a flip in my home town of Whitby, Ontario. I purchased a former grow-op house and am doing a large renovation. The interesting thing is that it's not one of the more difficult flips we've done, and we aren't even gutting the entire place (which we often have to do).

Because the house had been used as a grow op, we were required to get air tests done. When we got the air tests back, the property passed the standard. At the time we purchased it, it was an illegal duplex, so it needed some upgrades to make it a legal duplex. The kitchens for both suites were in place, the bathrooms for both suites were in place, the windows, roof, and walls were in place. There was a lot in place, and I knew it was a good deal.

All we really had to do to make it a legal duplex was install fire-rated walls, interconnected smoke alarms, and add two fire doors. On top of that, we decided to add separate wiring and meters to each unit. It wasn't necessary, but I thought it would add value.

So that was my plan, and it was a great plan. Then the inspector said I had to insulate and add fire-rated drywall to the ceiling of the basement, which in my original plan we weren't going to finish. Our idea was to market the house with the basement as a potential third suite, and any investor (potential buyer) down the road would love the third suite.

Once the inspector told us that we had to make those modifications to the basement, I started thinking (and here's where the flexibility comes into play), "If I have to drywall the basement anyway, why don't I add the wiring and a third meter for the third suite?"

So that's exactly what I did, and I'm now waiting for the inspections that will approve the third suite.

You might be thinking that I wasted all that money having the basement wired and plumbed for a bathroom, even before I knew the third suite would be approved, but here's the thing: I estimate that having a legal third suite will add $60,000 to my final appraised value on the property. If the suite doesn't get immediate approval, then I have a basement with a wet bar and another bathroom. Even if the third suite isn't approved, I still believe that the property will appraise at $30,000 more, and I have market knowledge to support that belief.

The extra work in the basement cost me $25,000 total. In the worst-case scenario, I've added a $5,000 value to the positive side of the ledger ($30,000 value lift for $25,000 renovation expense). However, in the best-case scenario, I've added an extra $35,000 in value ($60,000 value lift for $25,000 renovation expense).

The only reason I was able to pull this off was because I was flexible. This also ties back into what I was speaking about earlier as to the difference between a fix and flipper and a speculator. On this property I have multiple exit strategies. Right now I haven't decided what I'm going to do with this property. I may sell it, and I'm confident that I'll get the appraisal I'm looking for (when the bank appraises it during refinance) and the price I need to make the basement renovation worthwhile if I do that.

But this property is such a great deal as a long-term hold investment, that I might utilize another exit strategy, something I call a long-term flip. In this case, I will refinance the property for 80 per cent of the appraised value. With that money I will pay *all* expenses that I incurred on the project *and* take some cash home. Then I will rent the place out and it will cash flow around $800 per month (if I end up with a duplex), and potentially $1,500 (if I get the triplex approved).

Again, I want you to be careful with this one. Typically, it's better that you stick to a plan until the end, but sometimes an opportunity like this will come up. Let's be honest, some people make $35,000 in an entire year, and I may have just made it in a couple of weeks because I knew when to be flexible.

What Does It All Mean?

There are many skills needed to do well in the fixing-and-flipping game. Obviously, your need for each of these skills is going to vary with any given project that you're doing.

What I mean by that is your skill will have to go up if you want to fix and flip more intensively. If you're only doing one property, and your timeline is longer, and you're doing the work yourself, and you have a low-interest-rate loan on the property, and the number of renovations needed is low, then you won't have to draw on as many of these skills as you would if you were doing multiple projects with multiple team members, etc.

Fix-and-Flip Profile: Wade Graham

Buy-and-Hold Expert Uses Fix-and-Flip Strategy to Supplement Portfolio

How He Got Started

Wade Graham didn't start real estate investing with big intentions. He was working in the computer science field and living in Calgary in 2001 when his contract came to an end.

With the immediate aftermath of the 9/11 terrorist attacks affecting the economy, Wade was having some difficulty finding another contract. When an opportunity arose to work in another town, he had some decisions to make. Wade explains his predicament this way: "I ended up elatedly moving to Banff. It was a dream come true for me. Sometimes, when things go wrong, you end up looking back—and it was a gift."

Having a love of climbing and skiing, Wade couldn't have been happier to land a job as a network engineer for a heli-skiing company. "Along the way," he says, "I got to ski my brains out."

While his new job brought him to the town of his dreams, among the mountains he loved, Wade now had to make a decision about the condo he owned in Calgary. "The market was soft and I didn't want to sell it, so I became a landlord. But I found myself in a situation that a lot of people do: I didn't know how to landlord, and I made a lot of mistakes," says Wade.

Rather than throw his hands in the air at the frustrations of being a landlord, Wade decided to get some education and learn how to do it right. He joined REIN (the Real Estate Investment Network) and read a lot of books in order to improve his skills as a landlord and investor.

After starting his basic education as a landlord and investor, Wade learned the practical side of the craft with his Calgary condominium. From the day he became a landlord until the day he purchased his next rental property, four years passed. Wade is a testament to the power of small, incremental steps over time. He's now known Canada-wide as an investor, and he's in constant demand for speaking engagements and media interviews. Wade's detail-oriented approach brought him from wannabe landlord to full-time investor in only a few short years.

After holding his first condo for a period of four years, Wade recognized that he had earned a solid appreciation on the property, so he decided to sell the condo and put the money back into real estate investments. With the cash he pulled out from the sale, Wade went back into the market and bought four more properties. "We bought a few more condos, some pre-construction condos, and did pretty well on some of them, and didn't do too well on some of the others," says Wade.

Ultimately, as most investors do, Wade ran out of his own money, "So then you're in the world of joint ventures," says Wade. "We started talking to a few people who wanted to play along, and that's how we brought in joint venture investors."

Becoming a Full-Time Investor

Soon Wade was attracting a lot of money for joint venture deals. He continued to manage his existing portfolio and steadily added more properties at the same time.

Not too long into this phase of his investing journey, Wade was still working full time. One day, just before he was about to leave on a sailing trip, the company he was with at the time brought him in for a meeting and laid out all the things they wanted him to do when he returned. "My response was, 'You know what, I'm going on a sailing trip, and I don't think I'm coming back to this job after my trip,'" says Wade.

Wade figured he was doing pretty well in real estate, so he decided to make the jump. "In hindsight, I probably left my job a little bit too soon. A lot of the financial burden for our family fell on my wife, who was doing well with her business at the time," says Wade.

His candour about this topic should be an inspiration for all new and growing investors out there. If there's one thing the real estate education world can be guilty of, it's selling easy answers. But the truth, as Wade puts it, is that "people see so-called successful people and they think it happened overnight. In reality, there is usually a long period of time that is put in behind the scenes before success comes."

Every new investor and fix and flipper could heed Wade's advice. Use your real estate for what it is, an investment. Real estate in general—and fixing and flipping in particular—are vehicles for putting more money in your pocket, and perhaps lessening the amount you have to work at your day job. But trying to jump full-time into real estate too soon can bring more stress to your life than you need. Wade is a great example of someone who *has* found enormous success, and even he says he'd have stayed in his job longer if he were to do it over again. The financial strain of quitting too soon wasn't worth it for him.

The First Flip

Wade's first flip project looked like this:

> Purchase price: $500,000
>
> Total borrowed: $535,000
>
> Sale price: $625,000
>
> Renovation expense: $35,000
>
> Holding cost (hard money at 14%): $37,450
>
> Agent fees: $22,750
>
> Closing costs: $1,500
>
> Profit: $28,300

After being a strictly buy-and-hold investor for a long while, Wade recognized that he was coming across some properties that didn't fit the buy-and-hold model from time to time. He knew about fixing and flipping, but hadn't tried it before. He thought if the deal was right, it could be a good way to put some more "beans in his jeans" and yet stay within real estate, where he was now an expert.

Wade knew a few things:

- He knew he was an expert at buying residential real estate for the right price.

- He knew from his experience renovating properties in Calgary that he wanted to keep his fix-and-flip projects local. (Wade now lived in Canmore, Alberta.)

- He knew that he was going to make money on his flips from the buying aspect, not the renovating aspect. He had no expertise in renovating, and he knew he was going to hire a general contractor for the job.

- He knew he wasn't an expert in the Canmore real estate market.

With that knowledge in mind, Wade got started on his fix-and-flip adventure. As was the case when he started buying and holding, Wade was not about to rush into anything. "I took out some marketing, got in touch with some motivated vendors, and I got in touch with some local agents. I don't consider myself an expert on the Canmore market, so I got started learning about the local market," says Wade.

He spent the better part of a year looking at properties before finally pulling the trigger on his first fix-and-flip project. In the meantime, he looked at about 40 properties. All the while, he was improving his market knowledge so that when a good property came around he'd be able to identify it as such. He was also building a strong relationship with an agent who had excellent local knowledge and whose advice Wade trusted.

"One day my agent called me up and said that he'd found a great deal. He said it would be gone today. The vendor was going through a divorce, it was right before Christmas, and the list price had dropped by $75,000 down to $500,000," says Wade. It was a townhouse condominium and other properties in the same complex usually listed between $650,000 and $725,000. The sales comparables were slightly lower than that, but still quite strong. Wade knew it would be pretty easy to spruce the place up and sell it at a nice spread, so he acted immediately. "We saw the upside based on the other properties in the complex and we were able to offer the seller the terms they wanted by closing quickly and by doing the deal over the Christmas season. The asking price was fair, so we offered them what they were asking and had the place under contract right away," he says.

Wade gives us a great example of how a fix and flipper and a motivated seller can work together to solve the seller's problem. In the case of this property, it had already been listed for quite some time at a higher price. Once the sellers realized that they needed to drop their price to move the property quickly, the deal was done. Notice that Wade didn't grind on the seller, trying to purchase it for $5,000 or $10,000 less. He saw a real opportunity and took it quickly, offering the full asking price. This is the essence of what a successful fix and flip looks like: decisive action taken at the right time.

It also shows that if sellers aren't stuck on one fixed price, they can move their property a lot faster. "Some of the properties in that complex are still for sale," Wade says. As fix and flippers, we must always work with the right kind of sellers and only buy at the right price. Failure to do this is the first cardinal error of fixing and flipping. When you pay too much, it's impossible to make the money back, but when you buy right, your chances of success multiply.

The Renovation

Showing a propensity for fixing and flipping beyond his actual experience level, Wade made a few key decisions that worked out very well for him. First of all, he knew that he was going to use a general contractor for the entire renovation. "I'm not a contractor," he says. "I'm a real estate investor. If I start swinging a hammer, things aren't going to look very good. Also, if the deal wasn't good enough to make money and still pay a general contractor, it wasn't a good enough deal," he says. This clarity about his renovation strategy served him well.

Second, he purchased a property that didn't need a ton of work. "It had good bones, nothing had to be restructured, and nothing in the way of major work had to be done," says Wade. The property was basically just dated, which meant that the renovation was, for the most part, cosmetic. It involved a fresh coat of paint through-out, new flooring, updated lighting, new appliances, and new countertops. He also added a third bedroom, which added a ton of value and separated the property from most others in the complex. Wade's renovation strategy can be summed up like this: he chose a property where a small amount of work would result in added value, and he focused on key renovation features that didn't cost him much to get there. It was a wonderful strategy.

Third, he put an inspection condition into the purchase contract. This meant that he was able to get all of his contractors through the property for quotes prior to remov-ing the inspection condition. Even though he'd estimated that he would need to spend between $30,000 and $40,000 on the renovation, he wanted proof of those numbers in the form of written quotes. The quotes confirmed his own estimate, and now he had price certainty. This is a very important factor, probably the second most important (after buying at the right price). Once you have renovation expense certainty, it becomes fairly easy to figure out how much of a profit you're going to make. Of course, there are still a few more stages to go through, but with purchase price and renovation expense out of the way, the two biggest unknowns of a fix-and-flip project are removed.

Of course, things can go wrong on the renovation that can cause a project to go over the renovation estimate, even with a solid quote from a great contractor. If you change the scope of work, the renovation expense will change. This happened to Wade when a hot water tank blew up. Even with this unforeseen malfunction, Wade's renovation expense still came in at $35,000. It's quite incredible that even with an untrained eye he was able to estimate so closely when he first walked through the property, and even with the unforeseen expense of replacing a hot water tank, he still had a good deal. If a small thing like that going wrong can cause your fix-and-flip project to be unprofitable, the deal is not a good one! Go back to step one and search for a different property.

The Financing

Wade is a buy-and-hold investor, so he had no interest in refinancing and holding onto this property. In fact, due to the relative cost of real estate in Canmore, it would not have made a good holding property in any case. In Wade's target buy-and-hold market of Calgary, he purchases properties for much less money than his Canmore fix and flip, and earns much higher rental numbers, so the Canmore property was always going to be a sale; he didn't want to hold it. This was another reason why Wade needed a significant spread for the deal to make sense. If the spread had been too tight to make a profitable sale, there was no chance of the safe and secure refinance-and-rent exit strategy.

Prior to buying the property, Wade had been seeking out hard-money lenders. He knew he could likely do a joint venture on the deal since he had the contacts and the track record with joint venture partners to pull it off. But in spite of his ability to do a joint venture, he estimated that he could actually make more money by borrowing from a hard-money lender, even at 14 per cent! Working with a hard-money lender also had the added advantage of speed. He knew the money would be available on very short notice, and that he wouldn't have the trouble of dealing with a bank during the Christmas season. "I didn't want the hassle of the bank asking me questions like 'Okay, Wade, how much do you have in your RRSP account?'"

True to form, Wade went to his lender with the deal and he had the money within 24 hours. "The lender did an afternoon's worth of due diligence and said yes immediately," says Wade. But don't get the impression that this lender was a free-flying amateur. He was actually a professional hard-money lender, so it wasn't someone's line of credit that Wade was dealing with, it was money lent from the pool of cash that the lender keeps available for private loans. The lender knew exactly what he was getting himself into, and he did not take any unnecessary risks.

Wade gave the lender a first mortgage on the property, so he would own the property through foreclosure in a worst-case scenario. But more importantly than that was the fact that *the deal worked*. The lender, who had a great deal of knowledge about what constitutes a good deal, saw the numbers and knew that Wade had a good purchase price to sales price ratio. If the lender hadn't liked the deal, he wouldn't have loaned the money.

But the most important factor of all wasn't even the fact that the deal was outstanding. The most important factor was Wade's reputation. When he started sniffing around for hard money months earlier, he put the word out from within his network. The search turned up a few key professionals who knew people who vouched for Wade. The previous groundwork he'd laid as a serious, professional, and meticulous investor went a long way toward the hard-money lender saying yes. The person who introduced Wade to the hard-money lender spoke of Wade's track record for buying properties at the right price, and of his integrity. The lender was convinced, and sure enough, when the deal came along, the lender didn't waste any time; he simply did his due diligence on the property and wrote a cheque.

It doesn't matter who your lender is. If it's a professional hard-money lender as in Wade's case, or a private money lender from within your circle of family and friends, your reputation will always be first and foremost in the lender's mind. In fact, when it comes to the less professional lenders, your reputation is everything because the lender might not even have the experience to analyze a deal in as much depth as a hard-money lender.

Keep this in mind and always remember when you're first getting started that you have to start small. There's a pretty decent likelihood that you'll have to finance the first couple of deals with your own money, either completely or along with a partner. Build small and steadily like Wade did, and yes, one day there will be a lender out there who won't think twice about writing you a $535,000 cheque! It doesn't actually take as long as you might think, but you must continually improve and make sure that each deal gets better and better. If you should have a couple of failures along the way, don't despair—just learn from them and improve.

The Sale

Once the property was renovated to a high standard, it was time to sell. At the beginning of the project Wade liked the fact that there was strong evidence for his deal.

He saw that there were other properties listed for $659,000 and $675,000. The properties were in essence the same as the one he bought, but there were a couple of major differences: 1) the owners had done some renovations on their places and believed that they were therefore worth more than the market price; and 2) they both had only two bedrooms.

Wade knew that by doing four simple things, he'd separate himself from the competition:

- **Add a Bedroom:** All of the units in the townhouse complex had two bedrooms. There's nothing wrong with two-bedroom houses, but in general there is greater demand for three-bedroom units. People generally pay more for a three-bedroom unit than they will for a two-bedroom if all else is equal. Wade was able to create the third bedroom by carving some space out of a large recreation room. The rec room was a nice feature, but Wade correctly estimated that adding a third bedroom would be more desirable.

- **Do Cosmetic Renovations:** Wade knew that he'd never retrieve his money by renovating the "bones" of the property and he had no desire to do so, since the place had a nice layout and design. Restructuring would have been pointless on this property, but doing cosmetic renovations separated his property from others.

- **List Well Below the Other Properties in the Complex:** Wade was under no illusions. He knew that to sell a property quickly, the most important thing you can do is price it below the competition. In this case, he was actually pricing it below *inferior* product because his unit had more bedrooms and more recent renovations! He knew from the start that the deal had to make enough sense so that he was able to list and sell below the competition and still make a profit. When he listed at $633,000, he could anticipate a quick sale.

- **Market the Property Well:** Wade took the tack that the place needed maximum exposure. He knew it was a superior product and that the price was right, so all that was needed to move the property was making sure the right people saw it in the right way. So he had professional photos taken (it just so happens that Wade's wife is a professional photographer), he got a professional videographer to create a virtual video tour, he listed the property on the MLS with the same great agent who helped him purchase the property, and he advertised the property on other sources to catch those buyers looking at alternatives to MLS.

The net result of all these actions was that the property moved quickly. In a market where the comparable properties in the same complex were sitting for months, Wade was able to move the property within one month of listing it. The next closest property for sale was listed $26,000 higher than Wade's townhouse. That, combined with the fact that Wade's unit was actually better, made the choice pretty much a no-brainer in the eyes of any potential buyer.

The fact is that even after Wade walked away with a nearly $40,000 profit, the buyer *still* got a great deal. The buyer is now the proud owner of a turnkey property that won't have to be touched for many years. Again, this illustrates the fact that when done right, fixing and flipping can positively impact everyone along the chain. Let's review who was positively affected by this deal:

- **The Seller:** Needed to sell fast, and Wade was the one to provide a solution.

- **The Agents:** A total of four commissions were paid out to three different agents. The total value of commissions was around $40,000.

- **The Contractor:** Got a good-paying renovation contract during the slow season with a total professional (Wade). It was stress free for the contractor and a great job to have.

- **Wade's Family:** When Wade made the jump to being a full-time investor, there was a bit of a financial strain. This fix-and-flip project augmented the family's income.

- **Wade:** Gained valuable experience and made a nice profit, which helped him keep doing what he was best at: investing in real estate.

- **The Buyers:** They are now the proud owners of a superior product. They won't have to do any renovations for many years, and they purchased their new home for an excellent price.

You've heard of the concept of a win-win relationship. This deal was a win-win-win-win-win-win.

Having Focus and Using Fix and Flips the Right Way

The biggest lesson we can learn from Wade is in how he uses fix-and-flip projects. Each person will go about it differently, and some of you might want to be full-time flippers. Wade knew that he was never going to be a full-time fix and flipper. He has a strong focus and there was no chance he was going to replace his main focus (long-term buy-and-hold real estate). At the same time, he was wise enough to understand that there is real opportunity in fixing and flipping.

For Wade it came down to a few stipulations. He would do the odd fix-and-flip project if it didn't cause a major disturbance in his life. That's why he was only willing to do fix and flips in the city where he was living, Canmore. Second, he wanted to earn more cash, quickly. Buy-and-hold real estate investing is notorious for providing wonderful long-term gains, but does not typically churn a great deal of excess cash in the short term.

With those stipulations in mind, Wade crafted his strategy to fit his goals. He started looking only in Canmore for properties that would work as simple fix and flips. He started putting together a team to help him (a hard-money lender, a real estate agent, and a contractor), and he knew that he'd be somewhat passive in his search. "To be a full-time flipper, you really have to be active out there in the market, churning things up. It's difficult to find deals like this, and I have no plans to search that hard for properties," says Wade.

The final lesson we can take from Wade is to make decisions based on lifestyle. He was happy to add fixing and flipping to his real estate activities, but only on the condition that it fit his lifestyle. He had no interest in chasing down deals or managing renovation projects in another town, day in and day out, for a few bucks. But at the same time, he was happy to take advantage of a profitable strategy that gave him something he needed: a larger active income.

In your own fix-and-flip adventure, please take some time to consider what you want to use fixing and flipping for. Don't overestimate the power of it, and don't underestimate the power of it either. It truly *can* be a wonderful tool for accelerating your life, but it is not a replacement for more important things (such as family, well-being, and happiness).

Formulate a plan that works for you, and take slow, consistent steps toward executing your plan. Know that there will always be a trade-off for your efforts, so if you plan on putting a huge effort toward your fix-and-flip projects, make sure you're trading the right things (useless activities or other forms of work, not family and friend relationships!).

Part 2

The Essentials

7

Set Up Your Team

In this chapter, Mark describes the various roles of the professionals you need on your team.

Remember that kid who you used to play hockey or soccer with who thought he or she was individually more important than the team? Some entrepreneurs make the mistake of thinking they're individual in their efforts, that because of their supreme ability to do everything, they'll be successful. They don't think they really need a team, and are a little bit upset when reality impinges on this fantasy.

As a fix and flipper, there is little chance that you'll find any success without a solid team. As entrepreneurs, we *are* independent in the sense that we come and go on our own schedule. We decide what we do, when we do it, and how we do it. But the truth is that we don't get much done without others. We need a strong team regardless of what our business is. Fixing and flipping is no different.

Don't be individual—be independent. Spend effort and resources building a better team. If one member of your team is not living up to his or her role, be quick to fire that person. Of course, you must make sure you give team members a chance, and that you've given them a clear enough direction. But after that, if they're not fitting into your system, don't waste any more time, let them go. You need your team, so treat them well, and you'll find that if you do this, they'll take care of you too.

As a fix and flipper, you'll probably need the services of more professionals than listed here, but the following are some of the most important members of your fix-and-flip team:

- agent
- inspector
- designer
- lawyer

- accountant

- bookkeeper

- mortgage broker

Contractors are another essential ingredient, but they will be treated separately because it is a bigger subject.

Agent

I am a real estate agent, and on top of doing my own fix and flips, I help a lot of investors purchase and market their fix and flips. There is much that I, and other expert investment agents like me, can do for our fix-and-flip clients, but at the end of the day the investors themselves have the final word on what happens with their project. If things go sideways on a deal, the fix and flippers themselves have to take care of their own business. You must understand the distinction between utilizing team members and putting yourself at the whim of team members. Regardless of anything else, you must retain the direction and leadership for your fix-and-flip projects.

An excellent realtor is a valuable member of your team if he or she can do the following for you:

- Locate deals and notify you of them.

- Provide you with an accurate after-repaired value (ARV).

- Have a solid understanding of the scope of work that needs to be completed.

- Provide ideas to add value and/or point out problems that need solving with property.

- Provide accurate rental amount estimates for the subject property.

- Be knowledgeable about fixing and flipping.

- Have regional expertise.

A good realtor will take a lot of the legwork off your hands, especially if they're a consistent source of good deals. However, it must be noted that often the best fix-and-flip deals are private ones—that is, properties not listed for sale on MLS. You must also search for properties yourself and perhaps have a marketing program dedicated to finding suitable fix-and-flip properties.

Still, a realtor with a fix-and-flip track record can be a consistent source of deals for you, and it's in your best interest to develop a strong relationship with one. When we say relationship here, it's probably not exactly what you might expect. It's not necessary to watch a hockey game with your realtor every weekend. You don't have to host your realtor for a dinner party every month, and your spouses don't have to be friends. Of course, some of these social aspects may happen, but they're not necessary.

In this case we mean a business relationship. There's no better way to have a successful business relationship than by knowing each other's business well and doing what must be done to serve that relationship with your best effort.

Both Ian and I do fix and flips, and in addition, I am often a realtor for Ian. The other day a really interesting thing happened that illustrates how a good business relationship works when two people know each other's business well. I was previewing a property for Ian. Ian's strategy, as always, was going to be to fix and flip the property with either a sale or a refinance-and-hold exit strategy.

Ian has done plenty of fix and flips and he's developed a renovations system that works very well. Most importantly, it's the *same* every time. There isn't much guesswork for Ian because every property that he purchases will be renovated according to his standard process, with a focus on the same features. The only variables are the extent of time and the number of renovations required from job to job. For example, if the house needs new shingles, then Ian will have to put on new shingles, but he only does that kind of renovation if it's absolutely necessary. When a particular renovation is not needed, it won't be done. With features such as flooring, kitchens, and bathrooms, Ian pretty much follows a similar plan from property to property.

So, as I was previewing a potential purchase for Ian, I was able to estimate the amount of the renovation, based on the renovations system that I know Ian employs.

Lo and behold, Ian saw the property and agreed with my assessment. Because Ian and I have a strong *business* relationship, and know each other's business and goals, we are able to work together in a mutually beneficial way.

Find yourself a good and knowledgeable realtor, work together in a mutually beneficial way, and you'll find that your agent is able to save you time, and provide timely and useful information that will help you with your business.

Inspector

An inspector is another valuable member of your team. For the $350 to $500 that an inspection costs, you should get immense value from the inspection and the inspector's assessment.

Here's the rub: you might not always have the time or inclination to bring in your inspector when you purchase a fix and flip. When you're buying a fix-and-flip property, you'll often submit an offer to the seller without conditions (such as an inspection condition) in order to close the deal quickly. If you put a property inspection condition in the offer, you might lose the deal, so many fix and flippers won't put a condition in the offer and they rely on themselves or a contractor (whom they work with) to assess the possible defects of the property and the repairs that *need* to be done and which repairs can wait or perhaps won't add value.

However, if you *are* able to use an inspector, that person can be a very valuable resource to you in your purchasing process. Inspectors are in essence an extra set of eyes as you assess all the various aspects of the house. In addition, having an inspection done is a chance to have three hours of unfettered access to the property before the deal closes.

An inspector's main job is to search for potential big-ticket items that you might not be able to see for yourself. Inspectors should test for moisture all around the house. They should look at all the major mechanical and electrical systems. The roof, the foundation, the windows, and every other possible major expense should be thoroughly looked over by your inspector.

When you're at the house doing the inspection, it's also the best possible time to get everyone else through the property who needs to see it before you make your offer and/or close the deal. Every estimate that you need done should be done during the inspection. If you need an architect, engineer, or designer to come through the property, the inspection is the time.

Being a good fix and flipper is largely about how you manage your renovation. In the details of managing the project lies the greatest risk of going over time and over budget (two downfalls that will cost you plenty of money). Preparation is one of the key aspects of managing your renovation well. Taking care of all your estimates, architect visits, and designer visits in the early stages saves you valuable time on your project, ensuring that you can have your plans, drawings and permits in place by the time you take possession. Use your inspection as an opportunity to prepare for the project.

A Poorly Done Inspection Costs Investor a Bundle

As with a realtor, it is important to have a strong business relationship with your inspector. A strong relationship nurtures an atmosphere of co-operation, commitment, and responsibility.

An investor I know recently did a fix and flip where inspector error cost him $5,000.

The investor purchased a fix-and-flip property and was able to insert the property inspection condition in the purchase contract. The inspector came by and did his inspection. He found nothing of major concern—but did not notice the moisture problem in the basement.

Now, in the inspector's defence, we must note that the problem was not easily detectable, and many inspectors wouldn't have noticed the problem. However, if the investor and inspector had had a history of working together, and if the investor had communicated clearly that in his view moisture is one of the most important things to test for, then perhaps the inspector would have pulled out the moisture tester more liberally and been able to find the problem.

The end result was that when the investor completed the renovations and went to sell the property, the next inspector *did* detect the issue. The buyer negotiated a $5,000 discount off the purchase price in order to fix the problem himself. My investor friend lost $5,000.

The moral of the story is to develop a strong relationship with all your team members and make sure they know exactly what is important to you so that they can serve you.

Designer

There is a chance you won't need a designer, but for many or even *most* new fix and flippers, a designer can add massive value as a member of your team. You might not need a designer if:

1. you have proven design skills yourself (not just your biased opinion, but a proven track record of designing to add rental and sale value); or

2. you have developed a consistent system (you do the same type of renovations every time, and your track record proves that it works).

Ian is an example of a fix and flipper who does not usually need the services of a designer. From time to time, when he purchases a different type of property, he will bring in a designer for a special aspect of the renovation. For example, he recently fixed and flipped a semi-detached home that was very narrow. He knew the structural design of the place wasn't maximizing the space properly, so he brought in a designer to help him solve the problem. Through consultation with his designer, Ian decided to move the staircase to open the property up, which made it appear more spacious. On the rest of the renovation, Ian used his systematic approach to the renovation by installing wainscoting, waffle ceilings, and tile scheme. His bathroom and kitchen were designed the same way that they always are. He did not need a designer on the rest of his renovation because he follows a proven system that saves him a ton of money.

If you're not as experienced as Ian, and if you need a little help figuring out what adds value, a designer might be one of the most important members of your team. What does a designer do? For those who are skeptical about the value of a designer, it might seem like a frivolous expense, but the reality is that designers have the training and the eye to see what *others* will value in a home.

One of the *least* successful ways of renovating a property is to do it to your own tastes, *unless* your own tastes are the same as what is valued by a majority of your target market.

One of the biggest mistakes that new fix and flippers make is renovating way above the standard necessary for the target market. Ian's book *From Renos to Riches: The Canadian Real Estate Investor's Guide to Practical and Profitable Renovations* covers this topic in greater depth. The trick is renovating in such a way that the property looks modern, spotless, and attractive, but without breaking the bank to do it.

A great designer will be able to help you come up with a renovations plan that fits these criteria. As with all the other members of your team, though, it is essential that your designer be an investor who understands the relationship between cost and value very well.

Designer Adds Immense Value to Rental Property

An investor friend and client named Jerry was working on a renovation project for an existing property. The goal of the renovation was to hold for the long-term, so Jerry wanted to raise the rental value of the property through targeted renovations.

Jerry employed the services of a fix and flipper (and designer) named Cindy Wennerstrom (who is profiled earlier in this book). Cindy is known among the Toronto real estate investing community for designing her renovations without spending much more money than a typical renovation, but she *consistently* achieves rental figures $400 to $500 higher per month than typical market value.

When Jerry hired Cindy, something remarkable happened. He was able to raise his gross rental amount from $1,500 to $2,500! The property was somewhat run-down prior to the renovation, so a chunk of that rental lift can be attributed to the basic renovation, but with Cindy's design genius on Jerry's side, he was able to bump his rental amount significantly. And guess what? That makes Jerry a genius too, for hiring the right designer.

I love this story because it illustrates the value that an excellent design team brings to fix-and-flip projects. I tell it to people all the time when they say, "Really? I need to hire a designer?"

Lawyer

A lawyer is perhaps one of the most underrated and misunderstood members of a fix-and-flip team. On one hand it's easy to understand their role—to execute the legal sale and purchase of properties that you fix and flip.

It seems straightforward, but as countless investors have experienced over the years, purchases don't always go as planned. Late closings are common and, quite frankly, they're painful. Nobody truly knows if a deal is going to close until it actually does. If it's your lawyer who doesn't get the deal done on time, the other party *will* be freaking out, and they *will* be putting all kinds of pressure on you to get the deal done. You do not need that kind of stress in your life (trust me on this one).

On top of stress, late closings can potentially cause the following problems:

- late renovation completion
- rescheduling problems with contractors (they'll be upset with you too)
- longer debt service if borrowing private money
- late move-ins for tenants

The way to avoid the stress is to find a lawyer who "gets it." A lawyer who gets it is defined as a lawyer who understands that the deal *has* to close on time. Get a lawyer who is a master in the art of "git 'er done."

The importance of your lawyer's expertise may well depend on the nature of the project. If you fix and flip houses that only need cosmetic renovations, and therefore are being purchased at 15 to 25 per cent below what the standard ARV (after-repaired value) would be, then the talent pool of qualified lawyers is large. On the other hand, if you decide to take on the truly mammoth renovation projects, then you might need a more specialized lawyer.

When a mammoth renovation project type of deal reaches the lawyers, the discount off standard market value is so great that the *seller's* lawyer often starts wondering what is going on. They don't have any experience in the realm of fixing and flipping, so they can't understand how a property could sell for similar to lot value. The fact is that lot value is exactly what some of these junky houses are worth. The fix and flipper will solve the problem of the junky house and will therefore bring it up to fair market value.

When you buy such a property, it will be essential that you have a lawyer who "gets it" because he or she will explain the fix-and-flip business model to the seller's lawyer. In essence, your lawyer is selling your deal and making sure that there are no hiccups with closing.

Ian's Lawyer "Gets It"

Ian is a perfect example of a fix and flipper who buys the kinds of junky houses that require specialized legal talent.

For example, after being delayed significantly on one deal, and actually losing another because a lawyer talked the seller out of doing the deal, Ian decided to take his search for a lawyer who "gits 'er done" very seriously. He hit upon a scrappy lawyer by the name of Mark Woitzik whose practice is based in Whitby, Ontario (Ian's core fix-and-flip area).

Since discovering his determined lawyer, Ian has never had a late closing, nor has he ever had a deal compromised by an uninformed lawyer on the other side of the deal.

Ian's lawyer understands the art of communication, clarity, and persuasion. These features mean he's of immense value to Ian.

Accountant

An accountant can help you answer some of your more important business-related questions.

For example:

1. **Active Income vs. Passive Income:** Active income is taxed more heavily than passive income. With the help of your accountant, you can set up a strategy to minimize your active income and maximize your passive income.

2. **Corporation vs. Sole Proprietorship:** Since much of your income as a fix and flipper will be active, it might make sense to set up a corporation, because corporate tax rates are lower than personal tax rates. Setting up a corporation requires cost and regular tax filings, so if you consider this route, speak with your lawyer and accountant.

3. **Taking an Income from Fix and Flips:** Perhaps you need to take an income out of your fix-and-flip deals, or perhaps you have a full-time job and you don't want to claim any income from your fix and flips. Your accountant will be able to help you set up a strategy for how much (if any) income you want to take from your fix-and-flip business.

When you're in the rush of getting started with fixing and flipping, you might not put enough importance on the accounting side of things. But trust me when I say that setting your business up with the *right* accountant at the beginning is important. Failing to do so can result in huge tax bills, which in some cases have been known to sink investors. Even if you only do one fix-and-flip project per year, you'll be putting enough energy into it that you do not want to see it all go down the drain due to improper tax planning.

As with every other member of your team, it's imperative that your accountant is an investor as well. When they invest themselves, they will want to know and understand all your issues intimately *for their own sake.* Say what you will about helping others, I find that self-interest is almost always the strongest reason to do anything. I like to know that my team members are driven to learn and know things because they're investors themselves. That's why I always seek team members who are also investors.

Bookkeeper

A bookkeeper plays a special role on your team. With an excellent bookkeeper on your side, you will gain an incredible knowledge of the *exact* expenditures and income that your fix-and-flip business produces and demands.

From the moment you start your fix and flip, you will want to give every single receipt to your bookkeeper. You want him or her to track and categorize every penny you spend and you want it all tracked *per project.* The reason for this level of diligence is simple: it's about helping you raise money and prepare properly for the next project. When the fix and flip is complete, you will be able to take your complete set of numbers and show potential investors exactly what the project looked like. This is especially important for numbers-focused investors and lenders.

Let's face it: investors and private money lenders don't care much about anything except the return they will make from your fix-and-flip project. Why should they invest with you unless they'll be able to achieve a substantial return? It's one thing to do a fix and flip well, but it's a different thing altogether to do a fix and flip well *and then* turn around and promote yourself as an expert fix and flipper to a pool of potential investors. Having the proof in your books will go a long way toward proving yourself to new investors. Well-kept books will clearly delineate:

- realtor commission expense

- carrying cost

- closing costs

- materials costs

- labour costs

- all other expenses

On top of showing them just how strong your returns are as a fix and flipper, your books also show how many different aspects of the job you did. Sometimes investors won't believe that you're worth 50 per cent of the profit for the active role that you play in your investment projects. Breaking all the jobs and tasks down into numbers will often help convince them why the money they're putting into the project should earn them 50 per cent of the income but no more. It shows them how much work you do, and why you're worth the 50 per cent of the profit that you're going to take.

Mortgage Broker

Your mortgage broker is essential to your team because he or she will not only help you get the funds necessary to purchase your fix and flips to begin with, he or she will also help you refinance your fix and flips if you choose the refinance-and-hold strategy.

Whether it be through a conventional mortgage or private money, your mortgage broker is the biggest influence on how well financed you are. From getting timely approvals to securing better rates, your broker will make life a heck of a lot easier on you—but only if you have the right one.

As with all other members of your team, it's essential that your broker understands your goals and that he or she is an investor too who wants nothing more than to know the industry inside and out. When helping you is the same as helping themselves, they're more likely to be excellent at what they do.

Relationship with Mortgage Broker Pays Dividends

Ian recently fixed and flipped a property where there was a big problem to solve, and in the process added a lot of value to the property. It was a legal (from the zoning perspective) duplex that was previously a marijuana grow operation. Of course, the property was purchased at a steep discount, and Ian had to apply much of his acumen to complete the project on time while still adding value.

When refinancing the property, the appraiser had a hard time seeing as much value as Ian knew there was in the property. This is where Ian's mortgage broker, Kevin, stepped in. He went to bat for Ian and had many discussions with the appraiser. After explaining the situation numerous times, Kevin was finally able to get the appraisal to where it was supposed to be.

The result was that Ian pulled out $40,000 more than he would have with the original appraisal. He was left with a property that cash flowed more than $1,000.

Ian has been working with his mortgage broker for years. Kevin knows all the things that Ian does to add value to his fix and flips. Kevin is an investor as well, and he understands how important refinancing is and how added value on an appraisal can make all the difference to the investor.

8

How to Find the Right Contractor

In this chapter, Ian talks about self-knowledge and its role in helping you to find the right contractor.

How well do you know your own skills and abilities? How correct is your assessment of your own level of involvement in the project? These are key factors in helping you to find and hire the right contractor.

In order to get it right, you have to know your own motivations, and you have to know the motivations of the contractor you're seeking to hire.

This might sound like bragging (though it isn't meant to), but I believe I'm the perfect contractor for my own flips. I run the jobs, I control the expenses, and I'm the one who sees creative solutions to complex problems. On top of that I have staff members who are learning to do these things. In a sense they're learning to be my perfect contractors.

Some of you reading this might be the perfect contractor for a fix-and-flip project. But for some of you, that's simply not the case. I don't want to scare you away from taking on the contractor's role, because many people can assume that role, especially if they're doing a cosmetic fix and flip. In such cases, you must take on the task of managing the project and hire knowledgeable and expert sub-contractors to do the specialist work.

For those of you who are gathering experience as an investor and can't handle the role of contractor for yourself, a skilled and creative contractor is a must. It's a matter of identifying one with the right credentials who is prepared to work with you and who will be of value to you. It's a matter of finding the right people that work for you and your level of involvement in the project.

Take Wade Graham from the profile earlier in this book: he hired a contractor to take care of all the necessary work on the project that we discussed. That worked best for him, but I myself handle the contractor's role in my fix and flips. I know other fix and flippers who hire sub-contractors, but handle the overall job organization of the contractor. This is more achievable for the average investor when the project is a cosmetic flip.

Whatever the case may be, you have to be crystal clear about your project in order to know what is right for you.

Driving to a New Destination — without a Roadmap or GPS

Have you ever driven around in circles looking for a destination you've never been to? If you have, then you understand what I'm talking about. It's frustrating. If you stop to ask someone on the side of the road, they'll give you a set of directions that make sense to them because they're locals, but in reality you need the right set of directions for you. You need a roadmap!

That's what it's like looking for the right contractor without a crystal-clear *scope of work*. Without it, you're doing the fixing-and-flipping equivalent of driving around without a roadmap. It will take you a lot longer to get to your ultimate destination and you will likely have used up all your gas along the way.

I can't stress enough how creating a scope of work will transform your entire fixing-and-flipping process. Most importantly, it will enable you to bring contractors and sub-contractors to a project confidently. You can only know how to find the right contractor if you know what you're looking for. The scope of work is like the roadmap to take you to that thing you're looking for.

A scope of work comes back to the materials breakdown, the jobs breakdown, and being highly educated about the costs involved in a fix-and-flip renovation.

To make a useful scope of work you have to understand the difference between materials cost and labour cost. The next chapter will deal with that in more depth, along with a detailed discussion of how to develop a scope of work. For now, I want to stress how knowing the scope of work well is the key to finding the right contractor.

The Differences between a Contractor and a Sub-contractor (and Types of Contractors)

It's important to know this difference and also to know where the lines get blurry. A *sub-contractor* is a worker or a team of workers that performs a single aspect of a renovations project. A sub-contractor is a painter, or a plumber, or an electrician, or a drywaller. They are also known as *sub-trades*.

A *contractor* is an individual or a team who can do certain aspects of a renovation project themselves, and on top of that, they have the general knowledge and skills to run all the other various sub-trades. They can organize the team, direct the team and complete the entire project. When you hire a contractor, you will agree on one price. The contractor will pay all the other people who are involved in the project out of the money you pay him or her.

Where the lines get blurry is when dealing with some of the smaller contractors. In reality they only have the ability to do, let's say, 60 per cent of the tasks necessary to complete an entire gut flip project. These types of contractors might be perfect for small cosmetic flips, but they probably can't handle an entire gut flip.

Their ability as contractors usually breaks down in the business aspect. Sure, they're handy at doing some of the work, but if they can't put together an entire project, they're not a general contractor in the truest sense. They're more like a sub-contractor who has developed a few more skills and can tackle somewhat larger projects.

In my opinion, as a flipper, you will need to utilize smaller contractors for certain jobs, and (depending on your own skills) a large contractor for others.

In my previous book, *From Renos to Riches: The Canadian Real Estate Investor's Guide to Practical and Profitable Renovations*, I broke down the various different kind of contractors into groups:

Two Guys and a Van (TGVs)

One of the two guys is a craftsman; he is handy and probably experienced. He's no specialist, but he can do pretty much anything, given enough time. The second of the two guys got laid off from GM and he just needs work. He does not particularly love his job, but he's a hard worker and does what he needs to do. Neither of them is a businessman. They approach their work like a job-holder, and they are used to being dictated to by their customer, whom they see as their boss. They will never say they can't do something for fear of losing the job; however, there are some tasks that will take them a long time and therefore cost them time, which, in the world of renovations, is money. Due to the uncertainty of where the next job (and therefore pay-cheque) is coming from, TGVs are driven by the need for stability. Their motivation is consistent income.

Media Darlings (MDs)

As the name suggests, these guys are driven by the media, particularly television shows about renovations. They watch shows like *Holmes on Homes* and try to emulate them. They position themselves as the saviour to all your problems, and tell anyone within earshot about the supposed poor quality of their competitors' work. They are very trend driven and have no qualms about paying top dollar for materials. They make big box stores' marketing departments proud, happily buying paint at $50 per gallon when it's a completely unnecessary expense. Unknowing customers are their bread and butter. They charge way too much for their work, spend way too much on their work, and don't make any more money for themselves than the TGVs at the end of the day. As an investor, letting these guys control your job will put you $20,000 over budget within a week. MDs' motivation is prestige; they don't want to be known as "just" contractors.

Professionals (Pros)

As the name suggests, these guys have figured out the renovations game. They are job facilitators, sometimes even actively swinging a hammer or installing cabinets. They know all the ins and outs of the physical work involved in renovating, but more importantly they have the business aspects of it figured out. They dictate their own terms and prices, and always deliver a superior product with speed and efficiency. They know how to maximize value, buying great deals in bulk, saving thousands on every job. Rather than spending $50 per gallon on paint as the MD will, the Pro will get paint of an equal quality at $10 per gallon. Pros will give their clients crystal-clear guidelines and in reality they don't need the consistent work or the prestige that the TGVs or MDs do. They get consistent work of their own accord, probably by flipping houses or renovating alongside a professional investor, so that is not their motivation. They don't seek prestige because they're doing well in business and this gives them prestige enough, or perhaps they just don't care because they're free of the need for others' approval. In any case, the Pro's motivation is business. Pros know what their business does for them, and they'll make decisions based on whether or not their business will benefit.

Your Skills and Involvement Will Largely Determine Who Is Right for You

I come from a contractor background, which means before I was flipping houses, I was doing renovation jobs for clients. I learned, struggled, and built my business up to what it eventually was before I went full-time into fixing and flipping houses. I basically started as a sub-contractor, as a painter.

I learned to become more proficient in different trades as time went on, and I developed my skills more and more as a project manager. In those early days as a contractor I was very much a TGV. As I went along my path, I learned a lot about the things that clients wanted. I saw that they were swayed by what they saw on TV and from the big box stores' marketing departments. So, at certain times, on certain jobs, I was an MD. Heck, I even worked on numerous reality TV renovation shows. I guess in some ways I was the ultimate MD.

From there I started doing whole renovation projects as a contractor. Not long before I stopped doing customer jobs and went full-time into my own fix-and-flip projects, I was running multiple crews and multiple jobs at once. I had become a pro. I was in high demand as a contractor, and I never had to worry about where the next job was coming from.

I think my experience shows that, with hard work and dedication over time, you can become an expert. For me, the route I took was to first become a pro contractor, and only then did I become a full-time fix and flipper. I am not suggesting everyone involved in fix and flips has to do it this way, but what I am suggesting is that by sticking to it and by focusing your efforts on adding value and minimizing expenses, you can become an expert fix and flipper over time.

A Mixed Bag of MDs and TGVs

My strategy is to employ MDs and TGVs for certain aspects of my fix and flips, but I always retain control of the cost and scheduling.

I control the entire job, organize it, and plan everything. But I will use a mixed bag of TGVs, MDs, and sub-contractors. I give them varying levels of responsibility in my project, but I always determine the scope of work and always control the expenditures.

Armed with this knowledge, and knowing that it's my job to control every aspect of the flip project, I use my scope of work to guide me through the hiring process when I'm looking for the right contractors. These are the right contractors for me, based on my skills, experience, and knowledge.

Training Contractors and Sub-trades

Whenever I bring on new contractors or sub-trades, I don't think of it as strictly a transaction. I think of it more as the beginning of a relationship.

Do my new relationships always pan out? Of course not. Not every contractor or sub-contractor is going to be the right fit for every fix and flipper. I'm no different from anyone else. Unless you try to develop a relationship and find a long-term fit, you never will. Thinking long term is—in my opinion—always the correct mindset to bring into a new relationship.

In the interests of thinking long term, I always train my contractors and sub-trades. Don't think of training like getting a job at a fast-food joint and wearing a "trainee" badge for a week while you shadow an experienced employee. It's much different.

There's really no education out there for this kind of thing. Sure, there are trade schools and apprenticeships, but those are just for the actual mechanics of the work involved. They don't include the specialized methods of a fix and flipper.

We create a family atmosphere around our projects. The guys who work on our jobs often take real ownership of what we're doing and what we're about. They often see fixing and flipping houses as something they could do, so they're automatically interested. This is the first step in training people, in my opinion. Without them buying in, they're not going to learn anything. I go out of my way to look for people who might buy in because they're interested in fixing and flipping one day.

Once they're bought in, it's really a matter of sharing my knowledge with them and letting them see the difference between how we do things, and how things are often done elsewhere. So I share my systems with all the new people who work with me. I share my control sheets and my scope of work too. I let them know that the systems I'm showing them are what separates an individual performing a task from a business owner running a business.

Through this process, I've seen significant change in some contractors. Of course I don't take credit for all those changes, but I know what I'm sharing with them makes a difference.

I'm not trying to paint an unrealistic picture here: yes, it's true that, through this education, there is room for a lot of growth in people I work with, but it serves a purpose for my self-interest as well. The better these people are trained to my system and my way of doing things, the smoother my jobs move along and the easier it is for me to expand my business.

I always have an eye toward training new people on my jobs because the benefits go both ways.

Partnering with a Pro

If you don't have the skill set to run and control your own flip projects, then putting your project in the hands of a TGV or an MD might lead to disastrous consequences for your business. Please understand that I'm not being disrespectful to TGVs and MDs here. Remember, I was there at various times. All I'm saying is that TGVs and MDs might not have an eye toward the bigger picture at all times, and this could sink your project.

If we eliminate TGVs and MDs, the only type of contractor left is the Professional.

So it's simple, right? Hire a pro, give him or her all the responsibility and let that person take your project into the stratosphere! Unfortunately, there is a major unseen roadblock here, and I really want to stress this point. I believe this is one of those things that most real estate wealth gurus never tell you when they pretend that flipping houses is easy: pros are what they are because they know how to succeed! This means that they know how to make money. They know how to make the money that you want to make for yourself! It's their expertise that allows them to make money.

Hiring a pro is not as easy as it might seem. They want to make money on the job, and let's be honest, there's only a certain amount of spread on each flip project. Sometimes there will be enough for you and the pro, but other times there will not be enough.

In my opinion, what a lot of would-be fix and flippers do is try to partner with a pro. In principle this makes sense because you now have a pro on your team, but rather than paying them out of pocket, you're paying them from the back end. They only get paid if you get paid, and vice versa. So there we have it, done story, right? That's what you should do, right? Not quite. I want you to ask yourself a very serious and solemn question here: *What do YOU have to offer the pro in this arrangement?* If pros already know how to do all the renovations and project management, cost control, and coordination of sub-trades, what exactly are you going to offer? If they know all the basics of how to fix and flip a house, what do you know?

It can be done. There are circumstances where this exact relationship makes sense. I just want you to make sure that if you're trying to make your business out of this model that you're not just another one of the hangers-on. So many people seem to think they'll just partner up with a pro, but they honestly don't bring enough to the table to entice the pro to work with them.

I know this from experience because people are always, always trying to lure me into partnerships because the simple fact is that I have the skills and knowledge they need. Again, I have no problem if they provide something I need as well, and I do partnerships based on that principle from time to time. But more often than not, the people who approach me for a partnership are limited in what they can provide me!

I don't want to discourage you, but just be aware that if you're going into a partnership, you have to provide an equal value to your partner. You really do have to have some skills that the pro lacks.

When Is a Pro Not a Pro?

If you're not a pro yourself and you're looking for a pro to partner with, you will need to find the right pro to be on top of your flip project. Finding this person is going to be the real trick. In order to find that person, you need to know exactly what you're looking for.

The problem is that all pros are not alike. The kind of pro required for a flip project is a specialist and is not the exact same kind of pro that does most renovation projects. You see, the renovations are not always self-explanatory, even to a pro. If the pro is an expert at renovating houses for owner-occupied homes or some other end user, they won't necessarily understand the finer points of flipping houses.

Perhaps they are accustomed to working on projects where materials (and suppliers) are dictated to them by the end user. If this is the case, they might not know how to be ruthless on their material costs.

Maybe they have billed-out labour at cost plus 20 per cent on their previous jobs. If so, maybe they'll have a difficult time creating a scope of work based on the time investment of tradespeople (see below).

Pros don't all come with the same skill sets because they don't all come with the same experience. A pro that comes with a history of running a tight ship will likely be able to adapt to flips, but only if their mindset is right and if they want to figure it out. But not all pros are alike, and you will need to be aware of that when you're looking for the right contractor to partner with.

The Middle Ground

Partnering with a pro is not the best solution for every flipper. But if there's one thing I love about fix and flippers it's the spirit of finding a way to "git 'er done."

For someone with that level of determination, when one door appears closed (partnering with a pro, for example), another opens. When partnering with a pro is too tricky based on the mismatched value of skill sets, many flippers choose the middle ground.

What's the middle ground? It means that rather than paying a pro to do everything that a pro might normally do, and rather than partnering with a pro, you're now hiring a pro as a consultant or managing the job yourself with targeted sub-trades. You're trading some money (and therefore some of your profits) for the expertise of a pro, or you're doing all the jobs of management yourself but remaining cognizant of your skills and limitations. In essence, this means that if you're self-managing, you don't take on too complex a gut flip if your knowledge and skill base don't allow for it.

When hiring a pro as a consultant, the pro can act more as a silent hand behind the scenes than a full-time presence on the project. The pro can help you with the planning, the scope of work, the list of materials, and the labour breakdown. The pro can come to the fix-and-flip site from time to time and give you valuable feedback on the progress of the project.

The pro consultant idea is a wise setup when partnerships are not really possible, and I don't think any gut flip project should be done without the guidance of a pro.

In the case of self-managing while using sub-trades, the fix and flipper also gains valuable knowledge as the project moves along. Again, the most important thing about self-managing is to ensure you take on a project that's not too difficult for your skill level. If you're unsure at the beginning, it would be a wise idea to hire a pro to help you develop a detailed scope of work.

Whatever the best arrangement is for you, I am certain that the place to start is an honest assessment of what you bring to the table, what your particular skill set is, and what you want to do.

From there, seek the right fit for you and only enter into arrangements and partnerships that benefit both parties equally.

Fix-and-Flip Profile: Gary McGowan

Fix-and-Flip Strategy Accelerates Leap into Full-Time Investing

How He Got Started

Like so many other real estate investors, Gary McGowan started out in a good job. Working for Bell Canada, maintaining a portion of its network for 10 years, had all the trappings of corporate bliss, but Gary knew he eventually wanted to move on.

Before joining Bell Canada, Gary spent the previous five years working for smaller companies building websites and an online presence for various businesses. In total Gary had dedicated himself to 15 years in the working world.

When the opportunity for Gary to join his parents (who had been involved in investment real estate for the past 30 years) came about, Gary was quick to jump on the opportunity. "About four years ago, my dad informed me that he was going to dive deeper into the real estate business, and I immediately told him I wanted to be involved," says Gary. They would become partners on real estate ventures going forward.

Being strategic and methodical thinkers, Gary and Richard decided that their best course of action would be to first further their education. To that end, they joined the Real Estate Investment Network (REIN) and deepened their knowledge. "We haven't looked back since," notes Gary.

After gaining the seminal knowledge of how investment real estate works and about some of the strategies that you can use to acquire, improve, and manage rental properties, Gary and his father hit the market looking for a deal . . . or two . . . or three.

The First Rental Properties

Demonstrating a fine understanding of real estate investing and fundamentals, Gary sought out deals that fit the following criteria:

- strong cash flow
- good price
- opportunity to add value
- little cash to purchase
- creative financing

After a bit of searching, Gary and Richard found an investor in the town of Lindsay, Ontario, near Oshawa, who had a large number of real estate holdings and was looking to liquidate some of his smaller properties, since he was now specializing in larger buildings. The seller had two five-plexes and one four-plex for sale, and after a short negotiation Gary and the seller agreed on the sale of all three properties. For your reference, LTV means loan to value, the percentage of total purchase price that is loaned. The numbers looked like this:

Property 1

Property type: Five-plex
Purchase price: $207,500
First mortgage (75% LTV at 5% interest): $155,625
Second mortgage (15% LTV at 7% interest): $31,125
Gary's cash in: $20,750
First mortgage payment: $905
Second mortgage payment (interest only): $182
Monthly expenses: $1,000
Monthly rental income: $3,085
Monthly cash flow: $998

Property 2

Property type: Five-plex
Purchase price: $212,500
First mortgage (75% LTV at 5% interest): $159,375
Second mortgage (15% LTV at 7% interest): $31,875
Gary's cash in: $21,250
First mortgage payment: $927
Second mortgage payment (interest only): $186
Monthly expenses: $1,000
Monthly rental income: $3,085
Monthly cash flow: $972

Property 3

Property type: Four-plex
Purchase price: $164,000
First mortgage (80% LTV at 5% interest): $131,200
Second mortgage (15% LTV at 7% interest): $24,600

Gary's cash in: $8,200
First mortgage payment: $763
Second mortgage payment (interest only): $144
Monthly expenses: $800
Monthly rental income: $2,468
Monthly cash flow: $761

Total

Property: 14 units
Purchase price: $584,000
First mortgage: $446,200
Second mortgage: $87,600
Gary's cash in: $50,200
First mortgage payment: $2,595
Second mortgage payment: $512
Monthly expenses: $2,800
Monthly rental income: $8,638
Monthly cash flow: $2,731

You may have noticed a few odd things about the numbers. At the time when Gary was putting together the deals, the lending rules were looser than they are today. This allowed him to get a second (VTB—vendor take back) mortgage on each of the properties for an additional 15 per cent on top of the 75 to 80 per cent that the bank lent him.

This allowed him to keep his own cash invested to a minimum. In total, only 9 per cent of the total purchase price came from his money. The net effect of the wonderful deal and the great financing was that Gary and his father were the proud owners of 14 strongly cash-flowing units for just over $50,000 of their own cash. In cash flow *alone* this amounts to a 67 per cent yearly return. Incredible! However, the properties were a little bit rough, and Gary knew they were going to need some work, so he wasn't done dealing yet. He went about making an already excellent deal even better.

Gary was still working full time when they purchased these properties, and he would continue to do so for several years. Between Gary and his dad, they were able to qualify for these properties by themselves, but to set themselves up even better for future investments they decided to take on a joint venture partner.

Joint Venture

Since the purchase of the first three properties (14 units) happened very early in his career, Gary had no intention of bringing in a partner on the deal. He knew that typically an investor needs to have a track record to attract partners, so he wasn't counting on joint venturing the deal.

He was a bit surprised when some money partners came forward. All he did was discuss the deal with people, and the partners seemed to come out of the woodwork. "We didn't have the track record in real estate, but we had two other things: we had a track record in life, and we had a good deal with a ton of upside," says Gary. The partner who jumped at the opportunity had known Gary and his father for many years, and he invested his money mainly on their reputation. They were known for keeping their word and for consistent success and attention to detail. A partnership was born.

The joint venture partner committed $100,000 for a 50 per cent ownership in the property. Since the financing was already in place and was providing an excellent cash flow with the current setup, the McGowans and the new partner agreed to use the cash for the following:

Cash back to the McGowans: $50,200
Reserve fund: $17,000
Renovations: $32,800

In addition to the $32,800 that was already allocated to renovations, the properties themselves were throwing off enough cash to continually build reserves for future renovations, which Gary knew they'd need to do.

Deferred Maintenance

At the start of the deal, one of the things Gary liked about the properties was the opportunity to add value through focused renovations and improving the tenant profile. It's remarkable that at the beginning of Gary's investment career, he had a solid enough understanding of how to effectively maximize his investment that he was able to see such an opportunity and then capitalize on it. The guidance of his more experienced father, along with their training through the Real Estate Investment Network, helped.

This long-term hold had all the earmarks of a long-term flip. On a long-term flip, the active investor (Gary and Richard) pulls all their own money out and retains the property for the long term, adding value while renovating. The one major difference between this deal and a pure flip is the timing of the renovations. Typically, the renovations are done upfront on a fix and flip.

You will remember the definition of a fix and flip is that all or most of the initial money invested is removed relatively soon. The fix and flipper can hold the actual property as long as the cash comes back out soon. Often this cash removal comes with a refinance but, at other times, it comes from a money partner.

Gary went into the deal with little of his own money due to the seller-financing aspect of the deal. Then he was able to pull all his cash out by bringing in a joint venture partner. While he had to give up half the ownership in the property to the joint venture partner, he gained the cash to ensure the property could be renovated and therefore be a wonderful property for many years, and add value at the same time.

"We paid $584,000 for all three properties, which amounts to just under $42,000 per door. But a fair after-repaired value (ARV) of the properties was probably closer to $55,000 per door. We negotiated a good deal, but we were able to do that because the properties had quite a lot of deferred maintenance," says Gary of his first purchases.

From the day of purchase, Gary knew that he would have to update the properties as vacancies came up, and that was his strategy going in. He knew that by doing focused renovations, he could bring the properties up to the fair market value.

Since the purchase of the properties, Gary has put about $40,000 into renovating. On the surface, that sounds like a lot of money, but as Gary says, "It's a great property, and we keep improving it, so it gets better as a long-term hold as time goes on."

The Result

Through the additional value added with the focused renovation as well as the magic of market appreciation, each unit is now valued at an average of $65,000. From a total appraised value of $584,000 to approximately $910,000 in about four years is remarkable. Give one checkmark to Gary's value-add strategy.

In addition, total rental income (per month) has gone from $8,638 when the properties were purchased to just over $10,000. By improving the appearance and raising the perceived value of the properties, Gary has been able to attract better renters who are willing to pay a higher rent.

Finally, when Gary first purchased the properties, the floating variable prime rate was around 5 per cent. The prime rate has dropped over the years, and at the time of writing, the prime rate is 3 per cent. This means that his first mortgage payments have dropped from $2,595 to $2,112—an additional savings of $483.

In total, the positive cash flow went from an already outstanding $2,731 to an eye-popping $4,576 on the 14 properties in this first set of purchases. This first deal had turned into a home run for Gary, and if he didn't know it before, he was starting to see the power of real estate. With the addition of value to the properties over the years, Gary is now in a position where he could take more cash out, either through a refinance or a sale, although he hasn't gone down either of those paths yet.

Gary learned a few things from those first properties. He knew he wanted more like them, and he knew that by adding value and buying right, he could create excellent results. He turned his attention from straight buy-and-hold real estate to value-creating fix and flips.

From Accidental Fix and Flipper to Purposeful Fix and Flipper

With his early experience behind him, Gary adopted a strategic approach to fixing and flipping. The first properties were actually bought with the buy-and-hold strategy in mind, but they ended up looking almost exactly like fix-and-flip deals. Once he saw the power of fixing and flipping, he decided to do more of it.

With the solid result of the first experience behind him, it didn't take very long for Gary to start thinking of ways to *get paid* at the beginning of a real estate project. He knew that, for the most part, he still wanted to hold on to his real estate for the long term, but he was only going to be satisfied with a deal if the property was set up for its holding period without any of his own cash in the deal and, on top of that, he even wanted to *take some cash out* as payment for himself and his father.

Gary knew all along that he'd eventually like to stop working full time with Bell Canada, so he was looking for ways to accelerate his path in that direction. He knew that he'd need some consistent income, and through his knowledge and his growing experience at adding value to properties, he thought he'd be able to earn that income by fixing and flipping.

While Gary does *sell* his fix and flips sometimes, he typically *refinances and rents.* In any case, he produces cash for himself early in the process, and is able to move on to the next deal without draining his own resources or leaving his family without an income. It's the essence of fixing and flipping: using multiple exit strategies (in Gary's case, refinancing, bringing in money partners, and selling) to accelerate a career in real estate investing and creating strong returns for investors as he goes along.

The Oshawa Fix and Flip

Purchase price: $150,000
Renovations expense: $23,000
Post-renovation appraisal: $210,000
Refinanced at 75% LTV: $157,500
Interest rate: 4.19%

Amortization: 20 years
Joint venture partner investment: $26,000
Cash pulled out: $10,500
Rental income: $1,325
Mortgage payment: $967
Other expenses: $300
Cash flow: Minimal

In late 2010, Gary found a property in Oshawa that he liked the look of. It had all the hallmarks of what he has since started calling a "McGowan deal":

1. **Motivated Seller:** "Above all, the seller wanted to close really quickly on the property. We gave him that, and in return, we were able to buy at a great price," says Gary. There are thousands of properties available on the market every day that will never make sense for a fix and flipper. Many of them need work, and so there could be value added through renovations, but unless you have the discipline to buy right, as Gary does, you'll never *add* value. Instead, you'll always remain stuck paying for the value that you should have added. A motivated seller is often the difference between a fix and flipper buying at the right price and spending too much. Gary found out that the seller of the Oshawa place wanted out of the property quickly and was willing to give up something on price to exit.

2. **Comparable Properties Were Selling for $30,000 to $60,000 More:** On the very same street as his subject property, there were other similar-size bungalows selling for between $180,000 and $210,000. Seeing this, and knowing that his own renovations wouldn't cost more than the $23,000 he ended up spending, Gary knew there was a real opportunity to not only hold a property with built-in value, but also to take some cash out for himself at the beginning. He knew he'd have to refinance up to the appraised value and take on a joint venture partner to do it, but with the ability to raise the value, Gary knew he had the foundation to achieve his goal of holding an excellent property, and also take cash out at the beginning.

3. **Simple Renovations Could Add Real Value:** Gary saw that the property needed work, but was nothing worse than just a bit rundown. The property did not need a lot of big-ticket items, and though Gary knew there are always *some* surprises, he was quite confident that there would not be too many on this property.

4. **Ability to Remove Cash for Himself:** Through an analysis of all the factors and knowing his numbers well, Gary thought there was a very solid probability that he'd be able to remove some cash for himself once the renovation and refinance were done and the joint venture partner was brought aboard.

Closing quickly on the property, Gary immediately went to work. He got his renovation crew working on:

- **Roof:** The shingles were in very bad shape, so they put a new roof on the property.

- **Paint:** The place was just old and dingy, so they repaired and repainted the entire interior of the property.

- **Floors:** They ripped up the nasty old carpet, revealing a gorgeous original hardwood floor, which they sanded down and refinished. Gary was blown away by this simple yet effective renovation, saying, "The refinished hardwood was probably the nicest hardwood floor I've ever seen."

- **Basement:** Showing a real nose for value creation, Gary spent very little money on the basement since it was not an additional suite, nor was it economically feasible to convert it into one. "The basement was just nasty, so we focused on cleaning it up," says Gary. The scope of work in the basement amounted to gutting everything, painting the floor, and making sure there was adequate lighting. While the basement wasn't living space, it also no longer left the impression that a monster or a bogeyman was hiding down there. Gary's most important renovation on this property might have been the one that he *didn't* do. "I recognized that the $30,000 or so that it would have cost me [to finish the basement] would never be recouped through additional value or cash flow, so I decided to leave it," says Gary. This is simple but powerful advice.

Always evaluate the renovations to be done through the same objective lens. The only time that a basement renovation will make sense is when it adds an additional suite, in which case, the value of the property will rise as will the rental capacity of the property. Since adding a suite was impossible in this property, and since it was going to cash flow even without the additional suite, Gary made the wise choice to forget about renovating the basement and just cleaned it up well.

- **Baseboards:** As part of cleaning up and modernizing the interior, Gary installed new baseboards throughout.

- **Kitchen:** Gary modernized the kitchen by putting in a new double sink, replacing the countertops, and *re-facing* (using the existing structure of the cabinets but making them look like new by painting them and installing new hardware) the cabinets. Notice that Gary did not get carried away buying and installing a whole new set of cabinets. At the end of the day, the property was going to remain a rental. A re-faced kitchen looks like new, and it's a lot less expensive than installing a new kitchen.

- **Exterior:** As with the basement, the exterior was in need of a good cleanup. Gary cut back all the overgrown trees, removed a decrepit garden shed, and cleaned up the yard. He also added a new number plate and mailbox.

The whole process, from the day Gary took possession of the property until it was refinanced, joint ventured, and tenanted, took just over a month. Not a bad month!

Why Gary Liked This Deal

As we saw with his original 14 units, Gary loves strong cash flow. Heck, who doesn't? From those first purchases to where he is today, Gary has consistently achieved excellent cash flow. But this deal resulted in only minimal cash flow. So what was different about this deal?

Gary has the same talent that a lot of successful fix and flippers seem to exhibit: the ability to be flexible. Of course it's wonderful to have a system, to have a set of rules that you always follow. But as a fix and flipper, you are an opportunist, and as such there are deals that you will be exposed to that might not fit your standard criteria.

As mentioned above, Gary was able to add significant value to the Oshawa fix and flip, so he liked that. The addition of value and his ability to bring on a partner who'd happily own half of a hands-free property meant that Gary was able to pay himself at the beginning. That reason alone was good enough to make this deal in spite of the low cash flow.

However, there was another excellent reason that arose while Gary was negotiating a mortgage. "This property happened to be the thirteenth one in my name. According to the bank's lending standards, I was a bad risk. So they only refinanced at 75 per cent of the value of the property, and on top of that only gave us a 20-year amortization," says Gary.

The downside of the shorter-than-usual amortization was that the mortgage payment was higher than Gary wanted it to be, which lowered the cash flow on the property. However, due to the short amortization, there was an upside. A much greater portion of each monthly payment would go toward principal rather than interest. Instead of the property producing cash like many of his others, this one produced equity at an outstanding speed. Instead of instantly available cash every month, this deal built equity. Gary and his partner would have to wait to access the cash they were paying down each month, but the property was a strong earner.

Starting from the first year of ownership, the mortgage pay-down was more than $5,000, which is excellent on a $157,500 mortgage. It means that, at the end of five years, there will be more than $28,000 of mortgage pay-down, which amounts to $466 per month. If you add that to the cash-flow numbers, the property starts to look a lot better.

In addition to the $37,000 of equity created through the targeted renovations, this property now looks pretty darn good. Without any appreciation happening in the market, Gary and his partner are looking at the creation of $65,000 over the first five years of owning the property.

Having an agile mind allowed Gary to see a deal here where others might not have been able to do so. Fixing and flipping is really the art of putting together deals like this one. The key factor of the creative deals is adding value where there wasn't any before. On this example, Gary did just that and helped achieve the objectives of everyone involved. The seller sold fast, the investor received a strong return, Gary got paid at the beginning, and the tenant has a wonderfully renovated property. Everybody wins.

The Fix-and-Flip Ability ("The Knack")

"I hate putting money into properties," says Gary. These are not exactly words you'd expect from a fix-and-flip expert who has utilized the strategy to great effect and accelerated his path toward full-time real estate investing in the process. He adds, "But once you get over the hump and realize that it's specific money into specific properties, and then you see the result of cleaning up something shabby and turning it into a nice property, you realize how powerful it can be."

Gary employs the reverse-thinking method that is so powerful to any real estate investor. He thinks from the end of a deal and works his way back to the beginning, so that he knows what the starting point is and what the steps along the way are. Gary explains it like this: "You start to do the math backwards and you say to yourself, 'Okay, if I have to spend $5,000 to renovate the property, and then I'll be able to raise my rents by $150 per month, how many months is it going to take me to recoup the money I spent renovating the property?'"

From this standpoint alone, Gary likes to renovate. It makes his holding period easier by attracting better tenants and higher rents, but more importantly, as a fix and flipper, he adds value. This means stronger returns whether selling or refinancing and holding, or bringing in a money partner. Knowing this trick, and knowing how to buy right, are the two biggest factors to Gary's success.

Finding Deals

For Gary, finding deals is just an extension of himself. Rather than cultivating certain methods for finding deals, he knows it is important to cultivate the attitude to find and capitalize on good deals. There are a few factors to developing that attitude:

Knowledge

When you know exactly what constitutes market value in a certain type of property in a certain neighbourhood, then you'll recognize a deal when you see it. You'll recognize it instantly, and this allows you to move on it quickly. Gary seeks opportunity in many places, but there are certain areas that he knows intimately.

Relationships

Gary will often speak to sellers for months or years before they finally sell to him. "I've been knocking on the door of this place in my neighbourhood every three or four months for the past couple of years. Let me tell you, when they decide to sell, they're calling me," says Gary. It's a matter of recognizing the seller's needs and staying in touch with them. Gary has gotten numerous deals just by being top of mind to certain motivated sellers.

In addition to having relationships with sellers, Gary has excellent relationships with real estate agents and other real estate professionals as well. "People know that we can make things happen, so it comes to a point where people are bringing you deals. If you get that reputation, people will know you can close quickly and take care of business, so the deals just come to you," says Gary.

Opportunism

Gary knows what an opportunity looks like. He's created the ability to see when a house's value might be lower and will require work to create value. He looks for a problem to solve, which doesn't always have to be difficult. "I was looking at the

MLS listings the other day when I saw a four-plex. It said in the comments, 'Tenants aren't co-operative, so you can't see one of the units,' and I thought to myself, 'This is the opportunity right here.'" Whereas a buyer less attuned to problem solving might forego a potentially good deal because of a tenant issue, Gary knew that taking care of that tenant situation could be the opportunity to solve a problem and make a strong return in the process. For the four-plex in question, evicting the problem tenant might be an opportunity to add value. Certainly the "problem tenant" would reduce the value of the property, so Gary saw a chance to add value by managing the property correctly.

Vision

If you're looking for "a deal," the definition is so broad that anything could potentially look good. But Gary thinks from the finish and works his way backwards. So, if he has a joint venture investor looking for a 10 per cent return, he simply has to reverse engineer the result. A specific property might produce a 9 per cent return at a certain asking price, but since Gary knows he's looking for a 10 per cent return, he also knows that he has to pay less for that property. Having the end result in mind allows Gary to say no to deals and also to negotiate with a definite highest price in mind. "On the Oshawa deal, I went to my joint venture partner and told them about the deal. I told them I was going to try and get the place for $150,000, but that I could go as high as $155,000. He said to me, 'What if the seller will only sell for $160,000 or more?' I replied, 'Actually, no, that won't work,' and I meant it," says Gary.

Negotiation

It's great to find awesome deals all day long, but if you can't negotiate the price and terms you want and then close on the property, finding them won't do you much good. Gary's approach to negotiation is simple but powerful. He always remains ethical and looks for ways to cater to the needs of the seller. In return, he asks for a favourable price. Whereas others will try to talk their way into a deal, Gary *listens* his way into a deal, finding out what the seller wants and looking for ways to provide it. With the Oshawa bungalow, the seller had just recently inherited the property from his mother. The seller was uncertain about how to go through the legalities of getting the property through probate. Gary gave the seller some pointers about how to do so and referred him to a lawyer who specializes in estate planning and wills. The seller called Gary when the property passed through probate, and they reached a deal. Gary was able to close quickly, which the seller wanted, and in return paid his desired price of $150,000. "There were others interested in buying the property, but none of them offered any assistance to him and they didn't listen. When it came time to sell, he called me first," says Gary.

A True Professional

Gary is a true professional in the real estate world. Fixing and flipping has helped to accelerate him into investing in real estate full time. While investing on a full-time basis is not for everyone, Gary's examples are applicable across the spectrum of fix-and-flip real estate. This is because adding value and buying right are universally important to the fix and flipper's craft.

Gary demonstrates these in spades and more importantly shows the importance of approaching the business ethically and through the development of relationships. Whether or not your goal is to be a full-time fix and flipper, take Gary's lessons and integrate them into your business.

9

How to Break Down a Contractor's Costs versus Materials Costs

In this chapter, Ian outlines the scope of work concept and a detailed approach to costing renovations.

In the last chapter I briefly touched on scope of work. In this chapter I'll go into greater depth.

The scope of work has a *lot* to do with breaking down a contractor's costs into materials and labour. Only by doing the detailed analysis of creating a scope of work can you clearly distinguish between labour and material costs.

The scope of work is your roadmap and your destination when you're looking for the contractor. In my previous book, *From Renos to Riches: The Canadian Real Estate Investor's Guide to Practical and Profitable Renovations,* I laid out the foundation for using a scope of work as a guideline for hiring contractors. You can't know which contractor to hire, how much to pay them, or even what you're paying them for, unless you understand the scope of work.

Since the scope of work will inform the fix and flipper about how much they will need to spend on the project, it's also an invaluable tool for determining a reasonable purchase price. As mentioned numerous times in this book already, the amount you pay for the purchase of the property and then how much you spend on the renovations are the two largest factors in having a profitable fix and flip (or an *unprofitable* fix and flip). Therefore, the scope is ultimately important to the fix and flipper. Below is a detailed discussion of how to create a scope of work.

How to Create a Scope of Work

1. **Work in Silence:** This first step is critical. Turn off all of the noise. This means external noise (smartphones, laptops, radio, and distracting people) and internal noise (cares, worries, concerns).

2. **Create a Detailed List:** Once all the noise is turned off, I go to the project site, often with my trusted advisor and lead worker, Adam. We take only a clipboard. This process takes half a day, or a whole day, or sometimes more than a day. We go through the property room by room and we jot down everything that needs to be done on the entire job. Each room will have its own page or pages, and each section of each room is given a plan of exactly what is to be done.

3. **Source Materials:** After the detailed list is complete, we go back to the war room and build our materials list. Based on our knowledge and our experience, we know what products we'll be using much of the time. We estimate how much of each product we need to use, and we make a materials list that includes the amount of product and its SKU number.

4. **Summarize Procedures:** When we hand this scope of work to another contractor, and even when we do the work internally, we need to be totally clear on not only what needs to be done, but also on the procedure of how it gets done. Imagine a car manufacturer who didn't have a set of procedures. Each car produced would be different, and the ability of the company to produce consistent quality would be compromised. With houses, it's impossible to recreate the same level of procedures as with cars on an assembly line, but we still must have procedures wherever possible. In this stage, each individual job is broken down into specific procedures. No contractor who works on my jobsite will be able to say that they didn't know I wanted something done a certain way.

5. **Build Scope of Work:** Once I have the first four steps complete, I'm able to make this actual thing called a scope of work. It's a small book made up of individual scopes of work for each job that is to be done. Each individual page will include the exact procedure and the exact materials that are to be used. Together, these individual pages make up the whole scope of work that will be used as the roadmap for the project.

Get Detailed Quotes

If you have experience dealing with contractors, you may have seen a quote before. Even if your only experience with contractors was that you had a small renovation done on your personal residence, then you've probably seen quotations before.

My problem with quotations is that they are often not detailed enough. For example, they don't always break down the difference between labour and materials. A quote may be only a price based on a job. As a person hiring a contractor or a sub-contractor, you don't always know what you're paying for. I've seen a lot of people pay for jobs where they just plain didn't know what they were paying for.

Moreover, the contractor may not provide an estimate of the amount of time the job will require. As a customer, not only do you not know if you're paying for labour or materials, but you also don't know how much labour you're paying for. On top of that, they won't state the hourly rate for their services.

A lot of people hire contractors without knowing any of these things, and unsurprisingly, they pay too much for the whole job. If only they knew how much the materials and labour were really worth, they could pay a more accurate price.

That's why it's so important that you get detailed quotes. Tell every contractor or sub-contractor that you're dealing with that you require costs to be broken down into labour and materials. This will include a materials list so you can cross-reference the costs. In addition, you must tell any contractor giving you a quote that you require a clear estimate of time for the project as well as a breakdown of time per task.

Using Scope of Work to Source Contractors

When you're fixing and flipping houses, it's imperative that you don't act like a normal homeowner. Your goal is different, and ultimately you want to be able to repeat your system. You can't just close your eyes, pick a business card out of a hat and hope for the best when sourcing contractors.

As with my method of creating a scope of work, I break down sourcing contractors into a series of steps.

Put Out the Scope to Your Network

Whatever network of contractors you already have, it's a great idea to use this resource first. This is how you build solid relationships and how you *train contractors* to do the kind of work that you need done. What the contractors in your circle will begin to understand is that you might be a regular source of work for them. All they have to do to take this work every time is follow your system and do the work to the specifications on your scope of work.

Advertise

If your usual network turns up nothing, it's time to go shopping for a contractor. As a beginning fix and flipper (or if your plan is to do flips irregularly), shopping for a contractor or sub-contractors will be an invaluable process. You want to write an ad that will entice contractors and sub-contractors to bid on your job.

I only advertise online. It just doesn't make sense to pay for print ads anymore when you get all the viewers you will ever need online. I utilize Kijiji the most, but in some parts of Canada, Craigslist is more effective. To get the maximum coverage, use every online advertising source that is practical.

In your advertisement, you want to weed out the contractors and sub-contractors who can't do what you require. You only want ones who can tackle the job at hand. This is why you must post a mini scope of work in your advertisement. You have to make a version of the scope of work that outlines all the different jobs. You can't post the entire scope of work with all the process descriptions and product specifications, but you can list all the jobs. This list of jobs will be enough to attract some contractors and sub-contractors.

Field Calls

Between your existing network and online advertisements, there never seem to be a shortage of people looking for work projects. The truth is that these simple steps have *always* provided me with plenty of interest. I field calls from the various contractors and I filter them based on what I hear on the phone.

I like to look for people who are open-minded, people who think they can do better than what they are currently doing, and who want to learn. If they want to learn how to fix and flip houses, I'm fine with that. I'm not concerned about competition, and I love sharing my knowledge. I actually title my ads "Successful House Flipper Looking to Build Strong Working Relationship." This attracts contractors who want to learn the ropes, and I like that.

Most people who answer your ads will be TGVs. You have to be able to spot which of those TGVs want something better and will serve not only your own needs, but their own needs as well.

Bring Selected Contractors Over for Quotes

After those initial steps, it's time to bring the contractors to the jobsite. I line them up for quotes, back to back.

Having all the contractors come through in a row achieves a couple of purposes. It allows me to finish the entire process in one day, and it also allows the contractors to see that there was someone quoting before them and someone after them. I don't do this to intimidate them into pushing their price down; it's to let them see how organized I am, and how much I treat this like a business. Having them bring their best price on their quote is an added advantage. In fact, I make a point of telling them I'm not looking for the cheapest quote; I'm looking for the best quote. I tell them what constitutes the best quote: organization, being specific, and attention to detail.

I tell each contractor that I have an exact materials list and I will provide the materials for the job. I show them the materials list on each scope of work.

I tell them that what I really want from them is an estimate of the man hours it will take them to complete each task, based on the procedures that I've provided and on their own viewing of the house. I tell them that in addition to their time estimation, I want a price.

Compare Quotes

Once you've brought in the contractors and told them what you want from them, it's time to collect quotes. I always tell them I want it by the next day. Since materials are separated from the equation, and you're asking for an estimation of time that it will take them to finish the project, you've now got a clear picture of how they value their time.

Using this system means there is no grey area. You know that you're paying each contractor a certain amount of money for time invested, and by dividing the price by the time, you know exactly how much each hour is worth.

When you're comparing your quotes, you'll see the differences in the amount of time estimated. If six contractors estimate that Job A will take 40 man hours, and two contractors estimate that the same job will take 65 hours, you know that the two are likely adding hours to add money.

Hire a Contractor

When you've seen all the quotes, or at least enough quotes, it's time to call the one that you believe is the most professional and provides value for the amount of money you'll be paying them. Then ask them if they want the job.

As I mentioned above, I don't choose the contractor based only on price. I want people who have an accurate grasp of what needs to be done. Using the same example as above, if the bulk of contractors quoted 40 hours for a particular task (and I know what's involved myself), and another one quoted 20 hours, there's a good chance the 20-hour estimate is unrealistic. Sure, his or her price might have been better as a result of the low time estimate, but it doesn't serve anyone if that contractor ends up taking 40 hours and therefore gets paid half of what he or she deserves.

Note that it's still a good idea to keep the other contractors in your back pocket. This does *not* mean promising them anything or deceiving them in any way. It means being honest with them and telling them that you didn't select their quote this time, but that doesn't mean you won't ever need them. In fact, you might need them on that job later if anything happens to the first contractor you hired.

Shocked by His Workload

On a recent job, I needed a labourer for a whole pile of heavy work that needed to be done. I needed him to remove garbage and carry building materials into the property. I followed the exact procedure that I just laid out for you above in order to find my labourer.

The young man seemed perfectly suited for the job; he was a big, strong, bright-looking young man, and he seemed eager to get to work. He worked for the first part of the morning removing much of the household and demolition waste.

At around 9:30 a.m., the delivery truck with all the materials for the entire job showed up and started unloading three skids of materials.

At 10:00 a.m., the young man said he was off to the store for snacks and a drink. Not a problem—except that he didn't come back!

> Luckily, I had a list of other labourers to call. By noon I had a new labourer on-site and he completed all the work that we required.
>
> Because of this kind of situation, I recommend that you always keep workers and contractors in your back pocket. Recruiting workers through Kijiji ads is a perfect opportunity to do just that.

Scope of Work Is Not Just for Advanced Flippers

Having a scope of work is wonderful for a few reasons. First, as we've been discussing, it's a management tool to help you find contractors and give them a clear picture of what you need them to do and how you want it done.

Second, it's a shining beacon for you in the rough times during a flip, the times you might wonder if it's ever going to end. You can use your scope of work as a marker. As you complete tasks, you can go back over the scope of work and see the progress you've made.

Third, it helps keep you on task. It's easy to go off the path from time to time on a large project, or even on a smaller one, and a scope of work will help reduce the chances of that happening. This is especially true if you're doing most of the work yourself. It's one thing having a boss or a project manager keeping things on task, but when you're self-directed, you need to use your own motivation to keep yourself on track. The scope of work is like your inner boss coming back to you and reminding you where you're going and what's at stake. It's a snapshot of where your mind was when you were thinking clearly, with your mind on the bigger picture, at the beginning of a project.

The scope of work may seem like a very advanced step, and some of the process that I laid out is perhaps a little bit too much for you at the beginning. *That's okay!* Think of your flipping self as a work-of-art in progress. You can be complete as you are now, and at the same time you can come back later with new colours and touch yourself up.

Even if your projects are small and you're a beginner, get into the habit of creating and following a scope of work. You will get better and better at it, but you'll never be perfect. My scope of work is now a complex document designed to keep control of complex projects, but guess what? I'm still improving every single time I take on a new project, and each time I improve it, I find myself running a tighter ship.

You guessed it: a tighter ship means more profit on your flip projects.

Having a Scope of Work Saved Me $500 and a Day

Actually, having a scope of work saves me many thousands of dollars on each job, without fail, *every single time*. I have no doubt about this, but I wanted to share one small specific example with you, so you can see exactly what I mean.

On a recent job, I hired a drywaller for some new drywall taping in a newly framed room. In most of the rest of the house we were repairing a few large holes and a number of mangled spots rather than installing new drywall.

So I created a scope of work, not only for the new area but also for the repairs that were needed elsewhere. There were two jobs for my drywall contractor: the new room, and the repairs in the rest of the house. My drywall contractor knew exactly what he had to do while he was there. He was happy to do it because it made the job more profitable for him.

For me, it was great because it meant that a task was done quickly, by the right person, at the right time, and best of all my in-house crew didn't have to be pulled off another job and put onto this little drywall repair job. I estimate that it would have taken two of my guys an entire day (split up over a few days) to finish it. That's about $500 of labour and it means whatever they were doing at the time would have been put on hold, which would have put us behind schedule.

This is precisely the kind of small task that gets lost in the mix when you're juggling multiple tasks, even on a not-so-big job.

Having a clear and detailed scope of work saved my bacon on that job and it saves my bacon time and time again. I urge you to create a detailed scope of work even if—especially if—you're a beginner.

Fix-and-Flip Profile: Jeff Reed

High-End Fix and Flips Bring High-End Results

How He Got Started

Jeff Reed is a Toronto-based fix and flipper who focuses on the higher-end Beach and East York neighbourhoods. Jeff's story—from his days as a licensed carpenter to becoming a full-time fix and flipper—is a study in consistent measured progress. Jeff has learned many of the valuable skills of a successful fix and flipper through years of hard work and continuous growth. Today, Jeff operates a successful real estate investment business with a focus on adding value through fix and flips called Priority Management Ltd. Through his abilities and passion for what he does, he's creating outstanding results for his investors.

One thing we've found by talking to numerous fix and flippers is that each one brings a different skill set to their fix-and-flip business. Wade Graham showed us the value of patience and earning money the day you buy. Gary McGowan showed us the power of partnerships and earning income up front while holding the property for the long term, and Cindy Wennerstrom showed us the value of design.

The successful fix and flippers are the ones who have identified both their strengths and their weaknesses. They focus on their strengths and work hard in those areas, and wherever they don't have a specific strength, they are not afraid to hire someone more knowledgeable or gifted than they are.

Jeff is no exception to this rule. Through his growth from carpentry to construction management to full-time flipper, Jeff has developed a rock-solid ability to manage construction projects. Understanding the scope of work on a project, budgeting correctly, and then sticking strongly to his budget allows Jeff to know which projects will be profitable and which won't. His *knowledge* is his best protection against loss of profit, and, on the flip side, it's his best guarantee of a profitable fix-and-flip project.

Through his knowledge and experience, Jeff has also been inspired to help educate real estate investors about how to properly renovate their own projects, and how to properly fix and flip real estate. He cites the flipping TV shows currently available as being a negative influence on the *reality* of fixing and flipping: "You see it on TV—they claim to finish a flip in two weeks and make a huge profit every time," says Jeff. Jeff's message is more realistic, but in the end, more positive as well because he believes there are real profits to be made fixing and flipping.

Jeff's own authority on the matter is derived from his experience and his success. He's been in the construction industry since he was 17 years old, and now that he's 40, the combination of hands-on business, project management, and design experience allow Jeff to work at the level he currently does as a fix and flipper.

Ultimately though, Jeff—like many fix-and-flip specialists—is an entrepreneur first. Throughout his working life, he's done something that many entrepreneurs do. "I find that entrepreneurs get bored, and they always want to switch what they're doing, but real estate has so many different skill sets and sub-fields that there are no limits to what you can do with it," says Jeff. Real estate in general—and fixing and flipping in particular—stimulate Jeff's need to always be learning and growing as a professional.

Jeff learned the carpentry trade at a young age. He enjoyed the work, and it was his training as a licensed carpenter that laid the groundwork for the next step, even if the next step wasn't totally planned. "I developed carpal tunnel syndrome from swinging a hammer, and rather than get out of construction completely, I got into construction management." Sometimes the best things that happen to us aren't planned. Without his training in construction management, Jeff would not be the same fix and flipper that he is today.

Jeff credits his long stint in construction management with playing a huge role in allowing him to grow into the role of full-time fix and flipper, saying, "Flipping is like second nature to me." He managed construction jobs for other companies for many years before striking out on his own.

Working as a project manager for other companies, Jeff learned the higher end of the market, managing projects in Toronto's Rosedale district. Most projects were in the range of $500,000 to $1 million, so Jeff got very good at a couple of things: 1) budgeting; and 2) cutting-edge design. He liked what he saw in the more expensive end of the housing market, and something stuck with him: the fact that more valuable houses breed larger opportunities. He also recognized that he liked to do very thorough renovation jobs. He always liked to leave his projects knowing that nothing about the property would be wanting for repairs once he left. High-end projects allowed him the margin to work this way.

After branching out on his own as a renovator, Jeff still focused on very large and thorough renovation projects, but most of them were under $500,000 in total cost. Obviously, this still represented a significant renovation, and his clients had an enormous amount invested. While owning his own business, Jeff learned the rest of what he needed to know about managing a project and providing massive value to a renovation project. With years as a general contractor under his belt, Jeff's education as a flipper was almost complete.

As he was honing his skills for project management, Jeff was thinking about getting into investment real estate all the while. He knew that, eventually, he'd make the move into doing his own fix-and-flip projects full time. Jeff had purchased his first home when he was 19, and through the years has bought and sold several homes. He was well aware of the power of real estate as a class of investments, and he knew how to add value through renovations. Jeff partook in numerous "live-in" flips prior to becoming a fix and flipper.

He always focused on buying a property where he could add value and where he could separate the renovations into different parts of the house. Ultimately, Jeff found that renovating while you live in a house is too disruptive, so he discontinued the practice, but it did serve to bring him up to speed enough on his real estate training that he was able to confidently make the leap into full-time fixing and flipping. It also provided him with the current home he lives in.

Jeff's Final "Live-In Flip"

The final "live-in flip" ended up being the home he has lived in since 2003. Jeff bought the place for its value as an investment. It was in rough shape, but the structure of the place was perfect for what he wanted to accomplish.

He did a fairly quick renovation on the upstairs suite, knowing that the rent from the upstairs tenant would carry the monthly expenses of the property while he completed the job.

Just as he planned, the upstairs suite was easily rented and the mortgage and other monthly expenses were covered by the tenant.

Once he had the upstairs tenanted, he moved himself downstairs while renovating the basement. "I continued to dig out the basement. I actually had Bobcats in the basement while people lived upstairs. I wasn't too popular with my tenants for a while." But he did a nice renovation downstairs that was long lasting and good enough for him to live in personally for three years. When the upstairs tenant finally moved along, Jeff took the opportunity to give the upstairs a more thorough renovation. Once the more thorough renovation was complete upstairs, he moved upstairs, and Jeff still makes the upstairs suite his home.

The basement has been rented out since he moved back upstairs. The suited house is a great place to live, and a great investment for Jeff. The renters alone have covered the property expenses for all these years, effectively giving Jeff a place to live for free.

Most importantly, through the experience of his "live-in flips," Jeff learned some important lessons about flipping, landlording, and the power of holding real estate as well.

The experience also brought home to him that his six-year dream of getting into real estate full time was achievable. Jeff had the evidence he needed as well as the proof to himself that he was the one to do it.

The First Real Fix and Flip

For Jeff, it wasn't too much of a stretch to make the transition from a general contracting business to a fixing-and-flipping business. The projects were almost exactly the same, but the biggest difference was that he was now the owner of the property he was renovating. For his fix and flips, he decided that he would take a property that was in rough shape and apply his knowledge, team, and expertise to transform it.

The biggest difference, of course, was that he was working for himself and not for a customer. But in so many other ways, the process was similar. He had to make a budget and stick to it, and he had to know his scope of work perfectly well. With the right business acumen, he'd be able to make his projects successful.

He'd also have to buy right, which was something he'd already had a little bit of success at through his "live-in flips." This was going to be a little bit different again because, on the "live-in flips," if he got the price a little bit wrong, he could write it off as a living expense. With this new full-time fix-and-flip project, Jeff would have to be profitable or risk having to go back to the general contracting business, which he certainly could do, but it wasn't the direction he wanted to take.

So Jeff set out looking for a good deal. He came across a fire-damaged house in the East York area of Toronto. Jeff says of the property, "The couple who were selling it were going through a separation. It's one of those things where, who knows, maybe the relationship went first and someone set fire to the house, I don't know." What Jeff did know was that at the price of $105,000 there was plenty of room to renovate the property and sell at a significant profit. At the time, he figured that he'd be able to sell it for about $375,000 after he did all the necessary renovations. He also knew that he'd have to invest about $175,000 into the renovation in order to bring it up to saleable standard. The renovations on this particular place were no small potatoes: "The fire had destroyed the roof, and all the rain and snow had been coming in for about a year," said Jeff of his prized new property.

Just as he purchased the property, Jeff was scheduled to go away for a month-long trip to the Caribbean. His plan was to begin the renovation as soon as he arrived back in Canada. But before he left, his realtor suggested that Jeff test the market while he was gone. The agent had the feeling that with the amount of money that could be made in the place, there might be a buyer willing to pay Jeff enough that both parties could make a profit. Jeff left his agent with these instructions: "I want $160,000 for it at minimum, otherwise I'm not selling it, and as soon as I get home, I'm going to start gutting it." The agent listed the house and Jeff left for the Caribbean.

While he was basking in the warm tropical sun, Jeff received a message from his agent that there were two offers on it, and the better of the two was for $165,000. When Jeff arrived home, the paperwork was completed and Jeff walked away from his first fix and flip without even lifting a hammer. "The only unfortunate thing is that it set the bar pretty high because I've done some six-month fix and flips and made the same amount of money."

Becoming a Full-Time Business – Jeff's Business Model

After his flip, Jeff realized all the more that he wanted to do real estate full time. He joined REIN (the Real Estate Investment Network) and upped his level of knowledge through focused education on real estate. He learned that there were so many different strategies and that REIN focuses on holding real estate long-term for wealth creation. He thought REIN was on to something.

Through his additional real-estate-specific knowledge and existing project management and renovations knowledge, Jeff was able to take his business to the next level. He developed more strategies for successfully fixing and flipping properties. He discovered a more advanced technique known as a "slow flip," and he learned how to renovate a property, refinance it, and hold it for cash flow and appreciation. The net effect of all the changes that Jeff has made is that he's a far more sophisticated fix and flipper now than he was before.

Jeff has now structured his company so that he runs his active income through his corporation. He has a holdings company and a renovation company. Whenever he holds a property, it remains in his holding company, and whatever properties he sells go through his renovation company. He ends up paying the Ontario corporate tax rate of 16 per cent when he sells a property instead of the huge capital gains tax (there is no capital gains exemption on fix and flips). Jeff's tax strategy allows him to show a strong enough active income, without having to pay exorbitantly high taxes. With his active income as it is, the banks look kindly upon him and continue to lend him money as long as his debt service numbers remain strong, something that Jeff, like many wise investors, pays close attention to.

In an ideal world, Jeff would like to sell one or two flips, and then hold on to the third, but up until now, he's profited between $30,000 and $40,000 on average. Understanding his local market has led him to adjust his strategy to hold on to a property for about a year after he's done the renovations. "The Toronto Beach district has been appreciating about 6 per cent per year lately, and most of my properties are worth between $600,000 and $800,000 once I've completed the renovation. If you do the math (6 per cent appreciation on $600,000), this means an additional $36,000 minimum once I sell a year later."

This means that Jeff has to have strong cash flowing on a property during his holding period while he plays the market growth, something that isn't a problem because of the strategy he uses to add an additional suite to all his properties.

The "Slow Flip" – One of Jeff's Favourites

Jeff is currently holding a property that he calls a "slow flip." As of this moment, he hasn't yet decided how he will exit the property, but he does have two sold options. He can:

1. sell the property; or

2. rent-to-own the property.

He's already refinanced it, and is planning on holding it for at least a year. The property details look like this:

Purchase price: $300,000

Renovation expense: $200,000

Appraised value: $600,000

Refinanced for: $480,000

Money left in: $20,000

Property type: Legal duplex

Where: Toronto's Beach neighbourhood

Remember that the power of fixing and flipping is derived from the fact that the investor can pull out all or most of the initial money invested in a property. On this deal, Jeff left only $20,000 of his own money in the property. Contrast this with a traditional buy and hold: if you were to purchase a $500,000 duplex using the traditional buy-and-hold model, the investor would leave $100,000 in the property (20 per cent down payment).

Because Jeff added so much value through his renovation, he was able to pull out all that excess cash and leave only $20,000 in during the holding period. Of course, Jeff will be able to pull all of that $20,000 out along with a healthy profit when he sells. In the meantime, he's okay holding a cash-flowing property in a prime neighbourhood.

Jeff expects the property to appreciate a further $36,000 during the year he holds it, but if the market should turn, he's okay to continue holding it for longer because he has solid financing on the property, and it cash flows as is.

At minimum, Jeff expects to pull $100,000 from the property when he sells it, and likely up to $136,000 or more. The current tenants have shown a strong interest in buying the property and Jeff may choose to help them ease their way into it via a rent-to-own.

Jeff's slow flip will likely earn him a profit that is ultimately equal to an entire year or more of income for many people—not a bad strategy.

Adding Value – Basement Suites

As with most successful fix and flippers, Jeff has tried-and-true methods for adding value to projects. Jeff's value-adding techniques focus on two major features: 1) adding space; and 2) modernizing design.

With a strong local knowledge of the North York district of Toronto, Jeff quickly realized the need for additional suites in older homes. The Toronto region is typically quite open to additional suites as long as they are built to code and have passed inspection. Jeff learned to fulfill the needs of the region by adding legal suites to existing older homes.

Adding the suite achieves two major objectives:

1. **It raises the value of the property:** Any investor looking for a property that generates a strong income will immediately see that having two suites in the same building will fulfill their need for a stronger income. This improves the market for potential buyers. Both investors and homeowners who are looking for a "mortgage helper" suite are attracted to a property with two suites. This strong demand pushes up the market value of a suited house.

2. **Raises rental figures:** If the exit strategy for the property in question is to refinance and then hold the property for an extended period, it will be absolutely vital that the property earn strong rental numbers. By adding a second suite, the property will nearly double in terms of rental income. Along with buying right in the first place and getting a good refinance, having a strong rental income is the major factor in ensuring the property will be a strong property to hold on to.

"Most of the houses that haven't been upgraded have basement ceilings that are just over six feet. So every time you dig out a basement, you're adding 33 per cent more usable space to a property," says Jeff. Space that was once a storage area now becomes a serious income generator.

Adding Value – Top-Ups

Another of Jeff's favourite methods for adding value is to do a top-up, which means adding a second floor to an existing bungalow.

Ask your realtor to send you a list of properties in the same neighbourhood. Ask for listings for bungalows with around 1,000 square feet of above-grade living space. Also ask for listings of two-storey homes with approximately 2,000 square feet of living space. You'll see that the bigger places are worth more! People pay for more living space.

Jeff realized this very early in his flipping days and he commonly applies this technique in his original focus area of North York. Now that he's working more in the Beach, he's more focused on semi-detached homes that already have a second floor. This makes the top-up strategy unnecessary for him now. Instead he focuses on adding the basement suite (as mentioned above) or on redesign and reconfiguring of the main floor (as discussed below).

As with the addition of a basement suite, Jeff's focus with the top-up strategy is to add livable space, something that people will pay good money for; in other words, he adds value through his focused renovations.

Adding Value – Open Concept and Modern Design Elements

"Most of the houses that I'm flipping are from the turn of the last century, and most of them come with a separate formal dining room," says Jeff, who sees opportunity to add value when he considers these separate dining rooms. Nobody wants separate formal dining rooms now. They want an open concept so there's no barrier between the kitchen and dining room. They want the rooms to flow and an open space concept to the property.

Jeff gives people what they want in terms of design, tearing down unnecessary walls and turning the whole main floor into an open concept. He also seeks out other hot design trends and delivers these to his future buyers. "I regularly go and look at the one-bedroom condos that cost over $800,000," says Jeff. This is where he finds the work of the most cutting-edge designers. He's also in touch with a couple of highly regarded architects who keep Jeff up to date with the work they're doing.

In addition to making his flips open concept, Jeff also likes to provide exposed brick, concrete floors, and exposed joists. All of these are part of what Jeff calls the "loft look" that most homebuyers (25- to 45-year-olds) are seeking in his target markets. Homebuyers and renters like modern design with an open concept and the loft look. Jeff solves the problem of homebuyers and renters' needs and provides a solution. In doing so, he creates an opportunity for himself.

Staying within Budget

Throughout his years as a construction manager and his time as a flipper, Jeff has developed a consistent system for staying within budget. It's almost become second nature to Jeff, but he always sticks to his system for creating and sticking to a budget.

"If you spend the time up front defining the scope of work well enough, it's not too difficult to stay on budget," Jeff says. He adheres to the belief that if everything is quantified, it's achievable within the project's scope. This means that any renovation can be profitable, so long as the numbers are verified in advance. This obviously implies buying right, which is always the first step to a profitable fix-and-flip project.

For pricing, Jeff uses the same crews of sub-contractors over and over again, so he's always certain that he's getting a fair price. That doesn't stop him from checking his numbers to make sure they all make sense. Jeff uses a few trusted websites that post unit pricing in the Toronto area to make sure he's receiving a fair price. "If an HVAC guy, for example, comes to me with a quote that's twice as much as it should be, I never get burned because a) I know my pricing well, and b) if I'm unsure, I can go to my unit pricing websites and verify. I'm always well prepared to make sure I get the right price," says Jeff.

Flipping Horror Stories and Jeff's Message to New Fix and Flippers

We are very grateful to Jeff for sharing his wisdom with us for this book. He brings a truly professional touch to the fix-and-flip game, and as a result he meets a lot of people who want advice and who want to share their experiences.

Jeff told us a story about a beginning fix and flipper who did pretty much everything wrong on his first flip project. "He came up to me to tell me his story, and basically, he didn't do his homework. He had bought in at $500,000 and thought he could do the renovation for $150,000. He went and got quotes from numerous contractors and the lowest quote was $250,000. He was complaining to me about contractors and how they're overpriced, so I asked him what the scope of work was. When he explained it to me, I told him that he was crazy to expect to do that renovation for $150,000."

The would-be flipper bought at too high a price, he underestimated his renovation expense by at least $100,000, he didn't have a clear scope of work, he didn't have drawings, he didn't have permits, and the list goes on and on.

Jeff sees the fix and flipper's failure as one of poor preparation. If he was well educated on the renovation costs prior to closing on the property, he would have realized that there's no way he could have spent $500,000 on the purchase and still make money. Everything else fell apart from that point. Once he'd overpaid by $200,000, there was little he could do to salvage the project, but he only overpaid because he wasn't educated on what his expenses would be.

Speaking to fix and flippers like this gentleman has made Jeff believe that education is the key for people to be successful in all their real estate investment renovations, especially fix-and-flip projects.

Jeff's biggest message to people wanting to fix and flip is to educate themselves on the finer points of the business so they don't end up like some of the horror stories he's heard. One horrible experience trying to fix and flip can be enough to turn someone off the business forever. On the other hand, if you get educated, know your scope of work, understand your market, and know how to work with contractors, you can be very successful fixing and flipping.

10

How to Set Up a Joint Venture

In this chapter, Mark talks about the mechanics of a joint venture and how it can be a successful business partnership.

The term "comfort zone" may be somewhat overused, but it is still meaningful. When speaking about partnering with someone else, you absolutely *must* step outside your comfort zone.

Practically speaking, what it means is this: most people will seek out people who have a similar—not a different—skill set. They may not know how to evaluate a skill set or experience that is unfamiliar. For example:

- Two brilliant hands-on renovators join forces.
- Two deal-makers create a joint venture.
- Two people with money and no knowledge get together.

What's the point of partnering with someone who has the same skills as you? You don't need someone else to be you! When you partner with others who have the same set of skills, your project will be put at risk. For example, if two brilliant hands-on renovators partner together, but neither knows how to put the deal together financially, there's a good chance the partnership will be at risk because of the possibility of overpaying for a property.

If you can find the deal, but you don't know how to finance the project, then you'll need someone on board who will be able to put together the financing to get the deal done. In reality, the same person who can architect a great deal is also the same person who will likely be able to put together the financing. But depending on where that person is in his or her own development as an investor, that individual may still be developing the complementary skills to supplement the deal-finding ability. In such a case, it might be best for the deal-finder to partner with a finance person.

Putting together the pieces of the puzzle (the skills needed on the project) will lead to orderly success of your fix-and-flip projects. In truth, most people figure out the hard way exactly what their skill sets are. They typically do their first fix and flip alone or with a brother-in-law (or someone else they have a relationship with) and they suffer through their weaknesses. Those who are able to find success in fixing and flipping will usually figure out that they can't do it all and they must partner with people who have complementary skills. Some of the skills required are:

- ability to source liquid funds
- hands-on renovation ability
- ability to manage a renovation project
- marketing
- deal-finding
- ability to qualify for mortgage
- ability to put together financing
- ability to raise money
- knowing what their exit strategies are

I recommend that you strive to be like the pros: focus on what you're best at and figure out how to partner or outsource the other things. Work on your area of brilliance.

"Creative" Partnerships and Strategies

In the real estate education industry, there is never a shortage of seminars and programs teaching creative investing strategies. Maybe some of these creative strategies work, but in general, I've found that it's better to seek simple, standard, and consistently attainable types of deals. Creative strategies often fail for a few reasons:

1. There is often less actual cash in the deal—the property can be financed 100 per cent or higher—which means there is more debt to service.

2. When negotiating with the homeowner, the seller has the right to demand certain terms, which can impact the investor's exit strategy. Practically speaking, this

means that you as the buyer might be bound by restrictive terms such as overly expensive vendor take backs or agreements that require you to provide a fixed return when your own return is unknown.

3. Often the only kinds of sellers interested in a creative strategy are the ones who can't get rid of the property through a normal sale. Typically it's a property that can't be rented. Beware: when you get a property through a creative strategy, you're often inheriting other people's problems.

Ian and I did a creative fix-and-flip deal that illustrates point 2 very well. The deal broke down like this:

- I raised the money for renovations and put the deal together, including financing.

- We set up a joint venture with money investors, us, and the homeowner.

- Ian managed the renovation.

- I marketed the property after the renovations were complete.

- The seller retained his ownership of the property through the process and was promised a certain price once the house sold after renovations.

- Ian and I got power of attorney for the duration of the deal.

- The seller registered a second mortgage against the property to protect the investor's money.

Everything looked to be going along just fine, until the day the property was listed on the market. It also happened to be the day that Lehman Brothers collapsed in the fall of 2008.

Needless to say, all money was running scared at that moment, and the pain didn't stop at the U.S. border. We had a heck of a time selling that property. The reality is that if we hadn't already promised the seller that we'd sell for a certain price *as soon as we completed the renovation*, then we would have had more options. Let's run through them:

- **Sell**: This became an unprofitable option when the market suddenly went soft.

- **Refinance**: The property did not have the value to get cash out to pay the seller and carry the rest.

- **Rent**: Because we had promised the seller that we would get him his agreed price when we were done, this was not an option.

The final result was that Ian and I ended up selling the property and taking home about $500 between the two of us. It was a four-month-long project that took some serious work on our part, and we barely broke even. The seller got his promised price, the investors got their return, but we made almost nothing.

Here's the kicker: within six months, we could have sold the property for $50,000 more than we did. If we could have had our way, we definitely would have held on to the property until we could have realized a stronger sale price. But since we had already promised the seller that we'd sell, we did not have the flexibility to use a different exit strategy.

The "creative" deal ended up being a great learning experience, and we've both discovered since then that getting enough money to *buy* a fix and flip is easy and we don't bother doing these kinds of deals, since they limit our ability to exercise multiple exit strategies.

Standard Purchases

There is more money looking for a good deal than there are good deals looking for money. Drill that truism into your head until you believe it. It simply is true. Talk to everyone about your deals, do one good one, systematize it, and then tell everyone you know about it. In fact, tell people who you *don't* know about it (without bragging, of course). With a small track record of success, rather than having to look for money, my problem has become *turning people away* who want to invest with me. Private money lenders in particular like to get their 8 to 12 per cent on a regular basis. When you pay them out and take a couple of months off, they practically beg you to get their money back to work.

I would consider a standard purchase to use at least one and likely two or more of the following sources of money:

- 20% down payment mortgage
- cash
- line of credit (yours)
- line of credit (your partner's)
- private loan

Standard renovation expenses are financed at least one and likely two or more of the following ways:

- cash
- private loan
- line of credit
- store credit
- credit cards

Credit cards are not the preferred way to finance a renovation, but if the timeframe is short, and you know you'll be able to pay it off quickly, it might be okay to use a credit card in some circumstances.

There's a simple reason why investors like to give their money to fix and flippers. By solving big problems, we *add* value. This necessarily means that the return is better than a standard buy and hold where the property is purchased at market value and no value is added. In those standard buy-and-hold deals, investors put their money in on day one and don't expect to see it back right away. They often receive a cash-flow cheque, but they do not get the bulk of their investment back right away.

It's a rule of fixing and flipping that most of the original money put into the property is taken out within six months, and it often happens that the investor *also* gets a tidy cash-flow cheque after his or her money is taken out. As a rule of thumb, I like to have *at minimum* 75 per cent of cash taken out of the property by the time the renovation is done and the exit strategy is executed. Let's run through the top three exit strategies again:

1. **Sell**: Take all the cash and move to the next project.
2. **Refinance and Hold**: Take most, all, or even more cash out and hold the property at a strong cash-flow position.
3. **Rent**: Without pulling cash out immediately, this is the least attractive option, but in a pinch it's better than selling at a loss or small profit.

So imagine you're an investor who wants a solid return. Imagine you had $100,000 to invest. Would you rather have: 1) your entire $100,000 returned to you within a few months; 2) your entire $100,000 locked up for years until you received a return; or 3) your entire

$100,000 returned to you within a few months, and *then* receive another significant return a few years down the road?

Options 1 and 3 are available to investors when they invest in a fix and flip. Option 2 is available to a buy-and-hold investor. Obviously, the one thing that could change that in the favour of a buy-and-hold investor is if the market appreciates substantially (enough to refinance and take money out). As fix and flippers we don't like that as much because we want to raise the value of the property and remove the cash invested (with return) quickly so we can go on to the next one.

You can see why I like standard deals. They are only "standard" insofar as they're the typical way to do a fix and flip. In truth, there is nothing standard about taking a rundown property and turning it into a legal cash machine.

Raised Value, Cash Flowed, Refinanced, Cash Flowed Again

An investor I met recently did a deal in Hamilton, Ontario, that tells the story of the power of the fix-and-flip strategy very clearly. Here's the setup:

Purchase price: $150,000

Renovation expense: $45,000

Money: 20% down payment on a mortgage and cash funding for renovations

Property type: Four-plex

Time frame: Four months

Strategy: Refinance and hold

New appraisal: $245,000

Refinance amount at 80% of appraised value: $196,000

This deal went very well. What's most impressive is the fact that, from the very beginning of the project, there was one tenant in the property *during* the renovation process. This means that the mortgage used to purchase the property in the first

---

place was being paid by that single tenant. For his renovation strategy, the flipper focused all his initial efforts on a second suite. By the second month of the project, the investor was making a positive cash flow on the property *while* renovating the other two units.

It took two more months to complete the project, at which time the fix and flipper refinanced and took almost all his money out of the property, including renovation expenses. The closing costs were about the only expense that wasn't covered by the refinance.

And what was the result after all the cash was pulled out? A newly renovated property that attracted great tenants and cash flowed $1,000 per month. This is a simply wonderful result. A standard buy and hold just can't compete with that, and that's why investors will learn to love you if you can systematize fixing and flipping and execute correctly.

Partnership Structures

Joint Ventures

A joint venture is a legal type of ownership. The main thing to remember about a joint venture is that both partners (and sometimes multiple partners) will be on title and legally own the property. Beyond that, there really are no limits to the kind of joint ventures that you can do on a fix-and-flip deal. However, a very common version, with some alternate scenarios, is presented here:

Partner #1	**Partner #2**
Puts deal together	Brings down payment
Manages renovation	Qualifies for mortgage
Markets property	Brings funds for renovation expense
Is totally hands-on	Is hands-off
Receives 50% of profit	Receives 50% of profit
Is on title	Is on title

On a fix and flip, or for that matter a buy and hold, this is a very common strategy, and there can be any number of combinations. For example, perhaps partner one actually does the renovation himself, and therefore gets a larger percentage of the profit.

Another example of a joint venture is where both partners put in some of the money, and both partners take care of some aspect of the work (both qualify, one or both handle the renovation, one or both take care of some aspect of the deal, one or both do the management, etc.). As long as both have ownership through a legal joint venture agreement, then it's a joint venture. Always get independent legal advice before you move forward with a joint venture agreement.

Private Money

When you use private money for a deal, it's not actually a joint venture since a joint venture is a legal means of ownership. Private money is where your lender simply loans you the money, with interest, to purchase and renovate the property. It may not be a joint venture, but make no mistake, it *is* a partnership. The lender will register a mortgage against the title of the property and will have full legal recourse to get his or her money if anything should happen. Full legal recourse means the lender can foreclose, just like a bank.

A private lender will have a vested interest in your deal going well. Your job as a fix and flipper is to systematize your process and create a track record so that investors (including private lenders) can trust that you'll provide a return every time.

Whenever using other people's money, I find that this is the best way to finance the deal. Typically I borrow enough funds for purchase and renovation, and I have to pay all the interest at the point of the exit strategy. Not every private money lender will allow this, but then again, not every money lender is right for you. You may negotiate a deal where you have to pay monthly or you may negotiate one large payment at the end. The project obviously has to have created enough value to pay the extra money for interest on the private loan and more importantly for your profit.

People often freak out about the notion of borrowing money at 8 to 12 per cent, but you really can't think of it as a standard mortgage. You're not going to be paying the interest on the private money for very long. I always try to shoot for fewer than four months on my projects. Let's be realistic: if the deal isn't solid enough to pay for two to four months of financing cost, it's probably not a very good deal to begin with.

You have to think of the value of private money and forget about the high interest rates. If you have a strong relationship with your private money lender, it will be available immediately, which means you can purchase properties very quickly, sometimes with no conditions. It gives you a negotiating advantage. When you're offering sellers $20,000 (for example) less than they want, it sure helps to push your deal through if you have no conditions attached to your offer.

Other Partnerships

There are any number of other types of partnerships you can use, such as the creative deal we already told you about (with the homeowner); however, as mentioned, I don't believe in them. What is the point when so much money is available using standard deals that almost always end up turning out better in the end anyway?

If you can do a deal all by yourself, with your own cash, or your own line of credit, or your own mortgage, this is probably the best option for you, but if you want or need to partner with others to achieve your goals of fixing and flipping, then we recommend using standard partnerships and standard purchase strategies.

Part 3

Searching for Properties: The Fundamentals

11

Identifying Areas and Homes that Make Good Potential Flips

In this chapter, Ian talks about developing your ability to find the right areas and specific properties to fix and flip.

Start with the End in Mind

You have to know what you're looking for before you can find it. This is true no matter what you're looking for, but it's especially true when it comes to fixing and flipping. It may sound circular and nonsensical, but think about what I'm saying. Oftentimes I see people who think the starting place for a good flip property is the online Multiple Listing Service (MLS). In my opinion, that's the last place. If you go out in search of a "flip," then you'll find any number of properties that could make sense (in your mind). On the other hand, if you have a series of specific criteria that are certain to bring a good fix-and-flip property, you'll end up saying no more often, but when you do say yes, you'll have a winning property.

As a solid starting point, you have to know a few of the key indicators of an excellent flip property:

Multiple Exit Strategies Could Be Used

If you have a plan, a backup plan, and a backup backup plan, you are off to a good start. Having only one exit strategy can be a recipe for disaster. The only time it might be okay to have only one exit strategy is if your one strategy is *very* strong—for example, selling a renovated property with $100,000 of spread between costs and sales price.

You can undertake a search for properties that align with the exit strategies that you've chosen once you know what your exit strategies are. Knowing your end goal (exit) is what gives you the right questions to ask. From there you build a detailed system of due diligence.

It Passes Your Due Diligence

To be a fix and flipper (as opposed to a speculator), it's imperative that you do your due diligence each and every time you fix and flip a property. It's true that you'll develop a sort of instinctive knowledge of what a good flip house in a good flip area looks like, but you can't rely entirely on that. I know exactly what kind of property, in which neighbourhoods, works for me, but I'm always checking up on myself to make sure that I don't get caught slipping.

When it comes to *neighbourhood and regional due diligence*, consider factors such as job demand, in-migration, income, infrastructure improvements, etc. Breaking down economic fundamentals like this is covered in Don R. Campbell's book *Real Estate Investing in Canada 2.0.* I highly recommend this book as a primer on economic fundamentals and overall real estate investing fundamentals.

You must learn at least some economic fundamentals in order to do your due diligence properly, and it will take you a long way in the fixing-and-flipping business. The important thing to remember is that just because you're flipping, it doesn't mean you don't have to pay attention to economic fundamentals. This belief is false. It's every bit as important in flips as in buy-and-hold investments, because without multiple exit strategies you're playing a risky game, and without strong regional and neighbourhood fundamentals you're limiting those exit strategies.

As mentioned above, the major fundamentals to consider are regional job demand, in-migration, average income, and infrastructure improvements. However, it would be misleading to suggest that these are the only ones. I highly recommend you read the above recommended book to get a better understanding of fundamentals.

If the property and neighbourhood have poor fundamentals, you should be very wary of buying it. If it has strong fundamentals, you should be more excited about buying it, knowing that a strong fundamental base will give you a much better chance of success as well as provide you with more and better exit strategies. This is because when you buy a fundamentally strong property, you can be reasonably certain that the future will bring better rents and better sales values.

Focus on fundamentals for success!

In my core town of Whitby, Ontario, there is strong housing demand. People moving into Whitby are typically young professionals. Perhaps they're working for the high-tech companies that have moved into the region, and they're ready to graduate from apartment living into nice houses. So I provide a nice rental product in the right neighbourhoods and I'm immediately provided with two strong exit strategies (sell and rent).

As for *property due diligence,* the same rule about starting from the end and thinking backwards applies. I think of my potential exit strategies and what I want to achieve in the end. I look for a property that will allow me to implement those strategies, either as a flip or hold (as a rental).

What would a good, hardworking family like to live in? What would any professional couple like to call home, and would they be proud to entertain guests there? Can the property in question achieve that goal? If so, I know I'm on to something. If not, the property is not right.

Doing property due diligence takes a bit of vision because the product you're buying is not the product you'll sell. It's a different product and you will need the vision to see what it will be in the end.

It Has a "Certain Something"

To have multiple exit strategies, there has to be something special about the property. That "something special" will permit flexibility with the property. The property could:

1. Be a great producer of cash flow for a buy-and-hold investor. This is why I like small multi-family buildings like duplexes and triplexes so much. I know if I buy right and add value, the product will be in high demand when I want to sell it, or I could hold it and maintain very strong cash flow.

2. Be a high-demand kind of property in a high-demand neighbourhood. To tap into that high demand, I have to have the property priced right, which means I bought the property at the right price, spent the right amount on renovations, and listed the property at the right price.

3. Be cheap, cheap, cheap. This applies especially to wholesaling. If wholesaling is an exit strategy, the pricing must be cheap, cheap, cheap. Also, if your exit strategy is to sell a renovated property and it's not in a particularly high-demand neighbourhood, and thus the property is not in particularly high demand, then you have to be ready to sell it cheap. This again means that you had to buy it cheap, cheap, cheap, if you want to sell it cheap. Being the cheapest is not my favourite thing to do, but it is a sure-fire way to stand out from the crowd and greatly increase your chances of a timely sale.

I see a lot of people out there looking to buy an *average* house and try to fix it up to be nicer than the others and then sell it. This leaves the fix and flipper with few exit strategies, a tactic that could sink their ship. There is nothing unique about thinking a property is worth more than it actually is. Buying right is the key to differentiating yourself from the norm. When you buy a gut-flip type of property, you have to buy at least 20 per cent below market value (after-repaired value), and if you're buying a cosmetic flip, you have to buy at least 10 per cent below market value (after-repaired value).

As a quick refresher on possible exit strategies, go back to chapter 2 where there is a description of some of the ones I commonly use.

✶ ✶ ✶

Whichever exit strategies you employ, it's imperative that you always, always have a backup plan. To develop that backup plan, go back to your neighbourhood and property due diligence. It's the knowledge of those two that enables you to formulate multiple strong exit strategies.

A property that has that "certain something" should get you interested in a potential fix and flip. As time goes on and you develop skill in fixing and flipping, you will be able to identify at least one of the three "certain something" qualities that I described above. These are what good deals are made of and will allow you to execute multiple exit strategies if necessary.

12

Types of Homes: The Pros and Cons of Townhouses, Semis, Detached Homes, and Condos

In this chapter, Mark talks about what kind of property is right for you in the context of your capabilities and goals.

When it comes to picking the property you'll ultimately fix and flip, it's imperative that you spend a little bit of time considering what will be a good fit for you. Each kind of property comes with its own benefits and drawbacks. The type of property that proves right for you will depend on your experience, skill set, the time you have, end goals, and a host of other factors. For example, how confident are you in what you're doing? What is your risk tolerance? How are you going to finance your project?

Consider carefully which type of property will be best for you in the context of your experience and capabilities. Here's an overview of different kinds of properties and a discussion of some of the pros and cons of each.

Condominium Townhouses

Pros

- **Entry Level**: A townhouse is the opposite of buying a luxury product where the potential reward is big but the downside is a higher risk. With a townhouse, there will always be the potential to rent it, and the entry-level buyer can afford to buy it.

- **Low Risk**: If you don't have a lot of experience, it's a good way to start out because there is not as much at risk: the numbers involved are typically smaller.

- **No Major Items to Renovate**: Again, if you're lacking in experience, this can be a major benefit. Lots of the major items involved in renovating are already covered by the maintenance fees. When you take control of the property you don't have to do roofs, windows, outside walls, and such major exterior repairs. By definition, a townhouse will almost always be a cosmetic flip. The only "bones" type of repairs you may have to do are electrical and mechanical.

Cons

- **Smaller Return on Investment**: I always found it difficult to make much cash flow with a townhouse. This means that if you attempt to fix and flip a townhouse, but are forced to rent it, you won't make much money during the duration of the hold.

- **Condo/Maintenance Fees**: One of the big reasons cash flow gets eaten up (see above) is that condominium townhouses are part of a condominium corporation, and as such they require monthly maintenance fees.

- **Difficult to Find Deals**: I've always had a difficult time finding really good deals on townhouses. Part of the reason for this is the fees I just mentioned above. If the building is well maintained, then the sales prices should typically be somewhat in line with the comparables. If you do find a cheap one, you're probably looking at a poorly managed complex. In such a case, a cheap price does not equal good value, and you could inherit big problems that you will want no part of. One cheap townhouse in a complex means plenty of other cheap townhouses in the same complex. It's tough to raise the value of yours above the value of the others in the same complex.

- **Politics**: Yes, politics within the complex is an issue. You can only work certain hours and make certain amounts of noise within the unit because walls are shared with neighbours. This can sometimes cause slow production on the renovation. Plus, condo boards often require you to have their approval to do renovations. This fact often slows down production.

Whitby Townhouse Flip

A good example is a Whitby townhouse flip project Ian did. Here are the details:

Purchase price: $99,000

Renovation expense: $10,000

Exit strategy: Sell (but he got caught in a weak sales market, so he rented it)

Monthly cash flow: $100

Tenancy for two-year hold: 100% (the same tenants lived in it for two years)

Sale price: $146,000

Profit after mortgage payout and closing expenses: $27,000

Ian's first exit strategy was preferable in this deal, but he didn't time the market well, so he had to rely on his second exit strategy, which was to rent the property out. The cash-flow numbers weren't as strong as he typically likes, but the circumstance was unique. So he kept the property as a rental and survived without feeling too much pain. When it came time to sell, Ian still made a tidy profit, but during the hold time his cash was tied up in the property.

I think this example illustrates both the pros and cons of townhouses. He didn't make a lot of profit, but at the same time, he didn't take on a huge amount of risk. The pain of having cash sit in the project was minimized by the fact that it wasn't too much.

Semi-detached and Freehold Townhouses

Pros

- **Entry Level**: Typically a semi-detached/freehold townhouse is more of an entry-level product than a detached home. This is true unless you're flipping a high-demand product in a downtown neighbourhood in some of the major cities in

Canada, where semi-detached houses/freehold townhouses are more common and desirable. But usually, like a townhouse, a semi/freehold is lower risk in terms of dollars invested.

- **Easy to Finance**: As with townhouses, a typical semi-detached/freehold townhouse flip will be much more cosmetic than gut, and that means there's a good chance that a bank will put a mortgage on the property. This is essential when you don't have private money sources. When you get into gut-flip projects, the banks prefer if you risk your neck, or a private money investor does so: the banks like to play it safe.

Cons

- **Lower Return on Investment**: As with condominium townhouses, the chances of big income with a semi/freehold townhouse are typically lower than with a detached house—high-end products in high-demand areas being the exception.
- **Politics**: As with the condominium townhouse, in a semi-detached/freehold townhouse you always have to remember that you share a wall with a neighbour. This could lead to complaints and general buffoonery on the part of the neighbour. There's something about a neighbour improving their property that a lot of people just seem to hate.

Proactive Steps for Flipping Semi-Detached Houses

Given the fact that there's always going to be a neighbour involved in flipping a semi-detached house, it's best that you start to think of that neighbour as a partner of sorts.

You're going to need their permission to do certain things (for example, work past 5 p.m.). On other aspects of the project you don't exactly need their permission, but without their blessing, they can make your life a living hell (see story below) if they choose.

You'll never fully remove the risk of a nosy or difficult neighbour, but by being proactive, you can lessen the risk.

I recommend you always speak to the neighbours in advance of your flip projects, but when it comes to flipping a semi-detached, it's even more important. Make sure you are kind to them, but at the same time make sure you're real. Let them know that there will be some noise, but that it won't last long, and that it's for the good of the whole block.

Tell them that you'll be a responsible renovator, and that you'll keep the yard clean. Let them know that you're working as hard as you can, so you might have to work a little beyond normal hours.

If you approach it properly, there's a good chance the neighbour will be cordial and even helpful.

Semi-Detached Flip

On a recent fix-and-flip project Ian did on a semi-detached, he ran into a couple of problems with the neighbour on the other side of the shared wall.

Even though he spoke to her in advance, and even though he took absolutely the filthiest house in the neighbourhood and made it into the nicest, she still tried to obstruct what Ian and his crew were doing and made the project more difficult for Ian as a result. The neighbour put up roadblocks wherever she could. As part of the restructuring, Ian needed to move the staircase and it was going to be up against the shared wall. The neighbour needed to sign off on the permits that would allow Ian to move the staircase. She threatened that she wouldn't sign the permits, but she finally relented and signed them. At one point she almost shut down the job by restricting work to between 9 a.m. and 5 p.m., and this greatly impeded progress for a week or so until she was convinced to let the crew get on with the project.

When the project was nearing completion, she started throwing up a bunch of small roadblocks such as asking to change the downspouts in the backyard. She threatened to make a formal complaint even though the downspouts were perfectly legitimate. It didn't matter at the time because simply dealing with the complaint, whether it was legitimate or not, was enough to slow down the project.

This is a very common story when dealing with a semi-detached fix and flip. Be aware of this potential roadblock when fixing and flipping semi-detached homes.

Detached

Pros

- **Upside**: There is typically more upside on the sale price, and therefore a bigger spread between what you spend and what you make.

- **Deals**: I find there are often better deals on detached homes. Generally, there is a greater opportunity to add value to a detached home.

- **Fewer Politics**: You don't have to answer to anyone else on many vital questions of the renovation. You can customize the exterior, work as late as you want (inside the house), there's more room for a garbage bin on the front lawn, etc.

- **Sale Proposition**: If you've done your neighbourhood due diligence (so you know it's a sought-after neighbourhood) and made the property nicer than most, you should have no problem selling it.

Cons

- **Expense**: A detached house comes with a detached-size to-do list. Unlike a townhouse, there is every chance that on top of the smaller interior renovations, you'll also have to do some of the bigger stuff. There will also likely be more bathrooms, bedrooms, and a bigger kitchen. All these add up to more renovations, more time, and more expense.

- **Expertise**: To flip a detached house correctly, you'll need to be able to manage your expenses closely, so it may take a higher level of expertise to complete.

Apartment Condos

Pros

- **Minimal Renovations**: Unless you want to restructure the kitchen or bathroom configuration, there will be no major renovations to do. Renovations are basic.

- **Lower Entry Cost**: Apartment-style units are usually much cheaper than any of the others.

- **Price Certainty**: Because there are usually so many direct comparables right there in the building, you're able to accurately gauge your after-repaired value.

Cons

- **Fewer Deals**: Since there are so many direct comparables, and all exterior maintenance is taken care of, there is not usually a big price difference between the most expensive unit and the cheapest unit.

- **Less Value Added**: Since there are fewer deals and smaller price differences, there's not often a chance to make a big impact on the value or the end sale price.

- **Logistical Nightmares**: Take all the concerns about politics and board approval that I raised with townhouses, and now add the fact that every single piece of material has to be lugged up one of the two elevators the building is likely to have, and it adds up to a logistical nightmare.

Which One Is Right for You?

Spend the time to figure out which of the property styles is right for you. I find that detached homes with multiple units (duplexes, triplexes, four-plexes) often allow the most flexibility in terms of exit strategies, since the rental income is usually strong enough to justify holding the property after the renovation and refinance are complete.

This does not mean that the same detached strategy is right for you. It might be best to start with a small townhouse to build experience and work your way up to small multi-unit buildings.

In addition to the pros and cons presented here, spend some of your own due diligence time thinking about how each property type might fit into your life.

13

Where to Add Value – And Avoid the Money Pit

In this chapter, Ian talks about the "wow" factor and goes against conventional wisdom.

Everyone seems to repeat the same refrain over and over when it comes to adding value in a flip. Over and over again they say "kitchens and bathrooms, kitchens and bathrooms."

But keep things in perspective. Whenever I do a fix and flip, I question whether kitchens and bathrooms are truly candidates for renovation, and as a consequence I take a more holistic approach as to which areas of the house to renovate.

I pay close attention to something you've likely heard of—the "wow" factor. I want people to realize right away that when they look at a property I've renovated, they're looking at a special product, and I take that approach from the front yard all the way through to the back fence, not just kitchens and bathrooms.

Just to clarify what I mean, I don't spend big money on prestige items in each and every room. In fact, I don't spend big money on any room, but I pay careful attention to design, and set the house up in a way that will be certain to impress.

Who Is Your Target Market: Investors, Homeowners, or Renters?

Always keep your eye on the bigger picture. Once you've bought your fix-and-flip project, you have to remember that you're eventually going to exit it. So, when you're exiting the property, who will take it over? Will it be a sale to an investor or homeowner, or will it be rented out to a renter?

If the target is investors, and they see that the units they're about to buy are uniquely designed and stand out from all the other properties they're looking at, and at the same time the cash-flow numbers are strong, then I know the investors will want to buy. Intelligent investors know that a higher-end product will allow them to rent their units more easily, and therefore do what is necessary to buy properties like this, so I provide that. The key factor here is that the property's cash-flow numbers have to be stellar. If the property is renovated to a high standard and will not command strong cash flow, then the prettiest renovations in the world aren't worth much.

When the target market is a homeowner, there is a true pride factor involved in purchasing decisions. Well-designed and well-renovated homes are in higher demand than the typical rental home. Selling to a homeowner is great, because the nice renovations have a better chance of impressing. Homeowners are allowed to be a little bit emotional about the home they're going to be living in, whereas investors by nature have to remain unemotional to invest well. I like targeting homeowners when I sell a fix and flip.

If my exit strategy involves keeping the property as a rental, I want to know that I'll have the easiest possible time renting the property. Again, I have to balance my expenditures versus my desire to renovate to a high standard, but with creativity it's possible to have the best of both worlds.

Whoever the target customer is, it's imperative to have the best possible design features that will facilitate whichever exit strategy I choose, while marketing the property to whichever end user I choose. The "wow" factor is always important.

Initial Entrance

On all my fix-and-flip projects, I want buyers to be "wowed" by their entrance to the property. The first impression often leaves the strongest impression. That's why I make living rooms and front entrances very nice. I invest in the "wow" factor as people walk in.

As with most successful entrepreneurs, I like to test my results. I know that investing in first impressions is working because people often walk up to the front of my flip projects and stare through the front window, anxious to see the inside. The feedback is always very strong on our "wow" factor, and history has shown that it pays off in quick sales, quick rentals, and strong sale prices. I'll go into more detail later in the chapter about exactly how we create this "wow" factor without breaking the bank.

Kitchens and Bathrooms

I apply the same rules to both the kitchen and bathroom. I make them very clean and very nice. I do not spend big money on expensive single features. I install basic toilets, basic bathtubs, and basic countertops.

I always install dual-zone lighting, which adds the feel of depth to a room. In the bathroom this means a pot light over the shower and sconce lighting on both sides of the mirror.

The floors are tiled in both the kitchen and the bathroom, so both rooms feel like higher-end rooms, but I don't spend big money on my tiling—I use basic 12-inch × 12-inch ceramic tile (or even larger), because it gives me the most bang for my buck. It gives a luxury look, without spending luxury money.

I put a tile backsplash behind the kitchen sink and mosaic tiling along the top of the tub tiling. These features offset the floor tiling and along with the dual-zone lighting just feel luxurious, even though I don't spend big money on them.

Kitchens and bathrooms must be clean, well designed, and have a great feel, but I rarely spend big money on specialty items for either room.

Bedrooms

I'm a firm believer that bedrooms should not be a big source of expense on a fix and flip. A bedroom is typically a room with four walls and a closet. Sometimes there is an en suite bathroom, and when possible, this is a nice feature. However, I don't recommend adding one onto a master bedroom. The reason for this is simple: most houses in a similar neighbourhood will share the same bedroom and bathroom characteristics. In a neighbourhood primarily made up of bungalows—typically, three bedrooms on the main floor and one bathroom—people shopping for a house in that neighbourhood will not expect to find an en suite bathroom.

If there is one, it's a great thing to have, but I wouldn't sacrifice a bedroom to make one. Removing a bedroom is the most likely course of action you'd have to take to build an en suite, but it's expensive and sometimes difficult (if you have to bring plumbing through structural walls, for instance), and it leaves you without that important third bedroom. It's not only unnecessary most of the time, but it's usually best avoided.

So, given that you're not likely going to add an en suite, there's no need to spend much money in a bedroom. As with the kitchen and bathroom, it's important that it be clean, with new flooring and perfectly repaired and painted walls. The closet has to be nicely painted and clean, and the closet doors have to be nice, new, and in perfect working order. The baseboards, doorframes, and door have to be nice, new looking, and clean as well. The biggest exception to this rule is if you're seeking to restore an old home with the original finishings. Often buyers and tenants are attracted to the original finishings when they're nicely restored, and you probably would not want to install new finishings when you can restore the old ones in certain properties.

The other additional feature that can be added to make a bedroom nice is crown moulding. Crown moulding is not too expensive, and it does add a touch of class.

Keep the bedrooms simple. Do a simple update to every feature and make sure the room feels inviting and warm. Don't spend big money on the bedrooms.

Basements

It's simple when it comes to undeveloped basements. Don't develop them unless there is a suite in them and you'll be able to achieve a better sale price or rent if it's a finished suite.

If the exit strategy is to sell to a homeowner, you'll never recoup the cost of developing the basement in the sale price. This doesn't mean, though, that you can ignore the basement. I always make sure the basement is well lit and the floor is clean and painted. Basements are one of the biggest money pits in a house. Don't fall into one unless you have a good reason to—that is, you're building a suite that adds value.

Major Electrical/HVAC/Roofing/Windows/Foundation

The rule here is simple. Only tackle these if you *have* to. Buyers will be turned off by a major renovation that hasn't been done to an acceptable standard, so you can't try to peddle a home with major faults in any of the large structural/mechanical components.

On top of that, you can't knowingly sell a house that might pose a hidden danger to the next owner, so there's a moral and legal imperative on you to make sure that anything that is hidden (but that you *know* about) is repaired. These are "latent deficiencies" in the legal lingo, and they can cause you enormous headaches after you've sold the house.

If you don't know about it, there is nothing you can do, so don't go ripping down walls just to find out if some major system needs repair.

Whenever these major systems are in good enough shape (for example: a furnace is not brand new but it's only halfway through its serviceable life), then you absolutely should *not* repair or replace them. There is simply no improved value for repairing these areas of the house.

14

Financing Your Fix and Flip

In this chapter, Mark discusses the ways to finance a fix-and-flip project and fix-and-flip models.

Chances are, if you're like most people, you won't have all the money needed to purchase and renovate all the properties you'd like, all the time. How to finance a property, especially a fix and flip, is one of the greatest skills for the fix-and-flip investor to develop. There are many ways to finance a fix and-flip project. Below, I will discuss some of the methods I use.

Undoubtedly, there are more ways to finance a project, but the ones discussed below are the standard methods. I recommend mastering the traditional methods of financing over seeking out all of the most unique and creative methods. There is often a reason that the standard methods are the standard: they work better, they're proven to be effective, and they don't fall into any grey area. The standard methods are as follows:

1. If you have a steady job and have some money set aside for the down payment and renovation expense, you might just call up your banker or broker and apply for a conventional mortgage to purchase your fix and flip.

2. There might come a time when you purchase fix-and-flip projects with cash from your own pocket or from your own line of credit.

3. You may joint venture with others who will qualify on a mortgage. In such cases, your partners may provide the down payment as well as the cash to renovate the property.

4. You may use a broker to locate and secure private funds for your fix-and-flip project.

5. You may borrow private money directly from the source, with no need for any qualification.

Building Your Financing Team

Because of all the variables involved in financing a property of any sort (especially a fix and flip), having a strong financing team in place will be one of your most valuable assets as an investor. Among the variables to note are interest rates (which are much higher for private money) and qualifying standards that differ from lender to lender.

There are three major setups that you may employ in building your financing team. Any of these three may be used on any given project. You're not limited to just one, and I don't recommend that you limit yourself to just one. Think of the three types like lines on a hockey team. If you're the coach of a team, you will have at least three lines that you can use at any point during the game. The choice is up to you as to which line you put on the ice at any given time. Rather than a first, second, and third line, though, as a fix and flipper you have the option of using a banker or a broker, or self-brokering the deal.

Banker

If you use the services of a banker to obtain a mortgage, it's important that you understand the role of a mortgage specialist within the larger framework of the bank. If you walk into your bank and ask to speak to someone about a mortgage, there's every possibility that you will end up speaking with one of the many *generalists* the bank employs. They may sell mutual funds to a customer one minute, and be speaking to you about a mortgage the next.

If you speak to one of the bank's generalists, there is a good chance they'll be able to take your application—and that's about it. They likely won't know all the mortgage products their bank offers, and they likely won't know which one is best for you. There's a limited chance that they will understand the fix-and-flip strategy very well, but they will be happy to put you into a mortgage with their bank as long as you qualify.

The *mortgage specialist* at the bank, or in some cases the *mobile mortgage specialist* that the bank employs to serve its clients, will have a very good knowledge of the mortgage products that their own bank offers and perhaps some influence with the underwriter that they're dealing with. They will be better at getting you the right mortgage than the bank's generalist would be.

But let's be clear here, banks will often only provide their own products with no flexibility, especially to a consumer who hasn't seen other options through a broker. The clients they generate from within their own branches are likely to get into whatever the bank offers rather than the best mortgage available. Sometimes the best mortgage available is the same one the borrower's bank is offering, but not always.

A *mobile mortgage specialist*, although an expert in the mortgage products of their own financial institution, will *never* be able to find you short-term, private money. The reason for this is simple: they work for the bank, and the bank's mortgages, by definition, are not a private source.

Some people really like having a relationship with a single banker, but most seasoned investors that I know prefer to at least have one mortgage broker on their team. They've seen that mortgage brokers can often find better rates and deals for them and their needs.

Broker

A mortgage broker has more flexibility than a banker. They can source you a mortgage from multiple and varied institutions. Good brokers will also develop a system where they curry the favour of individual mortgage underwriters at different banks. They often compile a bunch of different mortgages from different sources and shop them around to different banks. What this means is that a broker will take a set of files that he or she is working on at any given time and offer a specific mortgage provider the chance to provide mortgages for the whole set of properties in exchange for a favourable rate.

Never forget that banks are in the business of lending money. When a mortgage broker has an excellent record of bringing great borrowers to a bank, and is bringing multiple mortgages to the bank at once, that broker is more likely to get a deal on interest rates. And, from time to time, the same broker may be able to get an exception to the bank's lending criteria. This means that the bank *may* make an exception for an individual borrower. For this to happen, the lender needs a good reason.

A mortgage broker's job is to put the lender together with the borrower. This can include private money, something that you will never have access to through a banker. A standard mortgage broker who only deals with homeowners likely won't have too many sources of private money at his or her fingertips. But a mortgage broker who specializes in working with investors will probably have access to some private money sources. A mortgage broker who consistently serves and engages the fix-and-flip investor will likely have the most sources of private, short-term money available.

Such a mortgage broker will also understand the needs of qualifying for investment mortgages better than a standard mortgage broker who only deals with homeowners. There's a chance you'll develop the right relationship with a single bank and its mortgage specialist over time, but it's more likely that a mortgage broker will be able to serve your fix-and-flip needs better. I'm not denigrating bankers as a source of mortgage funding, but I do strongly believe in the value of having a mortgage broker on your team.

Be Your Own Broker

Beyond the banker/broker debate, there is another method for finding money that plenty of seasoned fix-and-flip investors are using. They act as their own broker to source private money.

Rather than going to a mortgage broker to find private lenders, they go directly to private lenders. As a result, they have greater flexibility with their loans than they would by sourcing private money through a mortgage broker.

Such lenders know the fix-and-flip investor well. In cases where this pro strategy is used, the lender knows and understands the investor's business model, and when the relationship is established the lender will often lend the same fix and flipper money several times.

In fact, the people who lend private money to a successful flipper often don't like it when their money is *not* out in the market. Their biggest beef is that they don't get to earn their plum interest rates longer before the fix and flipper pays them out.

To be your own broker, you'll have to develop a track record of success. Perhaps you'll have to do a successful fix-and-flip project with your own savings. Then perhaps you'll have to do a couple of successful flips using joint venture money. In any case, people with available cash will have to be aware of what you're doing and of your success rate. Once your strategy and track record are no secret, you'll be on the right path to becoming your own broker. The people with the money need to know you, they need to know what you do, and they need to know about your track record. As with all aspects of this business, it is all about relationships. Even if you understand the strategy perfectly and have a great track record, you won't make it work unless you have the relationships to do so.

The advantages of being your own broker are:

- **Availability**: As soon as you need it, the cash will be available (as long as you've developed the relationship with the lender in advance and have gotten him or her to commit). This will allow you to make condition-free offers, which usually allow you to negotiate a better price. Better price equals better profit.

- **Cheaper**: Since there is no broker fee, there's a good chance that you'll be able to secure a better interest rate.

- **Flexibility**: Knowing lenders directly may mean that they won't ask you to qualify. If they know the business model, they will understand that they're lending to the project, not to a person with a job.

Getting Money Sources to Say Yes

When it comes to getting financing, you will need someone, somewhere along the way, to say yes to you, to your project, or to both. In many cases, you may need two or more parties (money partner and lender) to say yes to you and your project in order to secure the financing.

Institutional Lenders (Banks)

If you're seeking a conventional mortgage to purchase your fix-and-flip project, then someone will have to qualify for the mortgage. It can be you, or it can be a joint venture partner. The bank will use its lending standards to assess if you're a good risk. It will base its assessment on your debt service numbers. The essential question the bank will be asking is whether you (or your partner) have a strong enough monthly income in relation to your monthly debt payments to ensure that you can pay for the mortgage you've applied for.

When all your monthly expenses are bundled together, could you still pay the mortgage that you're applying for? The bank will be very interested in the answer to this question because your ability (or your joint venture partner's ability) to pay the bank every month is the bank's greatest protection against the possibility of having to foreclose at some point in the future.

In spite of what some people think, banks don't like foreclosing. They're not in the business of owning, managing, and selling real estate. They're in the business of lending money. A foreclosure is considered a failure of their underwriting department and (due to the extra work involved) is a liability to the bank.

Getting a bank to say yes to you and/or your joint venture partner is a matter of proving to them that you have the wherewithal to pay them if something goes wrong on the fix-and-flip project. In fact, a standard lender will only assess you based on your ability to pay, along with the income the property could earn as a rental. They will never assess the deal based on the potential value of the property as a fix-and-flip project.

The rules of how to qualify for a mortgage are too many to discuss in great detail here, but there are many wonderful resources available that teach investors the basics of getting the bank to say yes. Don R. Campbell's *Real Estate Investing in Canada 2.0* is a wonderful primer on this and many other topics for the beginning real estate investor.

Joint Venture Partners

There's a good chance that you'll want to (or have to) work with joint venture partners in order to achieve your fix-and-flip goals. Oftentimes, the right joint venture partner is someone unlike you. Perhaps you'll be bringing the renovations expertise to the partnership, or perhaps you'll be bringing the deal-finding ability. Usually you'll be seeking money. If you're not seeking money, why would you be looking for a joint venture partner in the first place? Taking on a partner if you don't need one is not usually a good idea. It complicates things more than necessary. By their nature, partnerships are more complex than doing a deal on your own. But not all partnerships are equal, and doing a partnership with someone who has complementary skills is less complex than doing a partnership with someone who has the same skills. Therefore, don't complicate the matter more than is necessary by bringing in a partner with the same set of skills that you have.

The simplest way to attract joint venture partners to your deals is to tell absolutely everyone about what you're doing. Tell your neighbours, tell your friends, tell people you meet at investment seminars. There is a skill to this too: if you're too much of a blabbermouth or a braggart, there's a good chance that you will repel people rather than attract them. It's important you don't come across as a hard-seller in your efforts to attract joint venture money.

When I was starting to search for joint venture partners, one of the things I did was ask everyone I met if I could practise my joint venture presentation with them. I'd say to them, "I've done a couple of these, and I was wondering if I could practise my presentation with you. Could you give me some feedback on how I could make my presentation better?" I would actively solicit their feedback, and sure enough, they gave me practical ways to improve my presentation. At the end of the practice session I'd say to them, "I know this might not be for you, but do you know anyone who might be interested?" One thing led to another and, before long, I had a whole stable of joint venture partners prepared to invest money with me.

It seems easy based on my description. The truth is that it was simple, but not easy. It's always a tough job to start anything new, and raising money from scratch is no different. You have to deal with a lot of rejection, and that's never easy. That's why I liked to set up my joint venture presentations in such a way that the people I was presenting to weren't really being presented to. They were just giving me tips. Of course, the practice presentations that I did led to the real thing, and to referrals.

For anyone who has ever done a sales-type job, you might be able to relate to the fact that the beginning is the hardest. The same goes with attracting joint venture money. At first it seems an insurmountable task, but after you do a few successful joint ventures, you'll attract more and more money with less effort. Success and a track record breed more money available for your projects.

Get the first couple of fix-and-flip projects done, and focus on doing them well. Make sure they're profitable. You will attract money with greater ease.

Private Lenders (Self-Brokered)

Many of the same rules that apply to attracting joint venture money also apply to attracting private money. Since self-brokered private money comes from people you know personally (whether prior acquaintances or new acquaintances), it is very similar to joint venture money in that people (in this case lenders) are often investing in your track record of success.

If you can prove to the private money lenders that you will provide excellent and stable returns, that acquaintance will be much more likely to write a cheque.

So who has the money? The first and most likely source is people with a line of credit. Because so many people have access to this source of money, you can never know who might be a potential lender. That's why, just like with attracting joint venture partners, it is wise to be very open about your activities with everyone you talk to.

Think of it like this: anyone who owns a home is a potential source of private money. This is because if they own a home, there's a chance that they have significant equity in their home. If they have significant equity, there's a chance they have a line of credit. If they have a line of credit, they're a potential source of private money. I promise you that you'll never know who has the money, and many people will surprise you. *Never* judge a book by its cover. The flashiest, wealthiest looking people may be the ones with the least capital available to invest (they may have spent it becoming flashy), and the simplest, most unassuming people might be the ones with the most cash.

Remember that private money lenders are not only people with a line of credit. Others simply lend cash that they have sitting in a bank. While you may find that the line of credit is more common, it's not altogether uncommon to find the lender sitting on cash.

He Became a Full-Time Investor on Other People's Lines of Credit

I have a friend in the investor community named Gary McGowan (profiled earlier in this book). Gary made the jump from full-time employee to full-time investor in a few short years.

He first developed his investment skills by investing in his own properties. He honed his ability to find deals, manage rental properties, and raise joint venture money.

Along the way, he realized that fixing and flipping could be his bridge to being a full-time investor. This was very appealing to him because he didn't particularly love his full-time job. Once he realized that he could leave his job behind and get into something he loved (and make more money doing it), he went for it.

He learned the art of fixing and flipping houses. First he started with his own money, and soon he started looking for private money. Once he had a track record, he knew that others would be thrilled to get the kinds of returns that he was generating, so he started speaking openly about what he was doing.

Soon, he was inundated with investors wanting to invest their 3 per cent lines of credit with him. He gave them 10 per cent for short-term loans, and each and every one of them was thrilled with a 7 per cent spread on their money.

Now he has more private funds available than he knows what to do with. The biggest money challenge Gary has now is finding enough deals to put all his private lenders' money to work and being able to manage the multiple renovation projects at the same time.

With this excess of money available, Gary can put all his efforts to work on finding the deals and adding value through targeted renovations. In other words, he's a full-time investor—exactly what he wanted to become.

Gary's example shows what's most important when you want to start brokering your own private money deals. Build your track record. Build your skill, find good deals, and the money will follow the deals and your system.

Private Money (Through a Broker)

Based on my experience, I'd estimate that about half of all private money deals are brokered by a mortgage broker, and the other half are self-brokered.

If you have a real fear of talking to people about their money, or if you want to keep your borrowing practices more impersonal, then going through a mortgage broker might be the best thing for you.

If this is your strategy, then it's of the utmost importance that you have the right mortgage broker (or brokers) on your team. The right mortgage brokers can source private money for you to purchase the property and they'll understand all the various ways to secure financing for renovation properties.

Cash Back

The number one issue that most real estate investors come up against as they go along their journey is the dreaded cash crunch. Depending upon what market you're investing in, cash flow from a normal buy and hold might be rather tight.

Whenever we utilize a holding strategy for fix-and-flip properties, the goal is always to have an excellent cash flow. By having the nicest property available for rent, we raise the rental incomes for the properties. With the right renovations on the right kind of properties, it is not at all uncommon to get above-market rental rates.

But fixing and flipping solves another (perhaps even more important) issue: it solves the issue of cash being sunk into a property and being stuck there for a long time. By adding value, we create equity and through the sale or refinancing of our property, we are able to take the original cash out, often with a nice return in addition to the original investment. Sometimes, we leave that return on investment in the property in the form of equity. It can then be withdrawn later with a sale or perhaps another refinancing at a later date.

Not only do we receive our own cash back sooner on a fix-and-flip property (as opposed to a buy-and-hold property), but we also give our investor's money back sooner. This enables our investors to give us the same money back sooner to invest again, and again, and again. If they put the money into a property, and that same money is tied up for five or more years, then they're not able to invest with us again as soon as we'd like them to. Getting the cash back soon is very important to providing above-average returns to our investors. Savvy investors really like this feature of fix-and-flip investments.

Getting the invested cash back (plus return) is the main financial model of fixing and flipping.

Cash Flow

If the strategy is to refinance and hold the property, it is imperative that the property you end up holding is a very strong cash-flowing property.

Buy-and-Hold Model vs. Fix-and-Flip Model

To illustrate the basic difference between a standard buy and hold and a fix-and-flip long-term hold, let's take a look at two scenarios. The first is a standard buy and hold and the second is the fix-and-flip long-term hold.

Buy and Hold

- Purchase price: $300,000
- Mortgage: $240,000
- Down payment: $60,000
- Interest rate: 4%
- Monthly mortgage payment: $1,141.25
- Monthly rental income: $2,000
- Cash left in property: $60,000
- Total Costs: $1,500
- Total Cash Flow: $500

Fix-and-Flip Hold Strategy

- Purchase price: $230,000
- Initial mortgage: $184,000
- Initial down payment: $46,000
- Renovation amount: $30,000
- Total cash in: $76,000
- Refinance value: $300,000
- Refinanced mortgage: $240,000
- Monthly rental income: $2,000

- Monthly mortgage payment: $1,141.25

- Cash left in property: $20,000

- Total Costs: $1,500

- Total Cash Flow: $500

I wanted to give you a very conservative example of a fix-and-flip hold strategy because it's very achievable. I know fix-and-flip pros who always seek to remove their entire initial investment with their refinance. As a real estate investor, which would you rather have: $60,000 of your money sitting in a property, or $20,000 sitting in the same property? Investors and money partners will definitely prefer to have their cash back so they can use the same cash and invest again (hopefully with you). There is a dual benefit for investors here, they get the long-term return of owning the hold property, and in addition they get their money back to re-invest. It compounds their initial investment when they can pull it out, retain an interest in the first property, and plug the same money back into a new deal.

With cash flow being identical, the only thing separating the two deals is the fact that the fix and flip returns most of the cash back to the investor near the beginning of the project.

Developing "The Knack"

New fix-and-flip investors, and other investors who don't understand the process, often say that fix and flippers have a special "knack" for the fix-and-flip game or for finding properties under value, or any other number of aspects of fixing and flipping properties.

The reality is that there is no special knack; it's just knowing the rules, knowing your numbers, and doing it right. It's true that the more of these that you do, the quicker and more intuitively you'll be able to do it. Without the fundamental skills in place, though, you'll never develop the quick, intuitive "knack" that the pros seem to have.

I've seen deals that looked like this:

- Purchase price: $220,000

- Renovation expense: $60,000

- Sale price: $400,000

I've also seen deals that looked like *this*:

- Purchase price: $260,000

- Renovation expense: $10,000

- Sale price: $340,000

So which model is better? Well, that all depends on how you look at it. The first one brought a larger return, but it was also a far more complex, time-consuming renovation, and there was more risk taken. The second was still a darn good profit, but the renovation was simple and quick. Each is as good as the other: the difference is in the preference of the person doing the flip.

The problem with limiting yourself to only one model of fixing and flipping is that you will limit yourself to fewer deals. For example, if you refuse to take on a renovation project where the renovation amount will be greater than $15,000, then you would not have been able to touch the first example above. If you only want to fix and flip single-unit bungalows, then you might not be able to achieve the stellar cash flow numbers that you'll want when you refinance and hold a property.

Having the flexibility to fix and flip an up/down duplex might enable you to get a better cash flow than a standard single-family house. It's great to have guidelines, but when you're developing financial models for fixing and flipping, it's best not to limit yourself too much. Instead, learn the necessary skills, and soon other people will say you have "the knack."

Know Your Market

In order to have the knack for fixing and flipping, you have to know what your property would sell or appraise for once the renovation is done. From that final price, you can work backwards toward the amount you can spend on purchasing and renovating the property. Knowing your market allows you to:

- move quickly on purchases

- negotiate better deals

- know what to reasonably expect as profit

Being able to predict the after-repaired value (ARV) of a property is a simple matter of understanding how to read and utilize comparables. Having the right realtor will enable you to quickly compare your property with the others that have recently sold or are currently for sale.

What Are Comparables?

If you're just starting out in the world of real estate, you've no doubt heard the terms "comparables" and "comps" being used regularly.

Comps are very important to determining the potential value of a property. You may wonder how people come to the "magic" number when determining how valuable a piece of real estate will be. At the end of the day, the property will only sell for as much as a willing buyer will pay for it.

As a guideline, however, real estate agents and appraisers determine a potential value based on similar properties that have sold recently (that is, comps). A comp is a property that has sold recently, is close to the subject property, and is of a similar size and style.

Those features are fairly easy to determine, but the next major factor is what kind of shape a property is in. Obviously, a nicely renovated property will be of greater value than a dump. It does get quite subjective as to how much value should change based on the shape of the property, but it is a factor nevertheless.

Always be a little bit conservative on this, but don't be too conservative. Being overly conservative probably sinks as many potential fix-and-flip investors as being overly optimistic does. In the case of being too optimistic with final ARV, the fix and flipper ends up walking away with little or no profit. But being too conservative can limit fix and flippers even more because it can mean that you never even try to do a deal! Don't aim to be overly conservative or optimistic with your estimation of ARV, just aim to be accurate. It is the only way to truly plan for a fix-and-flip project.

Know your market well, be conservative but not too conservative, and, by using your knowledge of the market (with the help of an excellent realtor), buy your fix-and-flip properties for the right price. When you buy right, you have fulfilled one of the major requirements of filling in your financial model. Buying right is a natural outcome of knowing your market well and understanding the renovation and carrying costs involved.

Knowing your market allows you to say no to bad and mediocre deals in favour of excellent deals. Being able to say no at the right times and yes at the right times is the same as having "the knack," so learn your market first and start saying no when appropriate and yes when appropriate.

Dieting on Cake

One of the beautiful bonuses about fixing and flipping houses comes with selling a property *above* market value. For example, our financial model told us the house would be worth $325,000 when it came time to sell, but then everything works out perfectly and the property sells for $340,000.

This is a very possible outcome, but it's not one that I recommend you *rely* on as a fix and flipper. The market value is the market value. Never try to be smarter than the market. The bonus $10,000 or $20,000 is like having cake at the end of a meal. Sure it tastes great, but do you rely on it as your only form of sustenance? Never!

The meat and potatoes of your profit have to come from adding value, bringing the property up to the market value. You do this through your renovations, which, when done correctly, will bring the property up to market value while you spend less money than the value you raise it by.

Too many new fix and flippers don't have a realistic understanding that the market can only bear so much of a value increase. They get confused between the meat and potatoes of fixing and flipping, and the cake.

Sadly, new fix and flippers will often involve their egos and emotions in their deals. If you ever find that the market doesn't agree with the value that you think your fix-and-flip property should have, and you hear yourself saying, "But this house is way nicer than the other houses in the neighbourhood," then you might be guilty of confusing the cake with the meat and potatoes.

You're not smarter than the market, and you never will be. Learn that lesson now and it will save you a lot of future grief.

Take the cake when you can, but buy right and renovate right in order to ensure there's a profit without the cake (because there's a good chance you won't get any!).

Know How to Renovate

Along with knowing your market, you must also know how to renovate right. The two go hand in hand. You cannot do one without the other.

Think of it this way: if you buy right and your financial model says that you should earn a $40,000 profit, but then you overspend by $35,000 on your renovation, you will have eaten up all your profit.

It's not as hard as it might seem to overspend on your renovation. There are fix-and-flip investors who do it all the time. Don't be one of them. Learn how much you have to spend, and then be ruthless in your quest to stay below that amount.

Staying within a budget that works for your fix and flip project is doable so long as you've prepared your scope of work properly. The trick to developing the scope of work is to know what has to be renovated and what doesn't. There's a simple principle that describes this: if it's visible and important, then you must renovate it.

A 15-year-old furnace in good working condition is not worth replacing. By not installing a new furnace when the existing one is just fine, you'll be saving somewhere between $3,500 and $5,000 on your renovation. The same goes for mid-life shingles and any other number of the big-ticket items on a house.

On the other side of the same coin are the frivolous items like expensive tiling in a lower middle-class rental property, expensive sets of new kitchen cabinets, specialty features such as swimming pools, etc. There are countless ways to ruin a great fix-and-flip project by overspending, but there is only one way to make it work: stick to the budget.

Timing

You risk losing your profits by attempting to sell a property into a soft seasonal market. In most markets across Canada, putting a property up for sale between December 1 and January 31 will result in a reduced purchase price by $10,000 to $20,000.

If you end up getting stuck with a property during the depth of the winter season, your best bet might be to refinance the property and rent it rather than take a hit on the sale price of the property. But renting it presents another problem because (along with selling a property), renting is also more difficult during this time. The best precautionary measure you can take is to time your deals so that you don't have to try selling or renting them during the winter season at all.

If the deal is strong enough to begin with, then you may be able to sell the property anyway, taking the lower sale price as a cost of doing business. If this is the case, it's all the more imperative that you don't rely on that $10,000 or higher lift (the cake) that we discussed earlier, because not only will you lose that lift, you'll also lose value off the real market value.

Tax Issues

Working with a real estate investment specialist accountant is the key to figuring out tax issues. Always strategize with your professional team prior to making *any* big decisions. Tax-reduction strategies are no different.

The major tax issue is the difference between capital gains and active income. Many new fix and flippers make the mistake of thinking that since they've sold houses before and been able to claim a capital gains exemption, they'll be able to do the same with another house they fix and flip.

This is not the case, and you could be dealing with a significant tax bill if you approach your tax strategy this way. When you purchase, fix and sell a property, the Canada Revenue Agency (CRA) treats it as active income. This means you'll be taxed at the full rate as though it were normal income. Depending on the profit you make on the flip, it could push you up one or two tax brackets.

When people make this mistake, they often don't recover quickly. Imagine working hard for three to six months on a fix-and-flip project, only to have your entire profit eaten up by taxes. Now imagine you've already spent a bunch of that money.

Starting your fixing-and-flipping career in debt to the CRA is not a great way to start.

The best way around the problem of paying active income rates on your flip projects is to run the entire project through a corporation. You will then be charged at the lowest marginal corporate tax rate for your province. The rates vary, but they typically hover around 15 per cent. Your accountant and lawyer are the best sources for information on corporate taxation.

Setting up a corporation will be a learning process, and there is a higher degree of diligence that your accountant must undertake, so your accountant's bill will be higher than usual. But compared to the tax bill you can potentially be hit with for paying active income rates, you'll more than make up for it by running your fix-and-flip projects through a corporation. You can also refer to a fine book on this and other financial and legal aspects of investing called *Legal, Tax and Accounting Strategies for the Canadian Real Estate Investor* by George Dube and Steve Cohen.

There are two major things that you need to remember about tax issues for fix-and-flip deals:

1. This is a business. Make it your business to be informed about potential tax issues.

2. Hire an excellent accountant. Perhaps more than anyone, an accountant has the ability to help you save loads of money.

Speak to your accountant and develop a strategy that minimizes the tax you will pay.

Financial Models for Fixing and Flipping

No two fix-and-flip projects are the same. The best model you can have is a guideline that tells you you'll earn a certain amount of money from each deal. I like to make a minimum of $50,000 from each fix-and-flip project. That $50,000 may come in the form of a cheque upon selling, or in equity upon refinancing. Or, if the fix and flip added a lot of value to the property, the $50,000 (or more) may come back as a combination of cash and equity.

These combinations are perhaps my favourite because it means I get to keep the property and hang on to a great cash-flowing asset, but I also get cash for my own bank account as well.

But in terms of modelling fix-and-flip projects, there are two standard variations. There is the gut flip and the cosmetic flip, with plenty of variations on both, though some features are relatively consistent.

The great thing about flipping is that each individual fix-and-flip investor is able to put his or her own personal stamp on each property flipped. You can develop your own brand of flips, and the properties that you hold on to can be totally unique from anything else on the market. This allows you to earn stronger rental numbers and keep tenants more easily.

For example, consider Jeff Reed, who is profiled in this book. Jeff's "brand" is the "loft look" in some of the established neighbourhoods in Toronto. He favours exposed brick and beams. It looks outstanding, and, as a result, his properties generally perform very well in the market.

All fix and flippers need to follow one model more than any other. That's the model of making profit. In order to make a profit, you'll have to:

1. buy right; and

2. renovate right.

Buy Right

As with *any* real estate investment, your flip will be a flop if you don't buy right. Paying too much for the property is probably the biggest problem facing fix-and-flip investors, especially new ones.

The problem arises from people not understanding the market. People will hear that there's a ton of money to be made fixing and flipping houses, so naturally they jump in with both feet and begin searching for a new property. They falsely assume that as long as they renovate it and it looks really nice, they'll be able to sell for at least what they've put into it.

They believe this equation is always correct:

Purchase Price + Renovation Expense ≤ Sale Price

This belief is wrong. Every market can only bear so much of a price boost. Ensuring that there is a large spread between the total cost you pay and the after-repaired value is the art of fixing and flipping.

The equation is not so simple, and many inexperienced flippers get crushed believing that what they put in will automatically be taken out on sale day.

Typically, even if a property is more nicely renovated than the comparable properties in the same neighbourhood, it will only realistically be able to fetch slightly more. If it's listed *at* market value or slightly *below* market value, it will likely sell quickly because of the attractive qualities of a nicely renovated property.

The bottom line is that a nicely renovated property will typically fetch slightly more than a "normal" property of the same type in the same neighbourhood. But the cost of bringing the property to the high renovation level is often great. Fix-and-flip investors have to buy right and renovate right. If they don't, the automatic problem is that the cost of the fix and flip will be greater than the value lift of the property.

What Is Market Value?

Market value is one of the most misunderstood aspects of real estate investment. For lack of a better term, we real estate investors are often found saying "market value" when we speak of how much a property will potentially sell for, either now or at some point in the future.

The reality is that market value is simply the amount of money that a willing buyer and a willing seller agree upon. This implies many different things.

For example, if a seller has to move within 30 days, and in order to move, they must sell their home, then the price that particular seller agrees to may be impacted by the need to sell quickly. It will depend on whether the market is hot or cool.

If a property is in horrible condition, and the vast majority of potential buyers would never consider buying it, then the seller will have to agree to the price that a buyer is willing to offer. Likely not too many will line up at the door.

There is a belief that fix-and-flip investors buy "below market value," and we've even used this term in this book because it's such a common way to speak of the purchase value of a pre-renovated fix-and-flip deal. The reality is that the ugly property (pre-renovation) bought for cheap is actually purchased *at* the market value.

The market value just happens to be low. It's your flipping (buying/renovating/value-adding) acumen that brings the value of the property up to what it will be at the time you sell or refinance the property.

When a property is a problem, somebody has to fix that problem. Fix-and-flip investors play a helpful role in communities by taking a property that is unoccupied and bringing it back into the market. The reward is financial. When problem properties aren't saved by such a person, they will eventually become the problem of the bank and/or taxpayer.

When you buy a property that is perceived to be deeply discounted, remember that it's just market value. Your job is to turn it from ugly to nice and you have every right to profit by solving the problem that the property poses.

If you buy right, it will be easier to renovate right and sell/refinance right. Buying right is like taking the right route to work in the morning. If you don't do it, you'll have a hard time reaching your destination at the right time. If you do it right, getting there on time shouldn't be too difficult. Even if there is an unforeseen traffic jam, you'll still likely make it on time.

I can't stress enough how important buying a property at the right price is to the whole process of fixing and flipping. Many people don't have a sense of how many times they will have to say no before they find one yes. The great fix-and-flip property is not as common as most of us would like it to be. So, focus on finding deals before all else.

Renovate Right

The biggest key factor to renovating right is knowing what needs to be renovated, and therefore how much will have to be spent on the renovation. Knowing how much will be spent is a matter of preparing an accurate budget. If you follow a few simple rules, it should be relatively easy to create an accurate budget.

1. **Create a Detailed Scope of Work**: This step of the process brings you clarity around the work needing to be done and, should you hire contractors, will give

you a platform for communicating with contractors. In order to develop your detailed scope of work, you must walk through the property and write down every step of every job.

2. **Put Down Numbers**: Once every aspect of the job is listed, your next step is to put two numbers down beside each task. One number will represent the cost of labour for that item. The second number is the cost of materials for that item.

3. **Add Them Up**: The third step is to add all the numbers together.

4. **Add a Buffer**: Once you have an accurate number for each item and you've totalled the numbers up, add between 10 and 20 per cent for potential cost overruns. Does this mean we *expect* to go over the initial number? On the contrary, we try to go *below* it. But using the total and adding 10 to 20 per cent ensures that we don't go over budget. Our budget is the number we reached, plus the 10 to 20 per cent. Adding the buffer ensures we're never surprised, even if surprises arise.

Surprises Can Blow the Budget If You Don't Budget Correctly

On a recent fix and flip that Ian did, he was met with a nasty surprise the day before closing.

After coming to the property with a couple of his employees, he noticed a smell in the basement. Upon further investigation, he realized that the sewage system was backed up.

This particular project was a total gut flip. The entire place was renovated from top to bottom, and it looked outstanding. But even on a gut flip, the one thing you'll never renovate is the main sewage drain pipe.

In this case, there was a blockage in the main drain. All the new piping that was installed was in perfect condition, but the main drain was very old, and since the place hadn't been used much for the previous couple of years, the faulty drain was not noticed during the renovation.

Ian had less than 24 hours to rectify the problem, so he got his guys to immediately start digging in front of the house to locate and replace the faulty drain. In the end, the repair cost him about $800 for labour and materials. It was most definitely *not* in his budget, but because he'd left a large buffer on the deal, the deal was still very profitable. Surprises are inevitable, and by preparing for them, you'll be preparing for success.

Insurance Needs

The main thing to know about the insurance needs of a fix-and-flip property is that you must have vacant building insurance. Attempting to do a fix and flip without it is like playing Russian roulette. All it takes is one property to burn down to derail your entire life.

Whoever provided the financing for the property will still want their money, regardless of whether you have a standing house, so make sure you'd be insured if anything should happen to that house while it's vacant.

No matter how cheaply you can rebuild an entire house, you'll never do it cheaply enough to recoup your money. Don't mess around without insurance or with gaps in insurance coverage.

During the holding period (if you decide to take that route), you simply have to insure the property as a normal rental. If the property is sold, then you're obviously released from having to insure the property.

15

Getting Started in Real Estate, Making Money, and Joint Ventures

In this chapter, Mark and Ian invite successful and renowned investor Thomas Beyer to talk about getting started in real estate and the preliminary steps to raising money for a successful partnership.

We're big believers in borrowing private money and doing joint ventures as a way to accelerate a fix-and-flip career. At some point, you will likely need to put other people's money (OPM) to work to do bigger deals or multiple deals at a time. If either of those fit your goals, you'll eventually need to raise money.

But how do you go from Joe Average who has no experience in raising money to having the confidence and authority to ask others to participate? Just like fixing and flipping itself, raising money is not as hard as some people make it seem, and it's not as easy as others make it sound. Raising money and utilizing the resources of others is serious business. You will hear stories of some investors (even some of those profiled in this book) who used OPM on their very first deal. We would say that most of those people had some previous experience or other form of backing to help them do this more advanced step at the beginning. Take it slow and easy, build upon a strong foundation, and move methodically. It won't be as long as you think until you're using OPM yourself.

If you've never used OPM, you're probably asking yourself, "How do I get started?"

Let us introduce you to Thomas Beyer. Thomas moved to Canada from Germany back in the late 1980s to pursue an MBA from the University of Alberta. His professional career has been long and varied, developing skills and creating momentum along the way. About 15 years ago, he started acquiring real estate. He started small with one rental-pooled condominium. Now he is semi-retired and overseeing a real estate empire valued at more than $100 million.

It's remarkable to see the kind of success that slow and steady progress has resulted in for Thomas. We love his perspective and his great insights, so we invited him to share his wisdom with our readers for this book.

Thomas is mostly a buy-and-hold investor, but he has done some flipping along the way, producing some extra cash to further his path. His advice about getting started is applicable to all kinds of real estate investors, and we're grateful for Thomas's assistance in giving you guys some awesome perspective.

"How to Start Out in Real Estate Investing" by Thomas Beyer

Some of you have come from humble beginnings. We all have humble beginnings in some sense. We're thrown into the world, and we have to make it on our own. As children child we had our parents' help, but eventually we have to make it on our own.

My parents helped me with many things, but figuring out how to build a portfolio of real estate investments was not one of them. In fact, when I arrived in Canada, I was shocked and amazed to see kids my own age (mid to late 20s) who were attending classes with me at the University of Alberta and who owned their own homes! I had never owned a home; I was a tenant (either with my parents or by myself) my whole life, and never once imagined owning one. In fact, it had never even occurred to me that someone must have owned all that real estate in Germany, where I grew up, or in Canada, where I moved in 1986.

My dad was a manager at a construction company, managing HVAC installations for large buildings. He had a good job, and he taught me many things, but we weren't homeowners! Unlike North America, home ownership is not a rite of passage or a cornerstone of financial success in Germany, so when I saw those young men and women owning a home when all I had was a bike and some kitchen utensils, I started to wonder if they were on to something.

But alas, I had other things on my mind, and there were many steps between then and now. Today, my company, Prestigious Properties Inc., controls approximately $100 million worth of real estate, mostly in western Canada.

So, am I a great wizard seeing the future in my crystal ball? Or am I a super individual, smashing through barriers with a single flick of my finger? The answer might surprise you. I'm just like you. I started off like anyone else, with baby steps, but wanting something better. Getting from where I was to where I am now was a series of incremental steps. That's the path I recommend to anyone reading this book.

You might be thinking that fixing and flipping will provide you with a lot of money. Well, it can probably do that, but for you to be able to pull that off, you're going to need a few things, such as:

- A solid money foundation. (See the section below about the five ways to make money.)

- Knowledge about the basics of getting started. Any real estate investment, and this certainly applies to fixing and flipping, is only going to work with certain other fundamentals in place. (See the section below about getting started.)

- Other people's money. (See the section below about structuring joint ventures.)

- For fun, I've thrown in a story about the kinds of flipping opportunities that you *will* be able to capitalize on if you take the slow, certain road of incremental progress. After two decades of hard work, I too became an "overnight" success.

Ian and Mark asked me to share some of my knowledge with you. It's my great pleasure to do so. I hope that some of the lessons I've learned myself and am sharing with you here today will make a difference on your path. Happy reading!

Five Ways to Make Money

There are really only five ways to generate your own cash. Likely, if you're reading this book, you are probably wondering how to generate cash for your real estate transactions. Perhaps you're looking for ways to start leveraging other people's money. If you're new to real estate investing, you may want to focus on perfecting #1. This will be your foundation for a successful life as an investor.

Number 2 will be a wonderful step to take before you ask others for their cash. Focus on the fundamentals of work and investing, and one day you will be able to ask others for their money.

In fact, you can do all five in time, but you have to take each one of them seriously!

1. Earning an income

Working. This is the most common way to start. Working is exchanging your time for money. The more time you give, the more money you get. It's a pretty linear relationship that's been proven successful through the centuries. Work has a bad reputation in some circles, among people who believe it's beneath them to trade time for money, but it has its place, and you should never feel belittled by working for your money.

But many people already fail at this. They don't take work seriously. They show up late for work. They chat with friends online. They do personal business on the side. They don't understand the business they're in. They don't give 100 per cent effort to their employer.

Yes, you can hide for a few days or a few weeks, but most employers realize after a while who is an excellent worker and who isn't. If you work hard at your job, you get ahead. To succeed at your job, give the extra 10 per cent, or the extra four to five hours every week. Read up on your industry. Go to industry conferences. Seek a mentor. Read, read, read! Learn, learn, learn!

Eventually, you will get promoted. You will get more money per hour for your work. If you have more skill, you will get more money. Formal and informal education helps. If you work hard, and earn more money than you spend, you can save some money. Don't ever underestimate the value of your work. You might be sitting in a career right now thinking you just can't wait to get out and become a full-time real estate investor. Sure, that sounds sexy, but the reality is that your *job* will provide you with the financial foundation to actually *begin* investing. People often dream of the result before they even *begin*. How are you going to begin? Build a foundation through your hard work. This formula worked for me, and it has worked for every successful investor I know.

Take your job seriously, work hard at it, be wise with your money, live below your means. I didn't buy my first brand new car until 2005. Why? I lived below my means. I lived in a small, rented townhouse when my children were young. Why? I lived below my means. I worked hard at my job, I lived below my means, and I was able to save some money. Yes, we did go on vacations to Europe or Hawaii with the kids eventually, and yes, we did eventually buy a second car (a basic necessity in Alberta), but that was much later. In the early days, we lived below our means.

If you save money, you're on your way, and you can begin to invest your own money, which is the next step for many.

2. Investing your own money

When you buy real estate, mutual funds, stocks, exchange-traded funds (ETFs), guaranteed investment certificates (GICs), bonds, or whatever seems to fit your risk tolerance, skills, and timeline, then you're investing your own money. It takes time to find out what a good investment looks like. Take it seriously. This investment could be more passive (such as a stock, mutual fund, or ETF) or more active (such as real estate or active stock trading). What's important isn't the amount you invest, but rather the process of understanding your investments and seeing the power of money at work.

If you invest well, then you're not trading time for money. Now you're into the world of using money to create more money. If you invest well, then your investments will churn cash for your next investment; and if your goal is to leverage other people's money, then you'd better create a solid track record. Investing your own money first is the best way to build that track record.

3. Investing other people's money

Once you've mastered investing your own money, then you have the right to ask for other people's money. The source of the investment money could be people who know you well, or people who initially do not know you at all such as joint venture (JV) partners. It could be money partners, or people who control your access to mortgages or lines of credit.

Investing OPM always assumes a degree of risk. Don't believe anyone who tells you that it's not risky to invest money, especially other people's money. Even the best predictions are less than 100 per cent accurate. When you buy a property to hold or to fix and flip, you never know exactly what the outcome will be. Perhaps a war will break out and the entire market will collapse. Perhaps your three-month project becomes a nine-month project. Perhaps your inspector missed the fact that the property has major foundation issues. Things can happen, and that's called risk. But that doesn't mean we do nothing. Assess the risk involved, and go ahead, present the deal asking for OPM.

If you're investing with private money, you borrow at, say, 8 per cent, and you invest it for 12 to 150 per cent. You must pay the rate you agreed with OPM, but invest at a more uncertain yet frequently much higher rate of return. This is called risk taking. For any risk, there will be reward, and it's your job to assess them both and take the risk when the reward seems right.

If you're involved in a joint venture, then both the investor's return and your return are dependent upon you putting together a successful deal. It's not unheard of for both parties to lose money or just barely squeak by. If you're barely squeaking by, what's the point? Investments are for making money, not working hard to break even.

For most people, investing other people's money is a step to take only if they've already succeeded at: 1) working; and 2) investing their own money. Most investors aren't fools (although there are some) and they look at your previous career and track record to gauge the likelihood that you will make them money. A lot of people only dream of using OPM. Don't be a dreamer—be an action taker based on a history of (small) successes.

4. Using other people's time (employing other people)

This is like #1, except now rather than trading your time for money, you're trading others' time for money (for you). Obviously this involves risk too because the people whose time you're trying to leverage will need to be paid regardless of whether you're making money. To do this, you'll have to be well capitalized, and have a plan, a strong market, and a good product/service to sell.

You might have a small or large business where you pay people a wage or salary and then use their time to make money for yourself. Usually you have to work hard to lead by example. You will likely need to risk some of your own or other folks' money.

When you fix and flip a property, you will likely have to use other people's time in an effort to make money for yourself. Even if you're a real go-it-alone type of person, you'll likely need at minimum a mortgage broker, agent, lawyer, plumber, electrician, inspector, and probably more.

5. Earning money from intellectual property (IP)

Intellectual property or royalties make money for you once you have created them. Maybe you have written a book. Maybe you have written lyrics or music (Elton John and Sting make money in their sleep). Maybe you have painted a picture and it is copied widely for a fee. Maybe you have invented a name and copyrighted it. Maybe you have a patent or a system that can be used for a fee.

Anything can be done by anyone, but generally intellectual property is only developed by people who have certain knowledge. This will almost always mean that to develop intellectual property, you first have to develop your skill at work (1) at least, if not also (2), (3), and (4).

So there you have it in a nutshell: five ways to make money.

Are you aiming to fire on five cylinders? Are you currently firing on half a cylinder? Try harder, or try different ways, to fire on all cylinders.

The First Steps

Frequently, the question on any new investor's mind is: How do I start?

While it's possible that you may be able to use other people's money on your first transaction, it is not likely. Investors who *should* be using other people's money on their first deal are few and far between. Most likely they brought some other form

of experience to their first deal that allowed them to raise joint venture money immediately. With that disclaimer out of the way, let's talk about the steps to take when
getting started.

First of all, you should assess your cash situation. Cash is a combination of real
cash (in your bank account, or a sock, or under a mattress), or the cash of a committed friend or family member. If you don't have enough real cash, then the next source
might be a home equity line of credit (HELOC) or short line of credit (LOC). On a LOC
you have to pay interest only on the portion you use, which is good. So don't use it all
immediately to buy a yacht or a fancy condo in Hawaii. These luxury items can wait.
The likely result of spending cash or lines of credit on superfluous luxury items is a
lifetime of being behind the financial eight ball. On the other hand, if you invest your
LOC into a cash-producing asset, you will begin the process of getting ahead. But if
you're reading this book, I suspect you've already figured that out.

The next step is to research the market. Decide what area of the country you
wish to invest in and then what type of property you wish to invest in. This is a big
country, so will it be the Lower Mainland of British Columbia? Edmonton and area?
Southern Alberta? Rural Saskatchewan east of Saskatoon? Toronto and the GTA?
Kitchener-Waterloo? Ottawa? Montreal? You get the picture.

The key point is that you are not looking for a "deal"—you're looking for a very
specific deal in a very specific place, based on a very specific type of property. Only
once you know your market very well will you even know what a deal looks like. In this
book, Ian and Mark discuss finding deals, and they profile different investors who seem
to have a secret knack for finding deals. That secret knack isn't so secret—it comes
from first knowing what a deal looks like in a certain area, or having a team that brings
you those deals based on their very intimate knowledge of this very specific area.

It takes time to research any area. It also takes a little bit of money for driving time,
flying there (if it's out of your hometown), doughnuts, lunches, and materials to research.
The bigger an area is, the more time you will have to commit to researching it. The entire
province of British Columbia takes more time to research than the Lower Mainland,
which takes more time than Greater Vancouver, which takes more time than North Shore,

which takes more time than North Vancouver east of Highway 1, which takes more time than Deep Cove. More time researching could lead to good things, or it could lead to a paralysis of analysis, a condition where you are handcuffed from taking action.

I suggest you start with a very small area, for example one suburb of one of the Top 10 REIN (Real Estate Investment Network) towns in British Columbia, Alberta, or Ontario. Perhaps the best town to research is the one you live in. It will certainly reduce your management headaches when you eventually buy.

Then, once you've decided on a very specific area of a city or an entire small town, you must decide on a *type* of property. A representative list is as follows:

- townhouses

- condos with an ocean view

- single-family homes older than 50 years

- new subdivisions

- presales

- acreages

- horse farms

- trailer parks

- office buildings in crappy parts of town

- high-end luxury condos with high-end finishing

- land with subdivision potential

- strip malls

- defunct shopping centres

- warehouses

- storage facilities

- fixer-upper homes

Any of these property types allow you to make money once you know what you're doing.

Most likely, the best one to start with (as there is plenty of supply, and plenty of seller motivation) is a small house or a townhouse. I don't recommend you start with a condo, as you can't control costs of the condo association. It's probably not best to start with a big house either, as this type of property is usually more expensive and consequently puts pressure on cash flow, although in a fix-and-flip deal that might be okay—*if and only if* the numbers work very well for a successful resale.

Once you've chosen the area and the property type, spend a *ton* of time becoming an expert on that property type in that area. Then and *only* then should you start writing offers and buying. When you're starting out, it's better to have several smaller properties than one huge one. Having several properties allows you the leeway to sell one if you have to.

For example, if you focus on townhouses, you must know after your research (also referred to as due diligence) if a 1,200-square-foot townhouse facing north is worth more than a similar one facing south, how much more a 1,400-square-foot townhouse is compared to a 1,200-square-foot one, how much a finished basement is worth, what the rent would be for the 1,200-square-foot one facing north compared to the 1,400-square-foot one facing south, etc.

You have to be an expert, because you must be able to discern within minutes if a "deal" is actually a sound business investment. Thus, you must know if $138,000 for that 1,200-square-foot south-facing townhouse is market price, overpriced or a screaming bargain. You must assume you are not the only person looking for a townhouse, and if *you* know it is a bargain, $20,000 below market, so will others.

You often make the most money with properties that lack curb appeal and need repairs. Many prospective homeowners look for a pristine property that requires no work. (I happen to be married to such a buyer—maybe you are too?) Therefore, you can often negotiate a substantial discount for a property that needs TLC. Be careful, though! You must be able to accurately gauge how much it will cost to fix the visible, and frequently less visible, problems. This is where four (of my list of five) ways to make money come in, as you use your own cash, and that of others, to fix an asset, investing your own time and that of others, for your often substantial gain.

You have to decide how much time you want to spend in this asset—it may be several weeks of full-time work in a rundown property. Do you have the time? Early in my real estate career I was running a busy software consulting firm with frequent travel and I did not have the kind of time to devote to turning around such a property. That's why I eventually bought an entire apartment building where others would do most of the work.

If you make one mistake on a big project, it could be the end of your tenure as successful owner of that property. You may lose the property (and possibly the property that is securing the HELOC you used to buy it).

When you're starting out, you might be tempted to rush into a deal. But it's better to pass on a bad deal than to realize six months into your ownership that you paid too much for a property and it is a drain on both money and time.

For each piece of real estate, you have to hang in there financially and emotionally.

This means that you must make a realistic assessment of your cash situation (including closing costs, vacancies, and upgrades required in addition to "normal" expenses such as mortgage payments, taxes, utilities, condo fees, insurance, management fees, etc.). It also means that you must make a realistic assessment of your mental toughness or time commitment. Vacancies will arise. Basements will flood. Tenants occasionally have to be evicted. Perhaps the police will get involved. Furnaces break down (sometimes at midnight). Get used to it, or anticipate it. Be prepared to handle those things yourself, or (preferably) hire a property manager who does it for you, but then be prepared to pay this person or company well. This obviously implies that you've purchased a property that cash flows well enough to afford management.

Ask yourself: Who will manage this property impeccably? If the answer is "I don't know," or if doing it yourself requires you to neglect your family or health, then spend some time reconsidering, and hopefully you'll find a property manager.

✷ ✷ ✷

Cash-to-close on a property comes in two forms: real cash and a mortgage. To get a mortgage, you need various documents including property documents and personal documents showing the bank that you are credit-worthy. Do as REIN suggests and prepare a binder with all of this information in advance so that when you show up at the bank you're ready.

Spend a *lot* of time preparing this document, then find a mortgage broker to get you a mortgage, or at least tell you what kind of mortgage you can get, depending on the type of property you've targeted. Horse farms are treated differently than trailer parks, which are treated differently than condos.

Before closing, ensure you have someone in that market to manage the property impeccably. That could be you, although a professional with in-depth market insight, knowledge of legalities, and local knowledge is likely better. Spend significant time finding that special someone, as good property managers are *very* hard to come by.

Once the deal makes sense, you've got the money (cash plus mortgage), and you've got the property manager, ask yourself if you will be able to hang in emotionally and financially. If so, close on the property!

Happy hunting!

P.S. Many hours are wasted when hunting and walking through the mud or underbrush. Many more hours are spent just waiting in the right spot. Then one day: BAM! Hopefully you were awake then, as sometimes the moment is short, and perhaps the opportunity passed or a better-prepared hunter got to the target first. So, be prepared and ready when you should be ready!

Is a 50/50 Joint Venture Fair?

When you first begin to consider the notion of a joint venture with a money partner, some questions you might ask yourself are these: How much am I worth? How much ownership should I have? And how much ownership should my money partner have? There is a fine line between self-confidence, arrogance, and self-deception. Be aware of this line. Confidence is necessary to negotiate a good deal for yourself—but please be realistic.

Fifty-fifty seems to be the norm for a joint venture (JV) on a single-family home, but is this the right split? Why not 70/30 or 25/75? Why not charge a fee upfront when all the work is done? Why not charge a fee as you go along? Why not own more than 50 per cent over a certain price target or investor return on investment (ROI)?

Some of my investors have made more than 300 per cent ROI. In cases such as those, 50/50 seems like expensive money. But those investors referred others, so in hindsight that was the entry price to mutual success.

The first deal is always the hardest, the second is a bit easier, and the third deal is a bit easier. The fifteenth is easier still . . .

Usually you have to do your own deals with your own money to prove a point or to prove that you have expertise in a certain area. That's why it might be a good idea to sell *too* early on your first joint venture. It helps you show a track record. With the success of the first deal, you can do a second and a third deal. Then you can show off your track record some more. Then you have the right to ask for other people's money. People with money today, in a volatile stock market or with low bond rates, are always looking to invest their money wisely. Don't be afraid to tell your story. Treat every "no" as a "not yet." The JV money trail always looks like this: no, no, no, no, no, no, no, YES.

Like a stonecutter at work, it takes many hits on the same stone for the stone to crack. Seven times is a proven sales rule of thumb. It takes seven times of asking, on average, to get a deal. Ask again and again.

It may be hard for your ego, but it might not be a bad idea to give away a little too much on the first deal, take a little more on the second deal, a little more on the third deal, until the formula fits these criteria:

1. It has to be win-win

This means that both you and the investor win. If one of you wins and the other loses, then the whole deal is a failure. Both you and the investor have to feel it is a fair deal and no one gets ripped off.

2. It has to be repeatable

This means you have to make money while you hold the property, or shortly after you purchase it. If you fix and flip properly, you can create cash to further your life, or if it's your goal, perhaps you can become a full-time real estate professional, living off the cash your fix and flips produce.

This is rare, and a more common plan is to build your portfolio slowly, holding some properties and selling others. The ones you hold have to pay you too. You will be doing a lot of work. For example, you'll be getting the mortgage, finding the trades, and doing the upgrades.

It's a lot of work, and to produce an income for you, 50/50 often works *poorly*, especially when the cash flow is low. It can often be this way while you hold. You'll need additional income to wait for the big equity pop at the end, which is often years away. So why not charge a fee upfront (perhaps it is being credited against your future earnings or perhaps you call it a sales commission or an asset-acquisition fee)? Or perhaps you charge a fee while you go along (perhaps it's charged against your future earnings; usually it's called an asset-management fee). You can negotiate whatever deal is a win-win because no one minds that you make lots of money as long as they make a decent ROI for the risk involved.

3. It has to adequately reward the risk

This means that some deals need to show a higher ROI than others. Building brand new homes in brand new markets with no expertise, subdividing land, condo conversions, and flipping presale condos (especially if they wouldn't cash flow if you had to hold it) are all high risk, and you might have to offer a higher ROI if you do any of those. Whether you like it or not, fixing and flipping has a similar reputation as anything in the list above. It's more risky than a standard buy and hold, especially when you don't have expertise. Reading this book is a good start to reducing that risk.

Buying lower-priced townhouses or small multi-family buildings or apartment buildings with rental and equity upside in growth markets is fairly low risk. That's why Ian and Mark like to fix and flip small multi-family buildings. If they can't sell them, they can always refinance them and rent them out with good cash flow.

On a standard buy and hold, there is perhaps less equity upside, but you can use a lot of the bank's money and thus create a high cash-on-cash ROI. The potential to lose capital is very low, so you don't have to offer too high an ROI. In other words, you can take 50 per cent or more of the profits. Keep that in mind when you're fixing and flipping. If your property will be a strong rental, then you're minimizing risk for your partners, so you have the right to ask for more of the deal. That's why Ian and Mark tell you to always have multiple exit strategies. If you try to fix and flip a house that *must* sell at a certain price, and something happens to the market, you might be in for trouble. Always have an option B, so you can escape without loss of capital. Once you mitigate that risk for your partner, you can ask for more of the deal.

4. It has to be sellable

A great property, or a great deal, or even a great asset manager, isn't any good if you can't present it to your investor in such a way that he or she will understand it and buy into it. You have to have a properly packaged proposition with appropriate legal and marketing material (perhaps a website). You have to have some degree of salesmanship and team members who execute with you or on your behalf. Investors want a track record and assurance that they won't lose any money. They want a return *of* their money and then a return *on* their money. So, the track record, you the person, the risk, the likely or potential reward, and the packaging have to be aligned for the deal to be sellable. Talk about yourself and the specific deal—an investor always looks at both. Also, include numbers and pictures or graphs. Some investors are very analytical and like lots of numbers, some like pictures of the (soon-to-be) renovated house, and a particular number such as 18 per cent (if that's your target return). You'll probably never know which one your investor is. That's why you always use plenty of both.

Happy joint venturing!

How I've Used Flips

I've built my real estate business largely from buying class C properties in class B areas of growth markets, adding value through renovations and management during the holding period, having a strong cash flow, and then letting the market do its thing. Buying in growth markets, managing impeccably, and holding for the long term is a good repeat business. I tend to agree with Warren Buffett that the best holding period is potentially forever. Ian and Mark recommend a strategy of refinancing, pulling out most or all of the original cash investment, and continuing to hold the property with strong cash flow.

I love that because it allows you to have minimal cash tied up in a property, but still profit from it over the long term. Value is added through targeted renovations, and by holding the property, long-term wealth is created. In essence this is what we do with apartment buildings, but it might take us longer to get to the refinancing stage because we have to raise the rent rolls and renovate numerous suites (which can only be renovated when vacancies arise).

So the idea of a long-term flip is very consistent with our philosophy. And just like you might be doing (or planning on doing), I've been fortunate enough to profit from a few quick flips along the way.

As Mark and Ian recommend, it is always a good policy to have multiple exit strategies on your flip projects. That's exactly what Prestigious Properties did when we flipped a property into the great Alberta boom in 2007.

The Flip

One of the wonderful things about working hard and diligently building a reputation is that, along with a good reputation, come great opportunities.

Our reputation as serious Edmonton, Alberta, apartment building investors led to numerous opportunities in the Alberta boom time (2003 to 2008), and a couple of the opportunities turned into flips that we did.

The first was a property in Queen Mary Park, an area of Edmonton known to be a little bit rough around the edges. A real estate agent that we'd worked with in the past had just gotten a pocket listing (not yet public) on a property that (even by Queen Mary Park standards) was in bad shape. It was dilapidated, and on top of that it wasn't being managed very well.

In fact, it was the weirdest rent roll I'd ever seen in all my years of investing. When doing diligence on a multi-family building, we are used to receiving operating statements for the past two to three years, tax assessments, utility statements, appraisals, property condition reports, detailed computer-generated rent rolls, etc. On this property, we didn't receive any of those documents from the sellers; all the sellers provided was a handwritten sheet with 18 slots (one for each unit).

Each slot had a name (Joe, Mary, Tom B.), or in place of a name it just said "vacant." Beside each name was a number indicating the rent each person was paying, like this: Joe – 550, Mary – 480, Tom B. – 530.

All the tenants were lower on the socio-economic scale, most were new immigrants, and didn't mind the bad living conditions provided by the landlord, presumably because it was the cheapest option they could find and the landlord accepted cash as payment.

What it amounted to for us was a great deal. Finding great deals often comes when a property is in this kind of shape, and it bore all the hallmarks of a classic flip.

The Numbers

Purchase price: $612,000

Holding time: Six weeks

Sale price: $692,000

Profit: $80,000

When you get an opportunity to purchase a building well under market value, but in horrible shape, and you don't want to do any work on it (as was our situation at the time), you have to expect to sell under market value as well. That's exactly what we did when we offered to sell the place to Mainstreet (a very large, publicly traded apartment building company). They have a large and ever-growing presence in Queen Mary Park and at the time were looking to add to their portfolio.

They wanted to do what we decided *not* to do to the property, which was reno-vate it, change the management, raise the rent, and profit in the long term from a sta-ble, well-managed apartment building. For them it was a great investment because it was one of the few small walk-up apartment buildings in the area that was block construction rather than the standard Edmonton wood-frame.

So we offered it to them at a price they liked, disclosed all the issues with the building (among them a leaky roof), and sold it quickly.

The six weeks we held the property were relatively cheap and uneventful. The only expense we incurred was the cost of buying two massive tarps from Canadian Tire. It was raining heavily in Edmonton at the time and we wanted to minimize water damage. Permanent renovations were out of the question, so we strapped the two massive tarps over the building. It was true duct tape construction at its finest, but the ugly tarps served their purpose. We minimized the damage, and sold the property without incident!

Obviously, there were some closing costs, but our profit was quick and signifi-cant. Someone asked me at the time when we did the flip, "What business are you in, Thomas? The milk cow business or the beef cow business?" I replied, "I'm mainly in the milk cow business, but every now and again, I like beef." (I later opened a veg-etarian restaurant with a partner, but that is another story.)

I'm a firm believer that it's wise to add properties to your long-term portfo-lio. There is real wealth to be created by holding real estate over the long haul. In this particular circumstance, though, it was relatively easy to make quick money and move on. I had to ask myself at the time if a quick $80,000 was better than a slow $200,000. Ultimately, we went with the quick $80,000.

We did have an additional motivation at the time. It was essentially the same motivation that some of you might be feeling. I wanted to produce some immediate cash! Just prior to this, we had the unfortunate experience of being swindled. It's another story for another book, but the gist is that a crooked on-site manager stole many thousands of dollars from us—in fact, it was around the same amount we made on the flip.

At the time, we really didn't want to pay for the crooked manager's crimes with money we already had, so we set about finding a way to produce the cash. This flip did the trick for what we needed at the time. Perhaps you want to flip real estate because you want to reduce your workload in your current job. Or perhaps you'd like to do real estate full time.

If either of those scenarios fits you, then you have a similar motivation to me at the time. The cash had a purpose. I didn't expect or desire to become a full-time fix and flipper, but I got what I needed from the flip.

On this deal, opportunity met with our reputation and our ability to pull the trigger quickly. We desired quick cash as well, something we don't normally aim for.

Given the figures involved, well over $600,000 in this case, it assumes that you know what you are doing. You must know, very quickly, what the real value of the asset is and what it could be. I had been in the apartment building business in Edmonton for around six years by then. I knew what I was doing by that time. I certainly could not have engineered this deal early on in my career, due to lack of paperwork, experience, and contacts in the industry.

All aligned well, and we were able to solve our desire for immediate cash. These opportunities come along as you move through your real estate journey. However, I'd like to stress the importance of taking care of your fundamentals first (see above).

Master at least the first one (and preferably two) of the five ways to make money; figure out how to get started. Then start doing deals. Perhaps you'll find opportunities like the one I've just spoken about and buy them with a partner (at 50/50 or whatever provides a win-win for both you and your money partner), or perhaps you'll be able to close on them yourself and profit grandly. You can and will do deals like this if you take consistent and incremental steps toward success.

Happy flipping!

16

Preparing a Property for Sale

In this chapter, Mark discusses the exit: what you need to do to market a property and close the deal.

If your chosen exit strategy is to sell, then it's time to consider preparing your property for sale. When you're selling, you likely want to consider *price* and *speed* as you prepare the property. The two factors might be closely related, since listing the property at the right price will likely bring about the sale of the property much faster than listing too high.

Speed

Once you get this far into the project, you will undoubtedly be ready to exit as quickly as you can. Even if your project went perfectly and there were no unforeseen problems at all (unlikely), you'll be facing the pressure of mounting carrying costs. Just the knowledge that you have these expenses mounting will be enough to make you want to sell quickly.

More importantly, though, is the fact that you will want to get free of the deal you're selling, so you can celebrate and move on to the next one. Even one month can be excruciating when you're sitting on the sidelines raring to go and you can't because your last project needs to be sold and wrapped up.

Price

By the time you're ready to sell, you'll be carefully considering your sale price and whether or not you can fetch what you'd calculated at the beginning. Nothing is certain in business or life—and definitely not in real estate. Even with the most detailed market knowledge, the most accurate comparables, and the best real estate agent in the world, you will never know exactly what the property is going to sell for until the day comes when you actually sell it.

The fair market value of a property is *not* what you hope it will be. The fair market value of a property is *not* the price you paid plus the renovation cost (if this were the case, why fix and flip?).

The fair market value is one thing only: the price that a buyer and a seller agree upon. For this reason, you never know what you're going to achieve for a sale price until the property is *sold*.

What Do You Want?

The most common, and sometimes the most dangerous, answer to this question is this: I want the most money I can possibly get for it. This kind of thinking violates one of the most fundamental principles of real estate investing in general, and fixing and flipping in particular: always leave something on the table for the next owner.

If your aim is only the top dollar, then you might end up hanging on to your property, missing the next deal, and slowing your momentum. Let's put it this way: if your deal *needs* an extra couple of thousand dollars to be a good deal, then it wasn't a good deal to begin with. Even in that circumstance, you're likely better off cutting yourself free of the property before it becomes a dead weight.

Dead weight drags you down. It makes you tired, and it removes all your energy for the next deal, which is much more important than the last deal. Once you're free of the last deal, then you can put your creative energy toward the next one, a good feeling, and a positive feeling. It's what great entrepreneurs and business people have been doing for centuries, taking lessons from the last experience, applying them to the next one, and creating continued momentum.

What this means is that speed is more important than price. Think of it this way: if the next fix and flip you do will earn you $15,000 per month, and you can't start the next one until you sell the current one, then holding the current one is costing you $15,000 per month. If selling it is only a matter of dropping the price by $5,000, then it makes financial sense to drop the price.

Obviously, you have to make your money, but when the time comes to sell, and if your property isn't selling as fast as you thought, then it's time to drop the price in favour of speed. Let me lay out a scenario that's all too common among fix and flippers.

Greed Puts the Brakes on Progress

Some new fix and flippers hold a deep belief that perhaps they will "get rich" from fixing and flipping on the first deal. Sadly, they have been confused by all the get-rich-quick schemes they've read about and false rumours of immediate fixing-and-flipping riches.

They may not check the comparables as well as they should and are a little bit unknowledgeable going into the sale.

Finally, they get to the sale phase of the project, are forced to check their comps closely, and are surprised when they see that other similar properties have been consistently selling for $30,000 less than they were relying on! Quickly, they reason to themselves that the other places must not have been renovated as well as the place they renovated. Not to worry, they'll just list what they originally thought, and when the buyers see how much nicer their property is than the others, they'll jump at the opportunity to buy.

When the buyers don't come, the fix and flippers get concerned. Over three months, they don't get any action on the property. Finally, they reduce their price by $10,000, and after three months of stress, mounting carrying costs, and pain, they sell for $10,000 below their (now reduced) list price. The fix and flippers throw their arms up in the air and assume that they've been duped. This fixing-and-flipping business is all a lie, they think. They start to think that it's impossible to make money at this business. They escape with little or no profit on the deal and decide that they're done, and that they're never going to flip another house.

The reality is that if they had listed the house for the right price ($20,000 less than they originally listed) at the beginning, it probably would have sold for close to list price, and they would have saved themselves the pain of those three months.

They would have learned the valuable lesson that buyers will pay more for a nicely renovated property, but there is always a ceiling to how much more they'll pay than the standard property in the neighbourhood. Every buyer is knowledgeable these days, and along with the property you're selling, they will be looking at others, wondering if they could just do a few thousand worth of renovations and make the other place nicer, all while paying less.

The new fix and flippers also would have learned the lesson that moving quickly onto the next deal is more powerful than hanging on, hoping for a home run every time. They should have listened to their Little League baseball coach when he said, "Just hit a single."

It's hard to quantify how important the small success of the first fix and flip is. It's more valuable than you can know. It acts as a huge lesson, teaching and training. You will be smarter and better on your second one, and third, and so on. Just taking a small success on the first one is often enough to breed a larger success on the second one.

In our example, though, the greedy first-time fix and flippers didn't allow themselves to get back into the game because holding on for the home run caused them to sour to the whole fixing-and-flipping experience.

This story is all too common. I want you to learn that speed is more important than price when it comes to fixing and flipping. Be prepared to sell for less than you want. Sure, try for the price you want, and sometimes you'll get it, but be prepared to sell for less than you want or use a different exit strategy. Move on to the next one and build momentum.

Being prepared to sell for less in order to move the property means that you have to do every other part of the deal well, and these other parts of the deal are where I recommend you focus your energies. Holding out for an unrealistic sale price is not the place to earn your money.

Do All the Little Things

Nothing is worse than a beautifully renovated and sharp-looking home being left unfinished. What I mean is that sometimes people will get to the end of a renovation and just run out of steam inches from the finish line. It's not uncommon to see light fixtures without bulbs in them or a dusty basement floor, or electrical outlets without covers on them.

If you leave any doubt in the buyer's mind, they will run with that doubt and imagine the worst. The smallest of things can leave a buyer focusing on the negative rather than on all the wonderful renovations that you did.

You want the buyer focusing on how wonderful the property is and how great it looks, so take care of the little things and offer a complete product to your prospective buyer.

I can't stress how important this is for marketing and selling a property. Think of it this way: would Coca-Cola put a bottle of their product on the shelf with half a label missing or a loose cap? Would Apple send you an iPad in the mail wrapped inside a plastic bag?

Of course they wouldn't, because packaging and having a complete product are important. You don't see major corporations selling an incomplete product, but altogether too many homeowners and even fix and flippers believe that they can sell an incomplete product.

I understand the rationale behind it: the fix and flipper has seen the property undergo such a dramatic transformation that he or she probably doesn't even notice the small touches that are left undone.

This is a failure to see the property the way that a prospective buyer does. They *do* notice the small touches. Nothing is more ridiculous than pouring months of effort into a fix and flip only to cut the smallest of corners at the end and achieve a subpar result on your fix and flip.

Take the time to finish every small detail. No dusty basement floors, no hanging light bulbs, and no missing light switch covers are allowed. Finish the job that you've worked so hard at, and you will achieve a better result.

Marketing a Property

Marketing a fix and flip is basically the same as marketing any property for sale. As a fix and flipper, you want to take every step possible to give your property the best chance to sell quickly and for top dollar. There are two major components to this: 1) you need to attract the maximum number of the right buyers to the property, and 2) when you get them in the property, you want them to be able to see themselves living in the property. If your target buyer is an investor, you want him or her to be able to see that the property would be problem free and profitable.

Attracting the maximum number of potential buyers is a matter of two things:

1. **Price:** We spoke about it at great length above, but the price of a property is hands-down the most important factor in getting warm bodies inside the door. The property can be the most nicely renovated place on the block and can have all the bells and whistles, but if the price is exorbitant in relation to the comparable properties in the same neighbourhood, it will not attract buyers. They will simply think the seller is being unreasonable and will not give your property a second thought. IMPORTANT: your fix-and-flip deal has to be strong enough that you can make a profit by selling at or perhaps slightly above or below market price. If your strategy is to sell well above market price, you will be left holding a property for a long time.

2. **Exposure:** Assuming the price is right, your next challenge is to get as many eye-balls on the property listing as possible. The major component is to make sure that the right people are seeing the right property. This means that if you're selling a high-rise tower in downtown Calgary, you wouldn't advertise the property in a local newspaper in Nova Scotia. But there are more than just geographical restrictions to where listing homes is effective—there are also different types of buyers, and marketing platforms for the different types of buyers. There are so many effective ways to expose a property to the market in this era that exposure should never be a problem.

Below is a list of many of those methods, along with my commentary about each one. Since we're mostly dealing with residential properties when we're speaking of fixing and flipping, I will keep my discussion relevant to these types of properties and their appropriate sites for listing:

- **Multiple Listing Service (MLS):** Hands down, the most effective platform for marketing a residential property. By far, the majority of homes in Canada are sold through MLS. The major benefit of MLS is that all realtors who are currently representing buyers will immediately see your listing if it fits the criteria of what their buyers are looking for. On top of that, the showing process is streamlined among co-operating realtors. If your fix and flip is listed on MLS as well as multiple other sites, chances are that it's MLS that will get it sold. But this doesn't mean we don't use other sources to expose the property.

- **Commercial Investor:** In my home region of Toronto, we have a magazine/website called *Commercial Investor*. I list with them whenever I sell a multi-unit building because it gets critical exposure to the investor market. Your local market will most likely have something comparable to *Commercial Investor* in which you can list your multi-unit properties.

- **Facebook Marketplace:** So many people use Facebook that it would be silly not to leverage that viewership. Marketplace is split up regionally, so buyers using Facebook Marketplace in your region will have a chance to see your property.

- **YouTube Virtual Tours:** For buyers to see your YouTube virtual tour, you'll first need to capture their attention elsewhere, such as any number of the other sites that we're discussing here. The advantage of the YouTube Virtual Tour is that it gives the buyer a better chance to really envision the property before deciding whether or not they want to see the property themselves.

- **Kijiji/Craigslist:** It seems that most areas are either Craigslist areas or Kijiji areas. Figure out which site is more widely used in your area and list your property there. These free listing sites just serve to widen your net. Why miss potential buyers if you can reach them through these no-cost sources?

- **Realtor Open Houses:** The realtors most active in your local region are most likely to come to the realtor open house. The best thing about this is that you'll get honest feedback from them about the sales prospects of your property. Ask your realtor to set up a realtor open house so that you can have many trained, professional eyes on the property, homing in on what's important.

- **Public Open Houses:** Only 1 to 2 per cent of homes sold are sold through public open houses, which is not a great success rate. Then again, 1 to 2 per cent of all homes sold are sold through open houses. There is a contingent of buyer that likes open houses, so when you're trying to sell the property, why not remain open to this form of marketing? As a seller of a fix and flip, you want to give yourself every chance to sell the house for top dollar, as soon as possible.

- **Private Sales:** There is a place for sellers looking to sell on their own, especially if the seller is experienced and knowledgeable. The biggest advantage of selling privately is saving thousands on commissions. In this age there are so many options for the private seller that it can often make sense. Many companies even provide MLS exposure by paying only a nominal fee. You won't get realtor services from these companies, but you will save a lot of money. Deciding whether or not you want to use a realtor or sell privately is a serious question that you will want to consider carefully. If you do sell privately, you will want to use every type of exposure possible, such as those on the list above in addition to an MLS posting service.

This list is not complete, but it is representative of the types of exposure you will need to get for your property. Again, exposing the property to the broader market is not difficult in the Internet era. So take good care of your marketing, and focus your extra attention on preparing the property well and pricing it well. Below we will discuss staging, which is a major component of answering this question for the buyer: "Can I live here?"

Focus your efforts on the overall deal. Then, so long as you price it right, prepare it right, and expose it right, you will be able to sell your property and move on without too much difficulty.

Staging a Property

The biggest factor of a quick and profitable sale outside of pricing the place right is staging it. I'm not an expert on staging, but I know well enough the value of it, so I hire Donna Ragona of Suite Design to walk me through the staging process. I spoke to Donna to get a rundown of the successful staging process that I've seen her perform numerous times for me and my clients.

The first thing Donna does is walk through the property during the consultation session and see it with new eyes. The property will always look different to the person who has been living in the property for years, or renovating it for months. Remember when we told you how imperative it was to finish all the small details? Donna and other professional stagers will always notice issues like that immediately. They will advise you to clean those items up. "I always tell my clients that cleaning is first and foremost. Even if you don't have the budget for anything else, just clean the place well," says Donna.

On the exterior, she's looking for the following:

- curb appeal
- overgrown bushes
- outdated lighting
- broken windows
- beaten-up garage doors
- chipped paint
- inappropriate colours
- dirty windows
- overgrown lawn

Inside the house on her initial walkthrough, she's looking for:

- cleanliness

- offensive smells

- chipping or inappropriate paint colours

- dirty or worn-out flooring

- fixtures and faucets

Obviously, many of these factors won't apply to your brand-spanking-new flip because you will have just finished renovating it. Still, the lesson of being aware of all the details stands. To properly stage a property, you must pay attention to the details: don't cheap out on some of the smaller things that make the biggest difference.

It's been said before, but it's worth stating again: the prospective buyers are focused on the visual, cosmetic aspects of a property. Luckily, those are often the most affordable things to renovate. Take Donna's advice and make sure the place is clean, looks good, and smells good.

Clean

It may be obvious, but if you're nearing the end of your flip project and haven't thought about who is going to clean the property, you should. If it's going to be you, make sure you have the energy and time to clean it. Otherwise, outsource the cleaning.

Smell

The best smell is clean. Donna says, "Some people like those plug-ins that release a scent in timed intervals. I'm not a fan of those things. Often they're too overbearing and when they put two different scents in one house, the smells compete with each other and it's a nightmare."

Donna recommends that rather than the chemical smell of plug-in scents, just make sure the whole house is clean, and if the weather permits, keep a window open for a fresh outdoor-air smell.

Furniture

Donna believes that the most important thing about furniture is to give prospective buyers a sense of what a room can look like. The furniture does not have to be designer, and it doesn't have to be too fancy or expensive. Of course, it's better if the furniture is not dated, and of course it has to be clean and smell clean, as does the rest of the house, but it doesn't have to cost you a lot of money.

One of Donna's greatest tricks as a home stager is to use cardboard furniture to stage homes. It's inexpensive compared to real furniture, and it's a lot easier to move around and arrange. When she deals with clients on a budget, they often choose the cardboard option. It saves them money, and at the same time accomplishes what good staging should: it shows the prospective buyers what a room could look like.

Walls

Donna looks around for dated paint colours and chipped or scratched paint. If possible, she recommends repainting anywhere there is a deficiency. The colours should of course be as neutral as possible. One person's "creativity" with colours is another person's ugly, so eliminate that problem and make sure you always use neutral colours when you paint your fix and flips.

Once the paint is taken care of, the next thing to consider is what to decorate the walls with. Donna recommends having some simple prints on the wall.

Bathroom

The bathroom is truly simple to stage. Since the "furniture" comes built in, you just have to worry about the little touches. Donna recommends some rolled towels on the vanity, and a simple white shower curtain. White always looks clean and never clashes with any other colour, so it will be your best bet. Place some brand new bars of soap on top of the towels.

If you've just renovated the house for your flip, hopefully you've considered lighting in the bathroom. If not, Donna recommends putting in the four-bulb "celebrity lighting" above the mirror. It lights up the bathroom nicely.

One print is plenty in a small bathroom. If you put too many, you will risk cluttering the space. And as a finishing touch, you can put some greenery in the room. Fake or live plants are both fairly affordable, but if you go with a real plant make sure it is low mainte-nance. If the plant doesn't get watered frequently enough and it wilts, it will be a turnoff rather than a pleasant accent. You don't want the plant to produce the opposite effect of what you intended, so make sure the plant is taken care of.

Living Room

The living room must have some form of furniture in order to give the buyers an idea of what the room can look like when it's lived in. Donna recommends not to fill up the room too much, but to put a sofa, an accent chair, and a side table with a lamp. A coffee table is also good, but in place of a big bulky coffee table, it's a great idea to get the small $25 cubes. They're light, easy to move, and inexpensive, yet they give the same impression as a coffee table.

Curtains on the windows are fine, as long as the actual curtain panels are clean and neutral. A simple curtain rod is best for the curtains. Blinds are fine as long as they're in good shape and they're clean, but the most important thing about window coverings is that they should be left open when the property is going to be viewed. The more light that is let into the room, the better it is going to look.

The same rule applies to any lamps in the room. Donna recommends leaving them on so that the room is well lit.

Kitchen

As with the bathroom, the kitchen is very easy to stage because most of the room is ready built. You will have to have a kitchen table and chairs. It's best not to have too large of a set for the room so that it doesn't look over-filled and cluttered. After the table and chairs, all you have to do is accessorize and keep it clean and simple. A simple bowl of fake fruit is fine for the countertop. It's great to use real fruit, but only if you're certain the fruit will never get rotten or off colour. As with every room, some simple prints also work in the kitchen.

The same rule applies to flowers. Real flowers are wonderful, but if there's any chance the water will get stagnant and smelly, don't use real flowers. If you do use real flowers, change the water and make sure the flowers don't wilt.

There are also sets of fake cheeses and breads, which give viewers the sense of a kitchen in use. Two bowls—along with cutlery—mimicking a nice breakfast setting on the table will complete the kitchen accessories.

Other than that, keep the kitchen completely clutter free. The cleaner it is, the fewer questions your prospective buyers will have.

Master Bedroom

As with the living room, the key element of the bedroom is that prospects see it as furnished. The most common question with a bedroom is "Will my queen-size bed fit in there?" When you stage it, you're removing that doubt from their minds. Keep with the simplicity of simple curtains (open), and a simple side table with a lamp, and the room is complete.

Second Bedroom

If the main floor has more than two bedrooms, it's great to have every room staged, but most importantly is the master bedroom and one other room. Donna says it's best to consider what kind of clientele you're targeting and stage the second room appropriately. If it's a family neighbourhood, then you're wise to stage the second bedroom as a child's bedroom. If you're targeting a professional couple, then it's best to stage the second room as a simple office with an office table or a desk and chair.

The same rules of lighting, lamps, and curtains apply.

Basement

Whether the basement is finished or not, the number one rule of basements is to have them clean and well lit. Make sure that it's not scary for prospects to go downstairs.

Results

Time and time again, Donna sees the results of staging a property. Like it or not, a lot of people don't see the potential in a property without a little help. Staging allows people to see it without having to use their imagination.

I recently had the occasion to witness firsthand how powerful staging can be. I had two clients who were both selling a similar property at the same time. In fact, the properties were both in the same neighbourhood and they were of a similar style. Both were in similar condition. The only difference was that one of the properties was left empty and the other was staged by Donna.

In terms of showings, the one staged by Donna did get more showings, although not drastically more. It seemed that buyers wanted to check out the competition. However, when it came to second showings, the difference was stark.

It wasn't that the non-staged home was ugly or in bad condition, it was just empty, and perhaps a little bit stale. But the staged home just popped and spoke to the prospects in such a way that they wanted to see it again.

The most important measure of all was the sale. The property staged by Donna sold within two weeks, whereas the other lingered on the market for three and a half months. The one staged by Donna went for 99 per cent of asking price and the other one sold for only 97 per cent of asking price. This is a significant difference. Both properties were listed around $450,000, so the 2 per cent difference amounted to $9,000.

Those of us in the real estate market see this kind of thing all the time. Staging makes a huge difference. Contact a good stager to help you sell quicker and for more money. Learn more about Donna Ragona and staging at http://suitedesign.ca.

Carrying Out a "Post-Mortem"

One of the best ways to learn from the fix-and-flip project that you just completed is to do a post-mortem. This means reviewing every aspect of your deal in methodical fashion. Ask yourself if certain renovations worked. Did they raise the value of the property, or did they bring a buyer to the property faster?

Ask yourself if your financing worked. If you used private money, did you spend too much on interest? Would it have been more profitable for you to joint venture on the deal and share 50 per cent of the profits with a partner?

Did you market the property well? Did you attract a lot of buyers to the table when the time came to sell? If you did, then congratulations! Celebrate and keep doing what you're doing, or tweak your marketing. If not, why?

Did you estimate your costs accurately? Did you stay within your budget? If you did, then keep doing what you're doing! Or, tweak your system and make it better. If your costs were higher than you wanted them to be, or if your estimation was wrong, why was that the case? Did you not follow your procedure for cost certainty? Did you fail to get detailed and concrete quotes from sub-contractors?

How was your stress level? If the process was relatively stress free, then keep doing deals like the last one. If you were stressed out during the fix and flip, ask yourself why. Was it caused by an unreliable contractor? Were your expenses too high? Did you pay too much?

Did you buy right? Was the most affordable renovation possible still too expensive to make the deal work for you? If so, you might have paid too much. Go back and learn your target neighbourhood better. Perhaps your paying too much was a result of not knowing the market well enough. Find out how you ended up paying too much and don't do it again.

A thorough post-mortem will allow you to slowly eliminate whatever errors you started with. By all means, ask your team what they think you could change. Ask the appropriate team member each of the above questions and keep digging (into yourself and your team) until you find your answers. Don't skip this step! This is how you improve as a fix and flipper.

Appendix

Flip Horror Story

Experienced Real Estate Professional Barely Escapes from Tricky Situation

Sean Greene is a true real estate professional. From fixing and flipping houses to owning and operating a real estate brokerage, to custom home sales, to custom home building, to subdividing raw land, to apartment building investing, he's done more than even the most seasoned real estate veteran.

This vast experience includes flipping, which he started at age 19. "I used flipping as a vehicle to supplement my real estate sales career for many years. I had been doing one or two flips per year for about 10 years—when the nightmare flip happened," says Sean.

Flipping houses is a more intense pursuit than traditional buy-and-hold real estate. Let's face it: when the business is good the rewards can be great, but nobody can deny that the risks are greater when flipping houses than when buying and holding. Sean's experience with the most difficult and problematic deal of his career is proof of this fact.

The Set-Up

Sean was running a successful real estate brokerage in Pickering, Ontario, in 2002, when he decided it was time to buy a commercial building as a base for his office. He spotted a building on a busy commercial thoroughfare and thought it would be a great place for his business. The building was a classic older home; the city had grown up around it and, as a result, the house had become a commercial space.

However, the property needed some work, and at the time, Sean didn't have the cash on hand to renovate the place before his move-in. As luck would have it, there was another, smaller property beside the larger one that was also for sale, and also needed some work. The smaller property was also a converted residential property.

Sean's business mind kicked in, and he envisioned a way to leverage the profits from fixing and flipping the smaller one into ownership and occupancy of the larger one. The plan was this:

- Purchase both properties.

- Renovate the smaller of the two.

- Move his business into the smaller one once renovations were complete.

- Sell the smaller one and take a profit.

- Renovate the larger one.

- Move his business into the larger one.

He kicked off his plan by renovating the first property right away and moving into it. At the time, Sean had a strong working relationship with a mortgage broker who was also looking to purchase a commercial space for his own business. Sean and the owner of the mortgage company agreed upon a deal (to sell to the mortgage broker) and got the property under contract. So far, everything was going according to plan.

That's when the proverbial stuff hit the fan. "The lawyer called me up and said they couldn't do the deal. I was thinking, 'What do you mean you can't do the deal?'" says Sean.

What had happened was completely out of left field and almost impossible to plan for. Due to an ancient and obscure law in Ontario, whenever you purchase two adjacent (side-by-side) properties that were surveyed and built prior to the new Land Titles Act coming into effect, those properties automatically become one lot with one title. When the buyer's lawyer had done a land titles search to execute the sale of the property, he found that the property was joined with the other (larger) property, and that the two properties could not be sold separately.

"The law is so obscure and strange. If I had changed the name of the owner in any way at all, then the law wouldn't have kicked in. In other words, if I had purchased the properties under different names, then I would not have had this problem," says Sean.

Incredulous at his bad luck, Sean did the only thing he could do: he kicked into action to try to solve the problem. His first course of action was to go to the city planning department and try to figure out if there was an easy fix to the problem. Unfortunately, they agreed with what the buyer's lawyer had told them and verified that the two lots were now one, and the property could not be sold separately.

Sean's next step was to apply for a subdivision of the property into two commercial lots. Again, he ran up against a brick wall as the city found, through its assessment, that the frontage on the property was not large enough to permit two separate lots.

Sean was starting to get concerned. He had to find a legal loophole to escape the clutches of an archaic law that was threatening to put his whole business into jeopardy. That's when he began the process of consulting lawyers. He went through four lawyers, none of whom wanted to touch the problem. Only the first lawyer had an idea that might allow Sean to escape the now nightmarish problem he was up against. The first lawyer contended that although the property hadn't technically gone through the "draft plan of subdivision" phase, there were surveys completed many years prior that could be interpreted as a draft plan of subdivision for the property.

If the first lawyer's belief was correct, they could in essence contravene the law that said the two properties had to become one when purchased by a single owner. But the only way to convince the land titles office of this was by getting a ruling from a very high-powered lawyer who had actually written all the planning law in Ontario.

If Sean could get a decision from this lawyer, he'd be able to claim the properties were legally subdivided and he'd be able to sell the small property to the mortgage broker as he'd planned all along. It was his final hope to salvage the situation before it caused him any major financial pain.

His first lawyer's opinion proved to be correct as the authority on the matter ruled in Sean's favour and said the original surveys acted as a sort of draft plan of subdivision. Sean was free and able to split the one title into two!

Luckily for him, the original buyer (the mortgage broker) still wanted to buy the property, and in fact had been leasing the place while all the drama was unfolding. Six months after the original sale was supposed to be complete, Sean was finally able to sell the smaller property, completing the first flip as planned.

The Numbers

- Purchase price: $169,000
- Renovation expense: $20,000
- Closing costs $\times$ 2: $2,500
- Sale price: $269,000

Disregarding the near catastrophe with the titles on the property, Sean had a great deal on his hands. Like some of the other fix and flippers you've read about in this book, Sean was great at seeing hidden value. On this particular property, Sean saw that there was a minor foundation issue that was scaring away potential purchasers. He knew that it wasn't actually an expensive issue to repair, so he did it. As with all the successful flippers profiled in this book, Sean saw a problem that he could solve and did so for a nice profit.

He hadn't counted on having to solve the land title problem as well, but on this particular deal, solving that problem was part of what he had to do to make the flip a success.

The Second Escape

Having escaped from the first major issue with the property (properties), Sean took his profit from the sale of the first property, plugged it into renovations in the larger property, and moved his office in.

After running his real estate brokerage out of the larger property for a couple of years, he found himself seeking a different kind of meaning out of his working life and ended up taking police officer training so he could change careers.

When he became a police officer, he effectively shut down his real estate brokerage. This meant that he no longer had any need for the commercial space for his own business. Rather than sell at that time, Sean had the idea to lease the office space; the tenant he found was an investment company.

When the tenant told Sean of their intention to put a sign up on the property for their business, Sean saw no problem with it and went about procuring the application for sign permits on behalf of the tenant. They sent away the application, thinking the sign permit would be rubber stamped.

Sean and the tenant were both shocked when the next communication they received from the city was a cease-and-desist order! Essentially, this means that the city was ordering the financial company to stop doing business from that location within 30 days. Although the property had been operated as a business for the previous 25 years or more, the zoning for that particular property had never officially been changed.

Again, Sean was blown away. What had happened was that, while a search for zoning on the property would show that it was zoned for commercial business, when the sign application came in, the city office did a search and found that even though the property showed commercial zoning, there was never an official rezoning completed. They sent the cease-and-desist order because the property was still officially zoned as residential.

Sean was now in another bind. Not only was he liable to lose the $4,000 per month rent that he was receiving from the tenant, but he was also potentially on the hook for the relocation expenses of the tenant. If a commercial landlord can't fulfill the conditions of the lease contract, they're liable for costs incurred to the tenant.

Again, Sean had to leap into problem-solving mode. The solution, it turned out, was to apply for rezoning immediately. Since there was a 30-day cease-and-desist order breathing down his neck, Sean had to apply for extensions while the rezoning process moved slowly along. After what seemed like the hundredth extension, the city finally granted Sean the rezoning that he'd requested.

Selling the Second Property

After finally moving on from the most recent red tape headache, Sean continued to lease the property. But approximately a year later, when the investment company that was leasing the property moved to a different location, Sean decided it was time to sell, realize a financial gain, and move on. The basic numbers broke down like this:

- Purchase price: $265,000

- Renovation expense: $75,000

- Sale price: $450,000

Remember that from the time he'd bought the property until the time he decided to sell it, he had left the property vacant for six months (while he was resolving the sale of the smaller property), then he'd spent six months renovating it, then he'd operated a business from it for more than two years. Finally, he had leased the property for a year, resolving the rezoning issue during the first part of the lease.

All in all, he had owned the property for more than four years when he finally decided to sell. "I recognized that there was an opportunity. The market had picked up, and I knew I could take a nice profit, so I decided to sell," says Sean.

Lessons Learned

Sean says that in all his years of fixing and flipping houses, he never did a single flip that went absolutely according to plan. He never experienced one quite as challenging as the two properties we've just discussed, but the lesson teaches new fix-and-flip investors that fixing and flipping real estate for profit is not an easy game. There are pitfalls all the way through, and it takes a more active approach than a traditional buy and hold.

When buying and holding, you'll rarely have to deal with city inspectors and permit offices. The tax issues will be less complex, and once the property has been purchased and rented out, there is much less to actively do. No real estate investment is totally passive, but a buy-and-hold model of investing is less intensive up front. On the downside, buy-and-hold profits take longer to realize. Depending where you are on your own real estate investing trajectory, you may benefit greatly from fixing and flipping.

In essence, this is exactly what Sean did for those years when he was fixing and flipping houses at a pace of one or two per year. The income he produced from his flips supplemented what he was earning on his other investments, as well as from his real estate sales career. Now he's at the point in his career where he's strictly involved in longer-term horizon investments. He now purchases apartment buildings with long-term strategy in mind, and builds equity slowly and surely through the holding period.

There's a good chance that your current goals to use fixing and flipping to produce income will be similar to what Sean's were when he was actively fixing and flipping. It's incredible the consistency of this point throughout the different investors we've profiled in this book. The lesson: use fixing and flipping in the right way. Take a measured approach to fix-and-flip projects. Have multiple exit strategies, so you're never left holding an un-sellable or un-rentable property. Use fixing and flipping to accelerate or supplement your income. Take your time to find excellent deals, and find a problem you can solve—for a profit. Learn to spot opportunities to add value. Follow these simple rules and you will find that fixing and flipping can serve you well along your real estate journey.

About the Authors

Mark Loeffler

In-between coaching students, mentoring real estate agents, guest speaking, and teaching online real estate courses, savvy entrepreneur Mark Loeffler runs a thriving business that has refined rent-to-own strategies and built a network of properties and experts across Canada. After graduating from the University of Western Ontario, Mark spent years focusing on real estate as his vehicle to financial independence. In addition to mastering his system of tenant-first rent-to-own, Mark is a firm believer in adding value to his investments through renovations. He practises the mantra that you can fix and flip a property and still keep it in your investment portfolio. This unique contribution to the fix-and-flip community promises to change the way investors think about fix-and-flip real estate.

As a result of his success and track record as an investor and realtor, Mark is a sought-after speaker and a Gold Member of the Real Estate Investment Network (REIN).

Being his own boss has meant that Mark has had time to share his information with other investors, lawyers, and mortgage brokers, who have benefitted from his expertise. Mark has appeared on television, and regularly contributes as a writer to the *Canadian Real Estate* magazine. His first book, *Investing in Rent-to-Own Property: A Complete Guide for Canadian Real Estate Investor*s, was a big hit and helped thousands of investor across the country. Mark has embraced social media by way of Twitter and a regular blog offering advice and keeping his readers up to speed on the real estate market.

Now independently wealthy, Mark is thrilled to give talks, courses, and mentoring sessions to anyone who is interested in learning about the real estate market and real estate investments.

For free bonus downloads and tons of other fantastic information, please go to www.markloefflerteam.com or www.theversatileinvestor.com. And for ongoing commentary and valuable information about real estate, please follow Mark on Twitter @mark_loeffler.

Ian Szabo

Ian is Canada's foremost expert on real estate investment renovations and house flipping. In addition to the current title, Ian is the author of *From Renos to Riches: The Canadian Real Estate Investor's guide to Practical and Profitable Renovations.*

In addition to flipping houses, Ian can be found teaching Flip School, his one-of-a-kind fixing-and-flipping education program.

Ian came to real estate renovations and flipping by way of the kitchen and the hammer. He was executive sous-chef at the Granite Club in Toronto before moving into the renovations business where he worked eight years prior to becoming a full-time investor and flipper.

In spite of his technical knowledge, Ian's greatest skills are his intuition and ability to think creatively about a problem, skills that he developed as a youth, when learning disabilities meant that he didn't fit the traditional mould of a future success.

A true underdog, Ian has shared his skills on numerous HGTV renovation shows as the lead contractor, speaks to large audiences, and trains the future house flippers of Canada through Flip School, which can be found at www.flipschool.ca.

Join the conversation on YouTube at www.youtube.com/user/renobible or connect with him on his Facebook page at "Flip School." Follow Ian on Twitter @Ibuyuglyhouses.

Zander Robertson

Zander is a writer and creative entrepreneur. He helps his clients to create their books and knowledge products with a no-pressure conversational style, intuitively drawing the information out.

From the age of 8, when Zander became editor of a newspaper (with a circulation of six), he has loved getting the story out. He loves to write and create, and he has a specific talent to help others tell their stories.

When not in the cold climates of northern Alberta, Zander can be found on the Reggae Beach on Jamaica's North Coast, where he lives and works from during the winter months.

Zander can be reached at zander.robertson@gmail.com.

Or, you can join the conversation with him on:

YouTube at www.youtube.com/user/zanderrob

Facebook at www.facebook.com/zanderrobertson

Twitter at twitter.com/zander_rob
His blog: zanderrobertson.com

Thomas Beyer

Thomas Beyer is a well-known, trusted, and respected real estate investor across Canada. Thomas started investing in real estate a mere 15 years ago and has built a substantial portfolio of real estate investments in that time.

Thomas is currently writing his first book titled *80 Lessons Learned on the Road from $80K to $80M*, giving readers a front-row seat to relive the journey of a highly successful real estate investor and his greatest lessons learned. The book will be released in late 2012.

Follow Thomas on Facebook at his personal page (Thomas Beyer) or at his business page (Prestigious Properties). You can also follow his blog at 80lessonslearned.blogspot.ca.

Index

property,
    marketing a, 228, 229, 230
    purchasing, 11, 33, 38, 60, 98, 193
    restoring, 12, 179–80
    selling a, 195, 197, 228, 230, 236
    staging a, 232–37
    turnkey, 90
    undervalued, 10
    wholesale, 16, 21, 26, 28, 29

Q
qualifying standards, 182
quotes, 86, 134–35, 137, 138, 151, 238
    comparing, 137

R
Ragona, Donna, 232, 237
real cash, 4, 212, 216
real estate, career in, 37, 123, 198
real estate agent, 57, 91, 96, 129, 194, 220, 225
    commission, 90, 105, 218, 231
Real Estate Investing in Canada 2.0, 19, 166, 186
Real Estate Investment Network (REIN), 26,
    39, 81, 117, 146, 213, 216, 245
*Real Estate Joint Ventures: The Canadian
    Investor's Guide to Raising Money and
    Getting Deals Done*, 58
real estate market,
    boom, 1, 220
    hard-charging, 2
    strong, 2, 34, 211
    weak, 1
reality TV, 75, 76, 111
recreation (rec) room, 89
redesign, 52, 150

Reed, Jeff, 141, 199
refinance-and-hold, 43, 59, 97, 105
registered retirement savings plan (RRSP),
    31, 87
rehabilitation, 35
rejection, 77, 78–79, 187
relationships, 28, 54, 92, 112, 129, 131,
    135, 185
refinancing, 59, 60, 63, 87, 106, 123, 128, 190,
    198, 220
region, 18, 39, 148, 166, 230, 231
renovation,
    expenses, 4, 28, 33, 34, 36, 61, 80, 84, 86, 147,
        152, 157, 158, 159, 171, 181, 192, 193, 199,
        241, 243
    key features, 86
    late completion, 102
    managing projects, 142
    phase, 43
renovations, number of, 45, 52, 53, 81, 97
rent-to-own, 1, 5, 147, 148
rental unit, 43
renters, 9, 41, 122, 144, 150, 177
repayment, 21
research, 4, 26, 31, 32, 212, 213, 214
resources, 95, 123, 186, 205
returns, 1, 31, 32, 105, 123, 128, 188, 189,
    190, 192
    fast, 1, 56
    stable, 188
rezoning, 243
risk,
    mitigating, 28, 49, 219
    unnecessary, 87
roof, 52, 79, 98, 125, 145, 222